MW00341666

EYE
ON THE *Sparrow*

EYE
ON THE *Sparrow*

The Remarkable Journey of
Father Joseph Nisari, Pakistani Priest

ROSEMARY COLGROVE

MILL CITY PRESS, *Minneapolis*

Copyright © 2010 by Rosemary Colgrove

Mill City Press, Inc.
212 3ʳᵈ Avenue North, Suite 290
Minneapolis, MN 55401
612.455.2294
www.millcitypublishing.com

All rights reserved. No part of this publication may be reproduced, stored in a retrieval system, or transmitted, in any form or by any means, electronic, mechanical, photocopying, recording, or otherwise, without the prior written permission of the author.

Author's note:
This is a true story. However, some names and identifying information have been changed, and some conversations have been reconstructed based on the memory of Father Joseph and others who were interviewed for this book.

Grateful appreciation is extended to the following for permission to reprint previously published material:

- Yasmin Khan (*The Great Partition: The Making of India and Pakistan*, Copyright 2007, Yale University). Reprinted by permission of Yale University Press.
- William Dalrymple (www.travelintelligence.com/travel-writing/lahore-blood-tracks, *Lahore: Blood on the Tracks*, 1997). Reprinted by permission.

ISBN 13 - 978-1-936400-87-4
LCCN - 2010940781

Front and back cover designs by Robbin Colgrove.
Typeset by Kristeen Wegner.

Family photographs courtesy of Father Joseph and the Nisari family.
Cover photo: Jehangir Kothari Parade, Clifton Beach, Karachi.

A portion of the proceeds from the sale of this book will be donated to "Missionaries of Hope," a project especially dear to Father Joseph. The organization provides education and health care to the forgotten children in Pakistan's rural villages.

Printed in the United States of America

For my High Priest, Jesus Christ, who called me, consecrated me, and appointed me to serve him and his people. For my parents, Mariam Regina and Barkat Joseph, and my brothers and sisters who guided and nurtured me in every way possible. And for my parish family at St. Cyril and Methodius Church, for their continuing love and support.

—Reverend Joseph Nisari

For my parents, who gave me the gift of curiosity—and so much more. And for Dean, who was always there (with your amazing technical support).

—Rosemary Colgrove

CONTENTS

Bishop John McCarthy

FOREWORD

Modern, twenty-first century communication has made virtually all of us conscious of the smallness of the planet. Economic systems, social systems, and cultural forces contradictory to traditions are inextricably interlocked. Even the continents themselves gradually become one awesome reality— the unity of the human family—over six billion people struggling for peace, prosperity, and the fulfillment of their dreams. When we view this planet from the moon, we realize what an amazing reality it is.

Despite all that diversity, many of us manage to live fully within our own zip codes. We recognize the various forces that are swirling around us; we read about them in our daily newspapers or we see them on the evening news. And, for the most part, we are able to glide by, year after year, buoyed up by the stability that comes from the shared economic and social forces that we have in common with those living immediately around us. The span of today's global community, however, is changing all our lives.

Joseph Nisari is a living example of both a unified local culture and an extraordinary internationalism. He was born a poor boy in a remote Pakistani village. Along with his family, Joseph suffered great discrimination because of his faith. Yet he had the vision and courage to secure an education in the face of overwhelming odds, and would go on to live the life of a Catholic priest, able to function in both the East and the West; a poor Pakistani village boy whose talents would be needed in many far-flung ministries, including Kings County Hospital and Kingsboro Psychiatric Center in Brooklyn, New York.

Eye on the Sparrow describes for us the remarkable journey of Father Joseph Nisari, Pakistani priest. It is an amazing story and one that is being repeated more and more in today's globalized world.

Joseph was born in 1942 in a small village in the province of Punjab, in what was, at that time, still India. Both his parents were adult converts and strongly committed to their new faith. Joseph was profoundly moved by the example and deep faith of both his mother and father.

At the age of seventeen, Joseph left home to attend St. Mary's Minor Seminary in Lahore. It was August 1959, twelve years after the Partition of India and the catastrophic agony that accompanied that process of establishing freedom from colonial rule. Ordained at the age of twenty-five, Joseph threw himself into the very difficult work of being a young priest who, while assigned only one parish, would be responsible for more than a hundred villages. Joseph's bishop was impressed with both his zeal and his talent, and would send him on to the Philippines for advanced studies. Later, Joseph would find himself a professor at the seminary, then off again for additional studies in Rome.

In 1997, when Father Joseph was fifty-five years old, the always-difficult situation for the Christians in Pakistan began to worsen. Anti-Christian mobs erupted around the nation, burning churches, destroying houses, and imprisoning Christians who were accused of the crime of blasphemy against Allah and his prophet, Muhammad. Joseph had already had a difficult life, born and raised in poverty, attending school after school in different parts of the world. He now found himself in a situation where he could be risking his life. Despite his difficulties, Joseph recognized that he also had certain blessings, and felt a responsibility to use those blessings for the Church and for the world.

Father Joseph got on the phone and reached out to his old friend, Father Oliver Weerakkody, with whom he had worked very successfully in a number of different situations in Pakistan. Father Oliver was, at that time, serving as a hospital chaplain in the Diocese of Austin, Texas. Knowing the need for priests in the rapidly growing area of Central Texas, Father Oliver wasted no time in inviting Joseph to cut his losses in Asia and come to the strange and wonderful world of Texas. Father Joseph responded positively and soon found himself in the office of John McCarthy, who was then Bishop of Austin. That was the beginning of the next chapter in the odyssey of this bright, determined, generous, and faith-filled son of Pakistan.

Father Joseph served in the Diocese of Austin for most of the next twelve years—years that were a real blessing for Joseph and, in a most special way, for the Catholics in Central Texas who benefited from his spirituality and loving concern for all those around him.

Now, approaching seventy years of age, Joseph continues to serve his Lord through his ministry at St. Cyril and Methodius Church in Granger, Texas. His professional background in counseling and social work have been great assets in his service as a parish priest in a number of different assignments. In these assignments, many of the people he served were initially taken aback: Who was this man from the other side of the world? Was he actually a priest? Could he really help them cope with their problems? These transitions were not without their difficulties, and each one required some adjustment, but Joseph never gave up. He pushed on, listening, wondering, praying, and giving of himself—as he continues to do today.

Joseph Nisari's life is a testimony to so much of the good of the late twentieth century and its openness to new situations, new realities, and a new way of being. Educated on three continents, serving effectively in multiple cultures, and struggling to understand his life and ministry for the mystery that it is, Father Joseph has truly been a success . . . and that success has been a great blessing for the rest of us.

—Bishop John McCarthy
Bishop Emeritus of Austin, Texas
September 2010

PREFACE

People need to see that, far from being an obstacle, the world's diversity of languages, religions, and traditions is a great treasure affording us precious opportunities to recognize ourselves in others.

—Youssou N'Dour

In October 2005, I received a phone call from a lady who introduced herself as Rosemary Colgrove. "Father, you don't know me, but you know my daughter, Shelly Martinka." Of course I knew Shelly, I replied. She had two children in our Catholic school and was a member of our school board.

But Rosemary didn't call to talk about Shelly. Instead, she told me that she had seen an article in the local newspaper about me. "I believe you have a story to tell," she said. "I am a journalist, and I would like to tell your story."

I wasn't at all sure that my story was worth the telling. Nevertheless, we began meeting weekly—Rosemary asking the questions, so many questions—and I, telling my story about a life filled with challenges, a life shaped, prodded, and guided by the Holy Spirit. And yet, in spite of all my faults and weaknesses, God has never abandoned me; rather, he has blessed me most abundantly—and continues to do so today.

And so then, this is my story.

—Father Joseph Nisari
Pastor, St. Cyril & Methodius Church
Granger, Texas
September 2010

AUTHOR'S NOTE

In January of 2009, I sat on a dark wooden pew listening to Father Joseph preach his homily. His was the only dark face amid a sea of white ones in the century-old church, and I couldn't help thinking about how far he had traveled to reach this place and time.

Eye on the Sparrow chronicles the extraordinary journey of Sadiq, a young Indian-born boy who overcame poverty, discrimination, and horrific historical events to become Father Joseph Nisari, one of the first indigenous Catholic priests in Pakistan.

Only five years older than his country, Father Joseph's life closely parallels the growing pains and difficulties of his young country. After his ordination in 1968, Father Joseph began his ministry in the remote villages of the Punjab, ministering to a largely impoverished, illiterate population— one that had no rights, let alone privileges or benefits. These were his people, voiceless people who faced daily injustices and discrimination.

Joseph embraced his mission of helping his people to better their lives through faith and education, ultimately earning a master's degree in social work from Fordham University, after which he spent eight years serving New York City's most wretched at Kings County Hospital and Kingsboro Psychiatric Center.

Joseph was working in Pakistan in 2001 when the terrorist attacks on the World Trade Center took place on 9/11. In the months after the attack, Father Joseph felt his mission was to remain in Pakistan, but too much had changed; his country was in turmoil, and his message was often misunderstood. He came to feel that the home of his birth was no longer his spiritual home, and he was forced to make a decision that would change his life forever.

Today, as Western governments struggle to balance democratic ideals with religious extremism, Father Joseph's story offers a compelling message of faith and hope in the face of terrorism and ignorance. He continues his mission today, ministering to the faithful in the little community of Granger, rich in its faith and heritage, and through "Missionaries of Hope," a project especially dear to his heart, which is providing education and health care to some of Pakistan's poorest children.

The experiences, perspectives, and views presented in this book are largely those of Father Joseph. Some events and timelines have been compressed or otherwise rearranged in order to better clarify the story. Any errors in fact, omission, or presentation are mine.

I am sincerely grateful to Father Joseph for his candor in sharing his experiences, and hope that his story will serve to increase insight and broaden understanding of cultures and issues.

—Rosemary Colgrove
Georgetown, Texas
September 2010

PROLOGUE
A Historical Perspective

India is the cradle of the human race, the birthplace of human speech, the mother of history, the grandmother of legend, and the great grand mother of tradition. Our most valuable and most instructive materials in the history of man are treasured up in India only!

—Mark Twain

The Islamic Republic of Pakistan is the sixth most populous country in the world and the second most populous Muslim nation. Pakistan is also a declared nuclear weapons state. But it was not until 1947 that Pakistan acquired nationhood during the infamous partition of India, which split the subcontinent into two independent nations, Pakistan (with a Muslim majority) and India (with a Hindu majority).

The recent actions of the Taliban and al Qaeda, as well as the potential threat of al Queda-controlled nuclear weapons have focused the attention of the international community on Pakistan, but most Westerners know little about the country, outside of media images of Islamic fanaticism and sectarian violence.

Located in the western part of the Indian subcontinent, present-day Pakistan is slightly less than twice the size of the US state of California. The country is bordered by Afghanistan and Iran to the west, India to the east, the People's Republic of China in the far northeast, and by a 650-mile coastline along the Arabian Sea in the south.

Endowed with spectacular landscapes, some of the world's greatest architectural monuments, and a rich history that predates most Western civilizations, Pakistan would truly surprise those unfamiliar with it. From the magnificent Himalayan, Karakoram, and Hindu Kush mountain ranges in the north, to the fertile plains of the Punjab, the desolate mountains of Balochistan, the sun-scorched deserts of Sindh, and the miles of golden beaches along the Arabian Sea, Pakistan offers a remarkable variety of climates and landscapes.

The Karakoram mountain range, which borders Pakistan and China, claims more than sixty peaks above 22,960 feet, among them K2, the second highest mountain in the world. And the next time you plan a ski trip, think Pakistan. The country offers impressive ski resorts and more glaciers than any other land outside the polar regions.

The people of Pakistan are some of the most generous and hospitable in the world, welcoming visitors into their homes with no expectation other than friendship.

More than 4,000 years ago, about the time the civilizations of Mesopotamia, Egypt, and Greece were flourishing, the people of the Indus Valley Civilization developed a remarkably advanced society that encompassed much of the modern-day Pakistan provinces of Sindh, Punjab, and Balochistan, building great walled cities with sophisticated sanitation and drainage systems—even flush toilets—that were centuries ahead of their time. Archaeological evidence at Harappa (southern Punjab) and Moenjodaro (Sindh) indicate that a highly developed urban settlement thrived in the area about 2,600 years before Christ.

Around 800 BC, the Indian mathematician Baudhayana produced his version of the Pythagorean theorem. Several centuries later, the Greek and Hindu scholar and mathematician Pingala (400 BC) developed the binary number system, which would become the basis of modern computer science 2,400 years later.

Three hundred years before Christ, Alexander the Great pushed through the Khyber Pass and sailed down the Indus to the Arabian Sea, meeting up with Rajah Porus and his army of 30,000 men, 2,000 cavalry, and 200 war elephants along the way to conquer what is now Pakistan's Punjab province. With his one dark eye and one blue eye, Alexander is said to have known Homer's *Iliad* by heart and slept with a copy under his pillow.

While Europe drowsed through the Dark Ages, Indian and

Islamic cultures were producing astronomers, scholars, poets, and mathematicians, whose pioneering philosophies would help shape our modern world. Chess was reportedly invented in the area known as Pakistan, and algebra and astronomy were studied in the region. Bhaskara, a seventh-century Indian mathematician, was perhaps the first to write numbers in the Hindu-Arabic numeral system using a circle for the zero, providing the foundation of modern mathematics. Albert Einstein once said, "We owe a lot to the Indians, who taught us how to count, without which no worthwhile scientific discovery could have been made." In addition to these contributions, many words in our modern lexicon, including *calico, apricot, artichoke, orange, rice, chintz,* and *shampoo,* trace their origins to the Indian subcontinent.

In the thirteenth century, Genghis Khan and his Mongolian hordes rode out of the treeless Asian steppes to conquer more than half of the known world. At one time, the Mongolian Empire was the largest contiguous empire in history, extending from the Pacific Ocean to the Caspian Sea.

The Mughal (an Indian spelling of Mongol) Empire (1526–1757) was one of the world's most glorious dynasties, creating splendid monuments, inspiring works of art, and magnificent architecture. They also developed an early version of a mail system and enjoyed the use of innovative technologies such as printing, the compass, and the abacus. For more than two centuries they ruled this dazzling empire until they were displaced by the British Raj, who would change the subcontinent forever.

Indeed, sixteenth-century India was a vast and amazing place. The 100 million people who lived under the patronage of the Mughal emperors were sophisticated, prosperous, and culturally diverse at a time when England was a relatively undeveloped nation, burdened by poverty and political and religious dissention.

In her book *Indian Summer: The Secret History of the End of an Empire,* Alex von Tunzelmann noted that, in 1577, the average

Indian peasant benefited from higher earnings and lower taxes than his successors ever would again.

Enlightened leaders like Jalauddin Mohammad Akbar, better known as Akbar the Great, advanced the cause of religious tolerance and democratic ideals, creating artistic, architectural, and literary masterpieces that still entertain, educate, and seduce us today. Widely considered the greatest of the Mughal rulers, Akbar ruled more than 100 million people during a time when the population of India was about 140 million and Western Europe only about forty million.

Some historians claim that Akbar possessed, for a short time, the celebrated Koh-i-Noor diamond, an immense stone weighing 186 carats (almost twice its present size). Over the centuries, the diamond was the property of various Indian and Persian rulers, and was eventually seized by the British as a spoil of war, ultimately becoming part of British Crown Jewels.

In 1648, another Mughal emperor, Shah Jahan, was completing work on what would become one of the Seven Wonders of the World, the Taj Mahal, the stunning white marble tomb he created as a memorial to his favorite and much-loved wife. And while Jahan was engaged in building his monuments, half a world away in the New England colonies, the midwife Margaret Jones was hanged for witchcraft from an elm tree in Boston.

The Raj

Arriving as traders in the Indian subcontinent in the early seventeenth century, the British would rule India for more than 150 years. In the process, they would transform the country, its culture, and its institutions, and it would not all be advantageous to India. Motivated by a confidence in their presumed moral and intellectual superiority, the British assumed it was their "duty" to reform and modernize India.

In time, the success that defined British rule in India would also be its downfall. The superior British attitude, along with their ignorance of—even contempt for—Indian customs, language, and traditions, greatly antagonized the Indian people, ultimately bringing about the collapse of British rule in the subcontinent.

Although the British introduced democracy, established a legal system, and made monumental improvements to agriculture and infrastructure, constructing schools, universities, hospitals, roads, irrigation systems, and more than 20,000 miles of railways, they did little to help India attain economic independence or preserve its multi-cultural traditions.

The British would rule India until August 1947, when the catastrophe that was partition carved up the subcontinent into two independent nations, the Republic of India (with a Hindu majority), and Pakistan (with a Muslim majority).

The Christians

Theologians seem to agree that it was the Apostle Thomas who first introduced Christianity to the Indian subcontinent around 50 AD, less than two decades after Christ's death. Early Catholic missionary efforts were organized by the Portuguese Jesuit, Saint Francis Xavier (1506–52), who is considered one of the greatest evangelists since the time of the Apostles. His remarkably preserved body is still on public view today, enshrined in a glass coffin at the Basilica of Bom Jesus, a World Heritage Monument in Goa. Although the presence of Jesuit missionaries in the court of Mughal emperors in Lahore is reported in the sixteenth and seventeenth centuries, the work of evangelization among local populations did not begin until 1889.

The Caste System

For centuries, Hindus have been born into the caste system, one of world's oldest surviving forms of social apartheid. Indian society has been defined by the caste system—which presumes that all men are not created equal—for more than 1,700 years.

There are four main castes. At the top of the social order are the brahmins (traditionally priests and scholars), followed by the kshatriyas (rulers and warriors), and the vaisyas (merchants, farmers). Laborers and domestic servants belong to the lowest caste, the shudras.

Beneath all of these were the darker-skinned "untouchables," who were not part of a caste at all, so called because if they touched someone from another caste, that person would become "contaminated." They were the outcasts, the poorest of the poor, the ones who would spend their lives performing the most odious tasks: sweeping, cleaning latrines and sewers, and disposing of the dead.

Caste was inherited at birth and determined a person's occupation, spouse, and most other aspects of life. To Indians, it was the "natural" order of things, and there was little one could do to change it.

Considered too unclean to be valued beings, untouchables were rejected, scorned, and banned from temples, schools, and many public places, denied access to wells used by the higher castes, and forced to eat and drink from separate utensils in public places. And if at any time an untouchable dared to use the utensils reserved for other castes and was found out, the utensils that he or she had used would be destroyed forthwith, and the cost charged to the violator.

* * *

Christian missionaries found abundant opportunities for conversions among the Dalits (a more politically correct term for untouchables), trapped as they were in an inescapable cycle of poverty, misery, and oppression. For the untouchables, conversion was an escape, a way out of their societal prisons. The church offered community, equality, and a place in a larger society. There was no caste; they were now the brothers and sisters of all other Christians. Converts found identity and relationship: in Christianity, they belonged somewhere. The churches also attracted the impoverished with offers of food and clothing, as well as the possibility of an education for their children. Thus, religious conversions of the time were often temporal as well as spiritual.

In the late nineteenth century, Catholic priests, primarily Belgian Capuchin Franciscans, dominated the Catholic missionary effort in India. They were apparently a resilient bunch and did not seem to mind walking (or cycling) under a scorching Indian sun or through drenching monsoon rains to minister to the faithful.

Some of the most enduring legacies of the British Raj are the renowned educational institutions established by the missionaries, including Gordon College in Rawalpindi, Kinnaird College for Women in Lahore, Forman Christian College in Lahore (alma mater of General Pervez Musharraf, the twelfth president of Pakistan), and Murray College in Sialkot, all of which continue to operate today.

There are currently two Catholic seminaries in Pakistan (Lahore and Karachi) and approximately one million Catholics (as of 2010), less than 1 percent of the total population. The first Pakistani Catholic bishop, Father John Joseph, was ordained in 1960, and appointed bishop in 1984. Joseph Cordeiro, Archbishop of Karachi, became the first (and thus far only) Pakistani cardinal in 1973. And, for the first time in the nation's history, Shahbaz Bhatti, a Catholic member of parliament, became the Federal Minister for Minorities in 2008.

CHAPTER 1

The Substitute Bride

*Even as thou seeketh a virtuous, fair, and good spouse . . .
it is fitting that thou should be the same.*

—St. Bernardino of Siena

In the 1920s, most marriages in India were arranged marriages, and they had little to do with love or affection, but rather a lot to do with cooking, commitment, and procreation. Marriages generally happened between boys and girls from different villages, and the couple customarily met for the first time only after exchanging their vows.

And so, when it came time for Barkat, a young Indian boy from the Punjabi plains, to tie the knot, his parents found him a suitable bride, negotiated a dowry, and arranged for the wedding ceremony. But Barkat's wedding would not turn out at all like anyone expected.

On the appointed day, Barkat set off on foot for the village of Pajian, the bride's home, accompanied by an entourage of relatives, friends, and a group of local musicians banging on drums and blowing on flutes. Barkat's father was a contractor who cleared the forests. With about one hundred men in his employ, it was presumed that he was a wealthy man, and there may have been as many as one hundred men and women traveling with him in the *baraat* (marriage procession).

When the group arrived in Pajian, the groom was already kitted out in his wedding clothes and *sehra*, a sort of turban with garlands hanging down that covered his face. The villagers, sensing the prospect of a celebration and a welcome diversion from their mundane lives, quickly joined the party. Coins were tossed out for the children to collect—the greater the number of coins, the more impressive the groom was thought to be. Amid much pomp and fanfare, everyone followed the groom to the bride's house, where the wedding party was welcomed with flower garlands and glasses of lassi and sweet creamy tea. The father of the groom and the father of the bride exchanged small gifts, usually cloth or a turban, and then the uncles and elder brothers met and embraced, playfully jostling each other in a feigned attempt to test each other's strength.

Shortly thereafter, the bride's mother went to summon her daughter, the bride-to-be. After some moments had passed, she returned, horrified. "There is no bride," she murmured, acutely embarrassed. "We beg your pardon. We don't know what to say, our daughter is gone."

Naturally, word went out almost immediately, and came to the ears of Bulanda, who was a friend of both families. Right away, he said to Barkat's father, "Dilawar, it would be a disgrace for your son to go home without a bride and I will not let that happen. It is a question of the honor of the whole village. So, let us become relatives. I am going to give you my daughter, Mariam, as a wife for your son."

Few people knew what had actually happened, but there was great curiosity in the village over what could be taking so long. The disappearance of the intended bride—she had eloped with someone else—was, of course, extremely humiliating for her family, but the shame was somewhat mitigated by Bulanda's generous offer of a substitute bride.

The bride's wedding outfit was traditionally a gift from the groom, so whatever clothes Barkat had brought for his bride were quickly taken to Mariam, who, only a few minutes before, had been looking forward to a wedding ceremony, never dreaming it would be her own.

Dressed in her wedding finery—a simple shalwar kameez, colorful dupatta, and heavy veil covering her face—the poor girl (there is no record of whether or not she was pleased by this sudden turn of events) was whisked away to a house that had been prepared for the ceremony. Afterward, the newly wedded couple returned to the bride's house, where one of the bride's relatives removed the groom's sehra. The bride's veil was lifted, and the couple saw each other's faces for the first time.

It was the custom for the wedding party to spend the night of the wedding at the bride's house, sleeping outside in the courtyard if the weather permitted. In the morning after breakfast, the groom's relatives would accompany the bridal couple to their new home, which was, of course, the groom's family home. In those days, most boys remained with their parents all their lives, and were expected to care for them in old age. The parting was often an emotional occasion for the bride and her family as she said farewell to her parents and siblings and left the only home she had ever known.

Mariam was transported to her new husband's village in a doli, a sort of palanquin supported by bamboo poles and carried by four men. The groom walked behind. Mariam's youngest sister, five-year-old Alhlakhi, had insisted on accompanying her big sister to the groom's house, so when no one was looking, she crept inside the doli. (During the journey, the men had commented on the weight of the doli, thinking the bride must indeed be a bit on the plumpish side.)

When the procession reached the groom's house about five miles away, everyone gathered around to get a look at the bride. It was a curtained doli, and the first thing the curious villagers saw peeking out from behind the covering was a tiny girl with a big tongue, which was stuck out at the crowd. The little girl then made a face and quickly tucked her head inside, an action that amazed and stunned the crowd until they realized that this was not the bride.

And so the two young people, who would in due course produce ten children (one of whom would become Father Joseph), began their life together, full of promise and portent.

CHAPTER 2

Sadiq

Before I formed you in the womb I knew you, and before you were born I consecrated you; I have appointed you a prophet to the nations.

—Jeremiah 1:5

When Sadiq was born on August 6, 1942, in the village of Pajian, in the province of Punjab, in the nation of India, the country of Pakistan did not even exist. As World War II raged in Europe and the British plotted the future of the subcontinent, the little village remained an oasis of peace and serenity, unaffected by time and world events. But in just five short years, all that would change. The tiny baby born in the little mud-walled house and laid beside his mother on the narrow rope bed that steamy August night would see changes in his country no one could have imagined.

Sadiq was the seventh of ten children born to dark-skinned, first-generation Indian/Sikh Christians. His father, Babu Barkat, was a catechist, his mother, Mariam, an illiterate homemaker. Born into the poverty of the ancient Hindu caste system, Babu Barkat and Mariam had come into the world with nothing more than a resilient spirit and a rich heritage. Baptized as adults, they embraced their new faith as surely as if they had been personally anointed by God.

At birth, he was named Sadiq, which means truth or righteous one. The name was derived from Melchizedek, the biblical priest-king of ancient Jerusalem, but the little toffee-eyed baby was not a king, nor would he be particularly righteous.

On the second day of his life, Sadiq was baptized in the name of the Father, the Son, and the Holy Ghost, taking the name Joseph as his baptism name. Since he was a catechist by profession, Sadiq's father had acquired the title of "Babu," which implied respect, and he was addressed by all who knew him as Babu Barkat (his friends would call him Babu-ji).

As a little boy, Sadiq was impressed by how much people loved his father, a gentle, devout man with a leathery face, a wide bristle of mustache, smiling eyes, and a large white turban, a mark of respectability rather than religious or tribal affiliation.

A Catholic convert with only a fourth-grade education, Babu Barkat managed well enough to read and write the countless records and reports required by his position as a catechist. Blessed with a rich mind and keen curiosity, Babu was a charismatic preacher and gifted storyteller who could hold a crowd spellbound, sometimes for hours. He could recite a Bible verse for every letter of the alphabet and had an amazing stash of anecdotes and folklore always ready for the telling. Once, when he was about to perform a marriage, he noticed the groom's party waiting idly for the meal to begin. Never one to miss an opportunity, Babu chided them gently, "Let's not waste our time. In the Bible, there is this gospel story about . . ." Often his beautiful stories would so captivate the audience that they would forget to eat. A counselor and a therapist of some repute, he could often be found sitting on the ground in the shade, listening to the problems of his people and imparting practical and prudent advice.

In the whole village, only Babu Barkat and a few others could read and write, which gave him a certain cachet among his peers. Illiterate villagers often came to him to get written receipts for their transactions. If a man was taking his animals from one place to another, the authorities might require some written proof that he was the rightful owner (and the animals therefore not stolen). Babu Barkat willingly offered his notary services wherever they were needed.

The gentle catechist put his faith before all else, traveling around the villages of his *ilaqa* (the territory assigned to the catechist) on a creaky old bicycle with a grain sack tied to the rusty rack, rosary in his hand, composing poems and songs as he traveled the countryside. He measured distances by the number of rosaries that could be said en route, as in, "Rangilpur is about five rosaries away."

Sadiq's brother Peter remembered his father as a man who taught not only religion, but also the social and moral values of life. "He worked as a mediator between the missionary priests and the impoverished, illiterate villagers, believing that he was responsible for their welfare. All his life, he worked to raise their living standard, convinced that the solution to their desperate poverty was education."

Sadiq's mother was called Baji Mariam or just mama-ji. A soft-spoken and intelligent woman, she was a sister to all in the village—Hindus, Sikhs, Muslims, and Christians alike. Whenever she went shopping in the bazaar, shopkeepers would greet her: "Welcome Sister, *salaam alaikum,* the peace of God be with you. Come and buy something from us and our business will be good all day." She was a kind of good luck charm for them.

Mariam may have been illiterate, but she was self-taught and well-grounded in intuition and common sense. She had a special talent for diffusing problems with a kind word, a bit of advice, or a small instruction. If a young girl was about to be married, Mariam would counsel her as to what was expected when she left home and went to live with her husband's family. If a husband and wife had an abusive relationship, she would let them know there were better ways to deal with their problems. "Don't start complaining as soon as your husband comes home. You will not like the consequences. He will pick up a stick and beat your neighbor or whoever is causing the trouble. Give him a good meal first, then tell him the problems of the day." She believed that if a wife was being mistreated, it was the wife's fault. Her advice may have been naïve but it made people think, and perhaps brought a measure of harmony where there was little.

Wise in the ways of village medicine, Mariam freely dispensed homegrown remedies and midwifery services to anyone who needed them. Doctors and hospitals were beyond the reach of most people in the villages, so the local women often came to Mariam with their complaints, receiving comfort—even cures—from her special herbs and home-spun treatments.

While Babu Barkat was his children's rock and inspiration, Mariam was their teacher and moral compass. When Babu was away tending his flock, Mariam taught her children religion, etiquette, and social proprieties. At home they spoke Punjabi, but Mariam also understood Urdu, the national language. And when the children worked on their school lessons, she would stop them if they made an error and make them correct the problem. Amazingly, she could solve math problems in her head, up through third-grade level.

When Mariam was a child, there were no schools in the small villages, and the missionaries often encouraged children to go away to boarding schools, sometimes even providing financial support for them to do so. Mariam dreamed of going to school and was eventually accepted at St. Joseph's in Lahore. But on the morning she was supposed to leave, while she was still sleeping, her older brother came to her bed with a machete in hand. "If you go to school, I will kill you," he threatened. And he meant it.

Her brother's reaction was not unusual at the time, fueled more by tradition and custom than any animosity toward her. It was a patriarchal society; women were viewed more as property than partners. An educated girl would have been a shameful thing, having gone into the world and been exposed to society—and other men. Girls typically left home when they married and went to live with their husband's family, so why spend so much money on education when the family would not benefit from it? Girls were meant to be mothers and remain in the home; all they really needed to know was how to cook, sew, and care for the children. And even if they did go to school, they could never aspire to be anything more than domestic chattel.

Even today, Pakistani women remain largely subordinate to men, primarily responsible for preserving the family's honor. And to make sure they do not disgrace their families, society restricts their activities and closely monitors their behavior. In the past fifty years, however, there have been dramatic changes in this dynamic. At least seventy percent of Pakistani girls now attend school. Yet, in many of the remote villages, girls still don't have a chance.

* * *

The early Belgian missionaries, who did not know the villages, the people, or the language, depended on the local catechists to help in educating the converts in their new religion. Indigenous lay people, mostly fathers of families, the catechists were the backbone of the Catholic Church in India (and later Pakistan). Taken into service as salaried employees, they were the ones who propagated the faith, maintained the records, and prepared the people to receive the sacraments. When necessary, they even assumed the duties of the priest, performing marriages, baptizing the faithful, and officiating at funerals.

There were no specific standards for catechists; if you were honest, married, literate, and could pray, you qualified. The priest would train the catechist in his specific duties and the especially gifted would even preach on behalf of the priest. Later on, most missionaries learned Punjabi and became quite good at it. Eventually, a catechist school was established and the standards were raised to include a high school education.

Gender taboos of the day required that all catechists be married. Most of the time, the men were away in the fields, and the women and children of the village were the ones who received the catechist. It would have been inappropriate for the women to be in the company of an unmarried man (who might also be looking for a wife). If the catechist stayed the night in the village, he would meet with the men in the evening when they returned from work.

Babu Barkat had a very large *ilaqa* (the catechist's assigned territory), with more than thirty villages, which he tried to visit at least once a month. He knew every family and kept track of all the marriages, deaths, first confessions and first communions (often for more than one hundred children per year). It was a daunting task for which he was paid the princely sum of one US dollar per month. To supplement his wages, fruit, vegetables, rice, and the occasional chicken also served as currency.

The missionary priests visited the ilaqas of their parishes as often as possible, frequently covering five villages in one day. But there were many ilaqas in a parish, so most villages only saw a priest once or twice a year. Most missionaries traveled by bicycle or motorcycle, but some used a camel cart or horse-drawn tonga. In the diocese of Lahore, a priest can still apply for a camel cart today.

The arrival of the priest was always a joyous occasion. Having been informed that he was coming, the people would sweep the roads and courtyards and hang palm branches to welcome him. The faithful would gather at someone's home, or at a chapel if the village had one. While the priest heard confessions, the catechist would lead the rosary. Afterward, the priest would celebrate Holy Mass and baptize the newly minted Christians. There was no electricity, no fancy vestments, no incense, and no choirs, but the little mud-walled house would be filled with God's presence and much joyous singing.

CHAPTER 3

Village Life

Come forth into the light of things, let nature be your teacher.

—William Wordsworth

A great sweeping plain about the size of Colorado, the Punjab straddles the border between India and Pakistan, stretching north from the province of Sindh to the lush foothills of the Himalayas. Once a bleak, arid desert, the region is now fertile farmland due to extensive irrigation provided by a large river system and the vast network of irrigation canals constructed under British rule.

Rising high in the Tibetan Himalayas, the Indus River flows 1,800 miles south through the broad Punjab plain to the Arabian Sea. Five rivers—the Beas (Indian Punjab only), Jhelum, Chenab, Ravi, and Sutluj, all tributaries of the Indus—give the Punjab its name, "Land of Five Rivers" (*punj* meaning "five" and *aab* meaning "water").

Babu Barkat lived with his large family in a small one-room, mud-brick house in the village of Sunder, in Punjab province, only twenty miles from Lahore, but a million miles from the rest of the world. The family shared their small but comfortable world with one dog, dozens of chickens and ducks, a few goats, and a water buffalo.

Perched on top of a hill born over the centuries by the flow of the Ravi River, Sunder was home to about five hundred families with an ancient Indian past (and a soon-to-be Islamic future). Hindus, Sikhs, Muslims, and a few Christians lived in the cluster of blocky, buff-colored houses with walled courtyards that lined the dusty road that fronted the village.

A dirt road ran beside the river and if the river was not in flood, a person could walk along the road and see the caves carved by the water over the centuries. Along the other side of the road, a canal ran for miles, irrigating the fields, which were the property of a few rich landowners. The villagers provided the labor pool.

Among its businesses, the village counted a tailor, blacksmith, cobbler, barber, carpenter, and several shopkeepers. It was a cashless economy, a sort of barter system—few rupees were ever exchanged. The merchants received their compensation in grain, chickens, vegetables, or rice, mostly paid when the crops were harvested.

Sadiq's uncles were businessmen of a sort, buying cattle, feeding them for several months, and then, they hoped, selling them for a profit. If a cow was weak or undernourished, they could buy it cheap, and if the cow cooperated, sell it for double the original price. There were no markets and if someone in the village slaughtered a cow or a water buffalo, it would be offered to the villagers on a first-come, first-served basis. People would take their pots and go wherever the slaughtered animal was, buying a kilo or whatever they could afford for a few rupees or bartered produce.

The area around the village was flat agricultural land plotted into fields of cotton, sugarcane, wheat, and rice. Goats, oxen, sheep, and water buffalo foraged the pastures; most prized was the water buffalo, which, in addition to the labor it provided, produced meat and milk, as well as dung for fuel and fertilizer. Farm tools were rudimentary and hand-made. Bullocks pulled the wooden plows that gouged, but did not turn, the earth. There were no fences; the livestock and their young tenders wandered freely over the countryside.

The village lived according to the rhythms of nature. At mid-day, when the sun was high, the men would seek refuge from the punishing heat under leafy peepul trees. Young boys led their water buffalos into the canal to cool down, their splayed hooves preventing the animals from sinking into the mud. Women rested in whatever shade they could find, rubbing *ghee* into each other's hair and chatting about village life. In the distance, the melodious creaking of the Persian well and the playful *tuk-tuk* of the Coppersmith birds accompanied the passing hours.

Sunder had four well-defined seasons. The village was dusty brown most of the year apart from the growing season, during which all was lush, the fields verdant. Spring arrived in early February and lasted until mid-April, followed by the hot dry months of summer. During the dry season, the sun rose early and simmered all day, drying up rivers, wells, and vegetation, sucking the life from the land.

The summer drought was broken abruptly in August or September when the monsoon season arrived with its torrential but beneficial rains. After a few days, the earth became mud, the rivers ran, and roads and railway tracks became impassable. Overnight, the landscape turned green and the trees sprouted new leaves. By the end of September, the days began to cool down from the summer highs of 120 degrees, and by December, frost was on the ground and a strong, cold wind blew down from the pine-covered slopes of the Murree Hills.

Topped by a white wooden cross, Sadiq's house was mission center, sitting between the Muslim enclave with its four hundred families, and the Christian enclave, with about thirty families. The Muslims lived on the "better" side of town; the Christians near the Hindu graveyard, where the bodies were burned. There were two houses in the small compound where Sadiq lived, both of which belonged to the Christian landlord, a laborer who worked the fields of a Muslim farm. The landlord lived in one, Sadiq's family in the other, rent-free, a catechist's perk. A four-foot-high mud wall enclosed the compound, and stubby steps crawled up the outside of the house to the flat roof.

Building materials—dung, mud, and straw—were plentiful and durable. The bare-earth floors of the mud houses were plastered over with a mixture of mud and dung that dried to an exceedingly hard surface that was easy to sweep clean. But mud was prone to melting in heavy rain, so the houses were particularly vulnerable during flood seasons. Every year, before and after the rainy season, the roofs would be re-plastered with the dung/mud mix.

The faithful from Babu Barkat's large ilaqa visited often for prayer services, counseling, and socializing. Whenever travelers stopped to ask how to get to such-and-such place, Babu would reply, "Come, sit down and relax. When the sun goes down and it is cooler, my son will take you there."

An excellent cook, Mariam never tired of hosting the family's many visitors, treating their guests generously even though their hospitality often exhausted their own supply of provisions. There was always a cup of tea, a sweet cake, or a meal ready, and if it got too late and the visitors could not go home, the family would accommodate them for the night. Their door was always open, and as is typical the world over, the poorer the people, the greater the hospitality.

The sun-baked courtyard served as the family's living area during clement weather, shared with their animals—goats, chickens, a buffalo, and always the lizards, which earned their residency by eating the mosquitoes. During good weather, the courtyard also served as a cooking area and a dung-fueled cook fire burned all day. A peepul tree and several large kikars grew in the courtyard; some believe that Jesus' crown of thorns was made from a branch of the prickly kikar.

The kikar tree was a most significant tree, a veritable cornucopia of domestic and medicinal supplies. The twigs made excellent toothbrushes, the leaves were useful in curing diarrhea, the foliage supplied food for livestock, the gum made a rather substantial glue, and the bark was reportedly useful in the treatment of eczema, snakebite, hair loss, earache, and sore throats. And in spring, the tree produced a lovely yellow blossom with a sweet fragrance.

Even without the cross on the top, it was easy to see that Babu Barkat's home was the home of a Christian family. Inside, the walls were adorned with sacred pictures and statues. There was little furniture except for the ubiquitous *charpoys* (four-legged bed frames strung with heavy jute) that were covered with quilts and arranged around the room. People sat on the charpoys, dined on them, and slept on them, as they had for hundreds of years. There was a kind of charpoy etiquette that required an honored guest or respected family member to sit at the head of the charpoy, while lesser guests and family members sat at the foot. When dining, several people would sit on the charpoy with a cloth spread before them, dipping bits of chapati into bowls of spicy curry or some other dish, their legs tucked beneath them. Exposing the soles of the feet was considered impolite.

Attached to the house was a separate room where Mariam cooked during inclement weather. The room had no sink and no stove—just a flat roof, four soot-blackened walls, and an open fire that, once started up in the morning, simmered all day.

Every day Mariam went to the Christian well (which was separate from the Muslim well) to draw the day's supply of water, carrying it home in an earthen jug on top of her head and a bucket in her hands. Women typically bathed by putting two charpoys next to each other and covering the top with a sheet for privacy. Sadiq's family, however, had the good fortune to have their own bathing area in the courtyard. It was a simple structure with five-foot mud walls and open at the top, the entrance covered with a sheet. Whenever you wanted to bathe, you brought a pail of water, some soap (if any was available), and a towel. Clothing hung over the wall signaled that the bath was occupied.

Alarm clocks did not exist, nor was there any need for them. In the villages, the people rose before the sun and had their own system of wake-up calls, reliably and unfailingly provided by nature. Before sunrise, the roosters would greet the new day, followed by the dogs, the goats, and the men leaving for the fields, who hoped to get as much work done as possible before the heat of the day. During the day, the hour was told by the animals' complaints, the position of the sun, and the length of one's shadow.

First up at dawn and last to bed at night, Mariam tended the children, the laundry, and the cook fire, making dung patties to fuel the little clay stove and then slapping them on the wall to dry in the sun. During the stifling summers when daytime temperatures hovered around 120 degrees, the family slept on the roof, or outside in the courtyard, lulled to sleep by the sounds of swooping bats, barking dogs, howling jackals, and the constant buzz of mosquitoes. To escape the bite of the insects, the villagers covered their faces and bodies with a sheet. There was no gate, no privacy, and no fear of wild animals or dangerous humans. The nearby fields or the graveyard served as an outdoor toilet. Always available, there were no plumbing problems, and the dead did not seem to mind.

When darkness fell, the kerosene lanterns cast long shadows on the holy faces in the pictures on the wall. In the cold of winter, Mariam would fill a heavy iron basin with old coals or burnt dung cakes that no longer smoked, and it would heat the whole room. Nights were warm under the heavy cotton quilts, and in the chilly mornings when they had to go outside to relieve themselves, they would wrap up in the warm quilts.

It was a simple world, one without electricity, plumbing, radio, television, or telephones, and where no one had ever heard of aspirin, insect repellant, sun screen, baby beds, or refrigeration.

About half a furlong from Babu Barkat's house was Babe-Sohne's well, an enchanting Persian-style contraption with buckets hanging off a vertical wheel that went up and down in the water. Bullocks provided the power source, plodding placidly in a circle with their eyes covered, seemingly unperturbed by the flies, the heat, or the frequent jabs by their minders. All were welcomed at Babe-Sohne's oasis, with its huge shade trees and cool refreshing water. The women came to escape the heat of the day, bringing small children to play while they washed their clothes and spread them on the grass to dry.

To Sadiq, the village was a tranquil, pleasant place altogether undisturbed by the harried distractions of modernity. Summers were long and hot, winters short and cold. Spring was green and beautiful with blooming fruit trees and blankets of wildflowers. In the evenings, shimmering clouds of dust announced the return of the shepherds bringing their sheep home, one leading the flock and the other following behind, softly playing a flute, its soothing melody floating through the dusk. The sheep seemed mesmerized by the flute, as was Sadiq. In fact, the music was so beautiful that Sadiq vowed to learn to play the flute. Because Babu Barkat was very strict and very conservative and the flute "a very romantic instrument," he strongly encouraged Sadiq to give it up, cautioning him that such action could only bring trouble; the flute was so enticing to women and girls. In spite of his father's counsel, Sadiq never lost his love for the flute and later on, the violin.

Very early in the morning when it was still dark, Babu Barkat and Mariam would wake their children and commit them to God's care, reminding them to begin the day with the sign of the cross, after which they greeted each other, "Good morning papa, good morning mama," and the same to all the brothers and sisters. Then everyone got up, washed, and until morning prayers were said, no one spoke. It was Babu-ji's "holy silence" (and the only time things were ever quiet in the household).

Joseph remembers the holy silence. "The only person who could break the silence was my father singing the beautiful verses of Psalm 121 in Punjabi: 'I lift up my eyes to the hills—from where will my help come? My help comes from the Lord, who made heaven and earth . . .'"

In the evening after the family had eaten, Babu Barkat would lead the family in the rosary and evening prayers. Sadiq knew all his prayers by the time he was three. Once when the priest was visiting, he asked Sadiq to make the sign of the cross. He did. Mariam said, "He also knows all his prayers." The priest did not quite believe this so Sadiq rattled them off, one by one, starting with the Our Father, all the way through the Hail Mary, Apostle's Creed, Act of Contrition, Ten Commandments, and Acts of Faith, Hope, and Charity, all recited by heart in Punjabi. It took several minutes. The priest was astonished.

God was a living presence in the house. The sign of the cross was made before each task and prayer applied to every aspect of their lives. There was nothing so insignificant that God could not be involved. Children were gifts from God and cherished above all else. Parental discipline was firm but filled with love and an abundance of laughter.

"It was a sparse life to be sure," Joseph recalls, "but it was more than enough. We did not know we were poor, and as children of a catechist, we were rich in the love of God and family, and better off than most. Our father always came home with his bicycle loaded with vegetables, rice, or grain, maybe a chicken or a few rupees that the villagers had given him. We did not inherit any material things, but since my earliest memory, my father's legacy was always the 'treasure of educating my children.' All my brothers and sisters had a high school education and most went on to college, found good jobs, and carried a wealth of knowledge and faith with them as they formed their own lives."

Sadiq and his siblings called their parents "papa" and "mama," or "papa-ji" and "mama-ji," -*ji* being a form of respect. *Papa* and *mama* were not Pakistani words, but a holdover from colonial influence and common among educated people. It was considered impolite to call older siblings by their names, so older sisters were called *bajian* and older brothers, *bhai*. Younger siblings were called by their proper names.

Enamored of the missionaries who came to the village on their big, noisy motorcycles, Sadiq would play at being a priest, using a stick as the motorcycle and chickpeas as communion wafers, ordering all the children to kneel and pray. He never forgot his fascination with the priests or with the motorbikes, which would bring him much pleasure—and much misery—later in life.

Sadiq and his friends had no real toys but their imaginations were fertile and inexhaustible. They ran barefoot and carefree through summer days and nights, caught insects, and sucked on watermelon, mangoes, and sugarcane stalks. On moonlit nights, they played hide-and-seek among the shadowy walls and trees and fought swordfights with powerful, spindly sticks. Sometimes they played *gulli-danda,* a game similar to cricket, or *khiddu,* a sort of hockey played with a rag ball and a stick. The national sport of Pakistan is hockey, although cricket, introduced by the British, is equally popular and played everywhere—wherever there is an available scrap of land—by children as well as adults.

Sadiq's sister Sabina remembers summers when all the children were home. "Because we were so many, we never lacked for playmates. My sister Maria had very long hair and once when we were playing outside, Maria's hair was flying about and she frightened the *subzi wallah's* [vegetable man's] donkey. The startled animal threw off his basket and ran away, leaving vegetables lying all over the ground. We gathered up the vegetables and put them back in the basket. Mother, of course, wanted to give them all back to the poor man, but he said, 'Take what you like, your children frightened my donkey and he has run away.' Mother did not reprimand us; instead she took a big bag of wheat and gave it to the man. She was not quite ready to admit that her children were responsible for his predicament, but she did not want him to leave without compensation."

In those days, a donkey or a bullock cart were the poor man's transportation, and in summer the dust churned up by the cart wheels settled everywhere—inside houses, on animals, on clothes drying on the ground, and in eyes, noses, and throats. Those with more resources had bicycles, which were not cheap; children never used bicycles for play.

When Sadiq was about nine, he decided he wanted to learn to ride a bike. One afternoon, Babu Barkat afforded him the opportunity on his own wobbly machine. "Push when your feet touch the pedals and you will go," he said to the eager young boy. But before his feet could touch anything, he was going. And he had no idea how to stop. That part of the lesson would involve hitting a tree. The thrill of this new skill was somewhat diminished when Babu, happy to have some help, asked Sadiq to go to a neighboring village and bring back several large sacks of grain on the bicycle.

Sometimes the family shared in local Hindu festivals, but they did not celebrate birthdays or any holidays other than Easter and Christmas. Sadiq never experienced a birthday party, never had a cake or gifts, no piñatas, balloons, or clowns. But his mother always remembered his special day and would make his favorite, rice pudding, which he also got whenever he was sick. According to Mariam, the pudding had medicinal properties.

Mariam was a culinary miracle worker, transforming ordinary food into delicious meals through the magic of kitchen alchemy and her special spices. In her courtyard kitchen, Mariam would squat on her heels tending the cook fire, maintaining the position for long periods of time as if she had no joints in her legs.

The staple of the Pakistani diet was (and still is) *chapatis,* a flat, unleavened bread made with whole-wheat flour and fried in a pan like a tortilla or pancake. Chapatis were especially tasty when spread with ghee and used to scoop up a spicy curry or stew. Spices are the heart and soul of Pakistani cooking. A generous combination of coriander, chilies, turmeric, gingery cardamom, or whatever was available added zest to otherwise bland food. Grains such as wheat and rice were everyday foods, along with vegetables; lentils were the poor man's meat.

A typical meal would include chapatis, stewed lentils, perhaps a vegetable curry, and hot, sweet tea, sometimes served with honey or cardamom. Locally grown fruit such as oranges, apples, watermelon, grapefruit, pears, apricots, and mangoes were cheap and plentiful. Even today, Joseph remembers the fruits of Pakistan as "the sweetest, most delicious fruit I have ever tasted."

Food was cooked outside, weather permitting, over an open fire, or in a special clay oven called a *tandoor,* a large, bell-shaped pot with sides that curved up toward an exhaust hole. Fueled by dung cakes or firewood, the tandoor produced an extremely hot, dry heat. To reach temperatures as high as 900 degrees Fahrenheit, women spent many hours squatting in front of a hot oven to ensure that the coals were kept burning. Foods prepared in a tandoor were generally crisp on the outside and moist on the inside. Tandoori chicken has been a Pakistani favorite since the days of the Mughal Empire.

The family ate together twice a day, sitting cross-legged in a circle on the floor, which was covered with a sheet or jute rug. No silverware or utensils were used; everyone ate with their fingers, seldom spilling even a grain of rice. Pakistanis eat with their right hand and avoid offering any food with the left, which is considered impolite, using a chapati to mop up curries and sauces. Breakfast was usually a *paratha,* a crispy chapati cooked in oil and stuffed with vegetables or an egg. The paratha was exceptionally filling and would keep hunger at bay all day. The evening meal consisted of more chapatis, perhaps a curry with some lentils or chickpeas, the ubiquitous rice, and strong, creamy tea or cups of greasy buffalo milk. After meals, Mariam or one of the older children washed the dishes squatting over a bucket, chin between the knees, using soap, sand, or ashes from the cook fire.

Flour was kept in pitchers or iron boxes, and rice was stored in sacks. Most food was eaten fresh, either purchased that day from a vendor or picked fresh from the field. Sugar was available in the shops, or villagers could go to the fields where the cane was processed and, depending on the person's relationship with the farmer, could sometimes take a piece for free. If meat was available, Mariam would cut it into small pieces, salt it, and hang it on a string to dry. There were usually chickens in the courtyard for special occasions, and a buffalo provided rich, fresh milk. Miriam did the milking, sitting on the ground with a bucket between her legs and small Sadiq beside her. Sometimes she would aim the teat at Sadiq's mouth and he would gulp down the warm, fizzy milk. And sometimes the aim of the teat would miss his mouth and he would end up with fresh milk in his eyes, nose, and ears.

In the fields, the sugarcane was crushed in large vats turned by oxen. The juice was poured into containers and cooked into a soft, sugary substance. Once it was dry, it became very hard and could then be cut up into sections and sold or stored for later use.

Babu Barkat traveled about the villages, usually for a week at a time, taking with him only a single shalwar kameez, the ubiquitous long tunic and baggy pants worn by both men and women, designed to keep the wearer cool and comfortable even in the heat of summer. At the end of the week when he returned home, his clothes would be filthy and full of lice, the result of sleeping in so many different beds. Mariam washed his clothes separately from the rest of the family's, boiling them in a large pot in the courtyard.

"When papa came home, we couldn't tell what color he was wearing," Sadiq's sister Maria remembered. "All of us were just happy he was home. We would bring him his slippers and mama would send him straight for a bath. Papa never came home empty-handed. Besides the offerings of fruits, vegetables, and grain, he always brought us little packets of candy."

Most village boys did not wear pants; instead they wore a *dhoti*, similar to a sarong, tied at the waist and worn as a long skirt. Women wore the shalwar kameez, along with a *dupatta,* a long scarf worn around the head or shoulders, or a *chador*, a sort of cloak that covered most of the body. Punjabi men wore turbans on their heads (some as long as seventy feet) and there were hundreds of styles and types, representing different regions and castes. Wrapping the turban on the head was an art form and required considerable skill.

Mariam made most of the younger children's clothes by hand, but when the adults and those in boarding school needed clothes, she would visit the tailor who could whip out very credible outfits for only a few rupees. Mariam herself never had any new clothes, wearing instead the castoffs of her daughters who were away at school.

* * *

Smallpox, malaria, typhoid, and dysentery were common diseases when Sadiq was growing up. There were no vaccinations, few effective medicines, and the diseases were highly contagious and often fatal. Many children died of smallpox; those who did not die were frequently left with scarred, disfigured faces, a stigma that often marked female survivors as unmarriageable, a cruel destiny in a culture where being female and unmarried was possibly the worst of all fates.

Smallpox has been around for more than 3,000 years, killing almost half a billion people in the twentieth century alone. Ramesses V was a victim, as were Mary II of England, Tsar Peter II of Russia, Joseph Stalin, and Abraham Lincoln, among others. Sadiq contracted the disease as an infant and bears the facial pockmarks to this day.

The nearest hospital was in Lahore, twenty miles away. Most hospitals in the large cities were run by Christians, a legacy of British rule. People seeking medical treatment usually had to walk great distances, which was difficult when sick, or travel by donkey, bullock, or horse cart if they had the means and were able to withstand the journey.

Despite contaminated drinking water and lack of sanitation, the villagers lived relatively healthy lives. Their diet was based on fruits and vegetables, and exercise was a way of life rather than an optional activity. People walked everywhere, and manual labor was how everything was done; wells were dug by hand, crops harvested by hand, and fields tilled by walking behind buffalo or oxen.

Sadiq's great uncle typified the physical strength and spirit of the day. He once ordered a bullock cart to be made for him in a village several miles from his home. A few months later, he returned to check on the progress. The cart was finished, so the uncle decided on the spot to take it home. Designed to be pulled by bullocks, these carts are extremely heavy even when empty. Undaunted by the fact that he had no bullocks, uncle simply put some cloth on his shoulders, hooked up the cart behind him, and off he went. Along the way he bought five kilos of apricots for the children back in the village, but as he puffed along, he ate a few here and there. By the time he reached the village, the apricots were gone and he was covered with dust. No one even recognized him.

* * *

Whenever people had a toothache, treatment was readily available for a small fee on the street corner. You simply squatted down on the sidewalk, opened your mouth wide, and the tooth-puller yanked out the offending tooth—without benefit of Novocain, disinfectant, or antibiotics.

There were also quacks who plied their trade on the buses. Whenever the bus stopped, they would climb aboard and shout, "Anyone have a loose tooth, sore gums, or a toothache? I can fix it in just minutes using only my fingers—no problem, no pain." There was a trick to this, of course, and a fee. And despite their claims, there was also some pain.

Dental hygiene was very basic. Toothbrushes were made from twigs, usually from the kikar tree, and since there was no toothpaste, people mixed salt and charcoal into a powder and rubbed it on their teeth.

Cataract surgery was often performed in the same way as tooth extractions, on the street corner, also without antiseptic or sanitation. The eye "doctors" would stake out a spot in the marketplace and hang up a little sign that said, "Get your eyes checked free. Surgery done on the spot."

"My father was troubled with bad eyes for most of his life and on one occasion, he encountered a 'doctor' sitting on a corner near a bus stop. He asked him for a free eye check and was told that he needed a small surgery, and then and there, the man performed the small surgery. Afterward, he bandaged my father's eyes, put a green cloth over them to protect from the sun, and sent him home.

"Some time later, my father went back to have the bandages removed, only to discover that his eyes were worse than before, but it is difficult to know exactly why. Today, I would characterize those practitioners as 'quacks,' but I guess you could say he got what he paid for."

* * *

When Sadiq was four years old, Nanni, his beloved grandmother, died. For the first time, she did not answer when he called her name.

The Christians generally followed the Muslim funeral customs, burying their dead before dark on the day of death. The death of an elderly or honored person was always celebrated, so Nanni's funeral was an occasion of joy and festivity. The body was washed, wrapped in a simple cotton shroud, placed on a bier, and covered with an embroidered mantle. The bier was decorated with stuffed birds, flowers, and dried fruits, and sweets were scattered over the body, along with coins for the children to gather. After the celebration, the men took the body to the cemetery, removed all the decorations, and lowered it into a freshly dug grave. Planks or bricks were placed over the body, and the grave filled with dirt. The more affluent had a wooden coffin made for their departed ones.

CHAPTER 4

Independence

May I be no man's enemy, and may I be the friend of that which is eternal and abides.

—St. Eusebius

A t the stroke of midnight on August 15, 1947, the largest empire the world had ever known was dissolved. Overnight, the Indian subcontinent was sliced up into two sovereign nations, the Republic of India (with a Hindu majority), and a two-part Muslim Pakistan (East and West Pakistan). Four hundred million people gained their freedom from colonial rule, ending nearly 350 years of British domination.

And in the blink of an eye, the country of Sadiq's birth had changed forever.

By morning, a brave new world had emerged beneath a brilliant blue sky, but within hours, violence exploded as Muslims, Sikhs, and Hindus clashed in unimaginable brutality and anarchy. Millions would be murdered and thousands more pushed from their homes as India's new leader, Jawaharlal Nehru, watched his dream of freedom and democracy descend into murder and chaos. Independence had finally come, but the cost would be far greater than anyone ever imagined.

At the zenith of its power in the early twentieth century, the British Empire comprised nearly one fourth of the world's population and one fourth of the earth's land mass. And in 1940, almost two-thirds of its six hundred million citizens were Indian.

The collapse of British rule in India was due in large part to its failure to manage its incredible success. India had become a lucrative enterprise, and the British were loath to share the wealth or allow the Indian citizens any power in their profitable new colony. The Indians found this attitude particularly irritating, and as time passed, talk of autonomy increased.

The idea of partition was not a new one, stemming initially from the basic ideological divide between the Hindu, Sikh, and Muslim populations. But for many years, the British had practiced a divide-and-rule policy in India, sorting citizens according to caste and religion, and their extreme insensitivity to Indian traditions and customs as well as their aggressive appropriation of land and wealth created such frustration among the Indian population that the end of British rule was unavoidable.

In 1885, the Indian National Congress was founded to give voice to the nationalist cause, and although the Congress tried to include the Muslim minority, most Muslim leaders had no faith in the goals of a Hindu-dominated organization. Most of the Congress leaders were against the division of India according to religious loyalties. Mahatma Gandhi, the spiritual leader of India's Hindus and the leader of the Congress, believed that Hindus and Muslims could and should live in amity. "My whole soul rebels against the idea that Hinduism and Islam represent two antagonistic cultures and doctrines," he said. "To assent to such a doctrine is for me a denial of God. For I believe with my whole soul that the God of the Quran is also the God of the Gita, and that we are all, no matter by what name designated, children of the same God."

With most of the political and financial advantages in the hands of the Hindus, the Muslims' frustration soon led to the formation of the All-Indian Muslim League in 1906 by Mohammed Ali Jinnah, a distinguished Muslim lawyer and statesman, and the man who would become known as Father of Pakistan. And while Jinnah supported the Muslim need for a homeland of their own, the Hindu leaders remained firmly opposed to partition.

To Jinnah and to most of the Muslim leaders, the disparity between the Hindus and Muslims was so divisive that any alliance under a partisan government seemed untenable. Two separate and distinct nations was, therefore, the only solution. Ironically, Jinnah was an advocate of secular government and proposed such a government for Pakistan—one in which religion would have "nothing to do with the business of the state." Jinnah's utopian dream would never materialize.

By 1946, the British were running out of money and the will to continue their mission in India. Faced with seemingly irreconcilable differences between the Hindus and the Muslims, the division of India into two separate nations seemed the only possible resolution.

On July 18, 1947, the British Parliament passed the Indian Independence Act, which provided for the creation of the Dominion of Pakistan (now the Islamic Republic of Pakistan) on August 14, and the Republic of India on August 15. Although at the time only words on a piece of paper, the fate of millions of people had been irrevocably sealed.

Unlike any other sovereign nation in the world, East and West Pakistan would be saddled with impossible geographical boundaries, separated as they were by more than one thousand miles of enemy (Indian) territory. About a third of the country's Muslims remained in Hindu India, while the remaining two-thirds migrated to Pakistan.

Although the Partition of India promised both political and religious freedom, the reality fell far short. In the ethnic cauldron that followed, nearly one million people would be killed, and ten to fourteen million would be dislocated in the largest human migration in history.

Once the new borders were established, more than twelve million people fled across them to what they hoped would be the security of a cohesive homeland. The Sindhis were the most negatively affected. Unlike the Bengal and Punjab regions, which were divided between both Pakistan and India, the entire Sindh area was given over to Pakistan, forcing the Sindhis to resettle in India. Overnight, the border had become an invisible barricade, dividing people who had shared the same land for more than a thousand years.

* * *

So how did Pakistan get its name? Choudhary Rahmat Ali, an Indian Muslim nationalist at Cambridge University in the 1930s, was reportedly responsible for the new country's name. The name was originally created as an acronym: Punjab, Afghania (Northwest Frontier Province), Kashmir, Sindh, and the last three letters of Balochistan. The *i* was added later, to enable the pronunciation of *Pakistan,* which means "land of the pure."

CHAPTER 5

Catastrophe

*Violence must sit at the core of any history of Partition.
It is the phenomenal extent of the killing during Partition
which distinguishes it as an event. . . . Grisly scenes of
violence in Punjab have been better described in fiction,
poetry and film. Children watched as their parents were
dismembered or burned alive, women were brutally raped
and had their breasts and genitals mutilated and entire
populations of villages were summarily executed.*
—Yasmin Khan, *The Great Partition: The Making of India
and Pakistan*

The political partition of India created one of the bloodiest and most violent upheavals in human history, plunging both countries into anarchy overnight. On a scale unequaled in modern history, the exodus began. Within days, millions of Hindus and Sikhs fled to India, and millions of Muslims poured into Pakistan, all fearing torture or death if they remained behind. Within a few months, more than a million people were dead, and about twelve million people had crossed the border between the newly abridged India and the newly created Pakistan.

The 50,000 Boundary Forces posted to safeguard the borders were powerless to stem the tide, as centuries-old hostilities and religious hatred boiled up in a fury of terrified, gratuitous violence. Wells were poisoned, homes incinerated, livestock burned, and people tortured, butchered, and roasted alive, their mutilated corpses stacked in the streets and thrown into rivers. Thousands more died from starvation, malnutrition, and disease.

Everywhere, the enemy lay in wait. Sikhs and Hindus attacked the Muslims remaining in India, while the Muslims massacred the Hindus and Sikhs left behind in Pakistan. Long caravans called *kafilah*—which seemed to stretch from horizon to horizon—marched east and west, each seeking safety on the other side, never to see their homes again. Piteous old men carried feeble old women on their backs, children supported infirm relatives, mothers cradled exhausted babies, desperate fathers comforted hungry families. Traveling by bicycle, bus, train, and on foot, people piled creaky bullock carts with bedding, trunks, sacks of grain—everything they could carry. Thousands of homes, shops, crops, farms, and farm animals were simply abandoned.

Silent trains arrived at the stations, their cars full of corpses. No one was spared, not Sikh, Hindu, or Muslim; none left alive except the driver and perhaps the fire tender. Relatives waiting for families to arrive found only bodies hanging from the doors and windows, slaughtered by neighbors they had known for decades.

In the midst of all the bloodshed, there were, however, numerous reports of Muslims, Sikhs, and Hindus who risked (and sometimes lost) their lives to save friends, who were now technically their enemies.

Scottish author William Dalrymple described the carnage in the Lahore train station: "On the night of Independence the last British officials in Lahore arrived at the station. They had picked their way through gutted streets, many of which were still littered with the dead from the riots that attended the Partition of India and Pakistan. On the platforms they found the railway staff grimly hosing down pools of blood and carrying away piles of corpses on luggage trollies for mass burial. Minutes earlier a last group of desperate Hindus had been massacred by a Muslim mob as they sat waiting quietly for the Bombay Express. As the train pulled out of Lahore, the officials could see that the entire Punjab was ablaze, with flames rising from every village. Their life's work was being destroyed in front of their eyes.

"Everyone you met had their story," Dalrymple wrote, " . . . the most horrific was told to me by . . . Khawaja Bilal who had had the unenviable job of being the station master of Lahore in 1947.

" 'One morning, I think it was the 30th of August, the Bombay Express came in from Delhi via Bhatinda. There were around two thousand people on this train. We found dead bodies in the lavatories, on the seats, under the seats. We checked the whole train, but nobody was alive except one person. There had been a massacre when the train stopped at Bhatinda. The sole survivor told us he had approached the train driver, an Englishman, who gave him refuge. He hid the man in the water tank by the engine. When the Sikhs arrived they could not see him so they went away and he survived. Only one man out of two thousand. After that every train that came from India was attacked. We used to receive one hundred trains a day. There were corpses in every one.' "

Observing the horribly burned victims at the Wah Relief Camp in Rawalpindi, Lord Mountbatten, then viceroy of India, was said to have remarked, "They seem to be very fond of tying whole families together, pouring oil on them, and then lighting them as a single torch."

In Amritsar, a group of Muslim women was reportedly paraded naked through the streets, raped by a gang of Sikhs, and then burned alive. Witnesses described women jumping (or being forced to jump) into wells or setting themselves on fire to avoid rape or worse—forced conversion—at the hand of the Muslims. Fathers murdered their children to save them from dishonor and humiliation. Death was preferable to whatever fate awaited them. Violence was understood; conversion was simply a fate worse than death.

Ironically, such acts of feminine martyrdom were widely regarded as the ultimate act of heroism and virtue. Suicide was believed to be infinitely preferable to the shame and disgrace of rape (which was, of course, rarely assigned to the perpetrator). Portrayed as courageous and honorable, the desperate acts of these women were rarely seen for what they were: the unspeakable horror of female subjugation.

* * *

Promising both political and religious freedom, the partition of India remains one of the great tragedies in human history, causing incalculable
human and economic agony. The preservation of national unity was an
objective that required much more than lofty dreams and impassioned
speeches. The leaders of the day failed their people and their countries
miserably, and the litany of blame is long, ranging from pride and political
duplicity, to shortsightedness, ego, and fanatical religious intolerance. In
the end, it is man's staggering inhumanity that must bear the lion's share
of the accountability.

Incredibly, and in spite of many warnings, the new governments
of India and Pakistan were profoundly unprepared for the catastrophic
tragedy of partition. Pakistan in particular, seemed blindsided by the panic
and chaos caused by the new border, which, created to safeguard and unify
a people, did neither.

By all accounts, Pakistan got the short end of a very short stick,
inheriting a largely rural economy with little or no manufacturing capa-
bility and millions of unskilled and impoverished refugees, while losing
millions of productive people. (An estimated twenty million Hindus left
Pakistan for India, and eighteen million Muslims departed India for Pakistan.) India, on the other hand, retained most of the educated population,
the bankers, doctors, teachers, and politicians. Adding insult to injury, India severed all trade relations with the struggling nation two years later.

Without a functioning government, with most of the manufacturing, commerce, and infrastructure remaining in India, and with Pakistan's
raw materials effectively embargoed from Indian factories, Pakistan's
very survival seemed, at best, precarious. Every aspect of Pakistan's existence—industry, infrastructure, commerce, currency, education—would
have to be restructured from scratch.

The original leaders of Pakistan's new government were largely
schooled in the liberal and democratic principles of the British government.
Although they envisioned Pakistan as Islamic in culture and tradition, they
also saw it as a moderate state that promoted religious tolerance. Ali Jinnah,

the founder and first president of Pakistan, had promised that all minorities would be equally represented, with equal rights of citizenship.

"You are free to go to your temples," Jinnah had said when addressing the first constituent assembly of Pakistan (August 11, 1947), "you are free to go to your mosques or to any other place of worship in this state of Pakistan. You may belong to any religion or caste or creed that has nothing to do with the business of the State."

Jinnah was, of course, a politician, and his vision may not have even been achievable. Ultimately, Pakistan's inexorable move toward Islamization has negated any promise of equality and religious tolerance.

The "solution" adopted by the leaders naïvely assumed that if hostile populations were separated, everyone would live happily ever after. But borders seldom resolve conflict, and centuries of history are not easily erased. And so, in incredible irony, the solution became the problem.

The sudden and permanent separation of Indian and Pakastani citizens—owing to the now impenetrable new borders—was particularly cruel. Places people had been visiting all their lives were suddenly inaccessible. For many, partition also meant leaving friends and family members forever.

Sadly, policy-making is generally the purview of those in power, but it is the ordinary citizens—the families, the laborers, the farmers—who must pay for the often misguided and naïve decisions of their leaders. They are the ones who endure, who toil, who hunger, and who die for a cause many of them don't even understand. One cannot fail to notice that, in the course of recent history, wherever conflicted nations have sought to reconcile their problems by means of partition—whether it be Korea, Palestine, Ireland, or others—the result has been violence and bloodshed. It seems somehow inconceivable that people cannot live in peace with those from different cultural and religious communities, and that borders must be established to protect them from each other.

In the end, of course, the remarkable spirit of the Pakistani people prevailed. The damaged and displaced people went to work sowing new crops, building new homes, and creating new lives. Half a century later, the two nations are still recovering from the trauma caused by the partition of a once-united nation.

Today, spectators gather daily at the Wagah Border crossing to watch rival border guards face each other in an entertaining, almost comical flag-lowering ceremony. The Indian Border Security Forces in their smart khaki uniforms, starched turbans, and jackboots, and the Pakistani Rangers with their black shalwar kameezes, rifles, and bandoliers, regularly cooperate in the military spectacle that is the daily border-closing ritual. There is much strutting about, stamping of feet, and bellowing of commands, as each side attempts to outdo the other amid loud displays of patriotic emotion, spectator shouting, and applause in support of each side's own troops. As the commanders meet at the gate and shake hands, the buglers play reveille, the flags of each nation are lowered in unison, and two sets of gates are slammed shut. A border is, after all, a border.

Today, the Hindus, Sikhs, and Muslims who share the subcontinent remain divided by social and cultural differences that go far beyond economic and religious prejudices. More than sixty years after partition, generations of Indians and Pakistanis have come of age—with no memory of a time not so long ago when all were Indians.

CHAPTER 6

Sadiq Becomes a Pakistani

*For us, our homeland is in heaven, and from heaven comes
the Savior we are waiting for, the Lord Jesus Christ, and
he will transfigure these wretched bodies of ours into cop-
ies of his glorious body.*

—Philippians 3:20

When Sadiq woke up on the morning of August 14, 1947, eight days after his fifth birthday, he was no longer Indian. He was now a Pakistani, and he had no idea what that meant. Although the events did not touch him or his family that day or the next, other areas of the country were boiling in chaos, terror, and death. Those who remained alive and made it across the new borders would tell the stories.

Partition caught most of the people in the villages by surprise. There were, of course, no telephones, televisions, or radios, and public announcements usually came from the local mosque, which was how the people of Sunder found out they were no longer Indians.

Partition sliced right through the heart of the Punjab. Half of the province where Sadiq's family lived became part of Pakistan; the other half remained in India. For hundreds of years, religious tolerance had been the basis of the Indian nation's peaceful coexistence with the other religions of the region, yet overnight, ancient differences bubbled up in incomprehensible hostility.

"My parents were not political," Father Joseph explained. "They did not really comprehend the fact that suddenly we were no longer living in India, but in a new country called Pakistan. They were distraught when partition became obvious, but like most people, helpless to do anything about it. Half of my mother's family remained in India, and the border was now closed, so they were lost to us. In a village where Sikhs, Muslims, and Hindus had always lived peacefully, partition did not yet mean much. 'Freedom' was for the politicians and the elite who had fought for it. Everyone else who had previously been subjugated by the British, were now simply subjugated by the new governments, who had decided our fate for us."

Few in number, the Christians enjoyed relative safety during the early years after partition, occupying a neutral position, neither embraced nor reviled. The Christians identified themselves by marking their homes with crosses and sewing crosses on their clothing. Ironically, having been persecuted for their faith by many over the centuries, it would be their very Christianity that would save them.

When the Hindu and Sikh families fled the new Pakistan, they left behind their houses, their crops, their livestock, most of their personal possessions, and their land. In order to accommodate the thousands of new Muslim refugees, the government simply divvied up the land abandoned by the Hindus and Sikhs and re-distributed it to the incoming Muslims.

Joseph remembers his uncles' stories of the devastation they encountered, villages with streets filled with corpses, reports of women throwing themselves into wells to avoid the unthinkable. "Not all the Muslims came to Pakistan," says Joseph, "but most of the Hindus went to India, leaving the security of their homes to go God knows where. The Muslims of Sunder fared better, this was now their homeland."

Sadiq's sister Maria was about eight or nine at the time. "I saw people running everywhere, looting, and leaving the village with everything they could move piled on bullock carts. Men were beating people with big bamboo sticks and my mother hid us in the house."

Initially, the Muslims had no quarrel with the Christians, and generally considered them, along with the Jews, to be "people of the book" (of the Bible), fellow travelers seeking a common salvation. All three religions advocate many of the same values, and venerate many of the same prophets. The Muslims worship the same God as the Jews and Christians, although they call their God Allah, and honor Muhammad, the founder of Islam, as Allah's messenger. They do not, however, regard Jesus as the Son of God, but rather as a prophet. The Muslim scripture is the Quran, which they consider the literal word of God as revealed to the prophet Muhammad, but the Muslims also acknowledge the Jewish Torah and the Christian Bible (although they regard the Quran as the most enlightened scripture).

For Muslims, religion and politics are the same—it is who they are. More than just a theology, Islam is a highly defined way of life. Alone among the religions of the world, Islam has its own legal system based on the principles of Islamic *sharia*, or law. Widely accepted as one of the three most common legal systems of the world, Islamic law is the basis of the constitution of Pakistan and governs all aspects of a person's spiritual, personal, and physical well-being—from politics and economics to sexuality and hygiene. Each Muslim country makes its own laws autonomously, according to its own interpretation of sharia.

Islam is a religion that requires much of its followers. According to the Five Pillars of Islam, every Muslim must profess his faith in God and his prophet Muhammad, pray toward Mecca five times every day, give alms to the poor, fast from dawn to dusk during the holy month of Ramadan, and, if they are able, make a *hajj,* or pilgrimage, to the holy site of Mecca, once during their lifetime. (Many of the hotel rooms in Pakistan have small arrows on the ceilings or the furniture pointing toward Mecca so guests will know where to face when praying.)

Islamic civilization was once far more advanced than the Christian empire, but by the nineteenth and twentieth centuries, the West had surpassed the Islamic world in many areas. Seduced by Western modernization and technology (like cell phones, iPods, computers, and weapons, all of which fly in the face of the fundamentalist values of Muslim society), many Muslims were convinced that Western values and education held the promise of a better life. Others believed that it was the widespread influence of Western greed and materialism that contributed to the decline of the Islamic world.

The growth of Islamic fundamentalism is, in part, the result of an effort to return to the original teachings of the Quran and the sanctity of Islamic history. Aside from the influence of the decadent West, fundamentalists blame the breakdown of the Islamic nations on the failure to follow implicitly the tenets of the Quran. As with other Holy Scriptures, the Quran has been subjected to widely varying interpretations by various factions, and the fundamentalists are often in opposition to the more moderate approaches to Islam. And, as is often the case, the majority are decent people, overshadowed by the terrorist tendencies of the few.

* * *

Prior to partition, the Punjab had historically been regarded as the homeland of the Sikhs. Overnight, the Sikhs found themselves without a land of their own. They, along with the Hindus, were now unwelcome in this new Muslim country.

For many Sikhs, conversion to Christianity represented a way to survive, to avoid persecution, and to remain in Pakistan. These conversions were often guided more by pragmatic impulses and a desire to hold on to their property than by any spiritual epiphany.

Sikh men are required to have five symbols of their faith on their person at all times: uncut hair and beard, a sword or *kirpan* (ceremonial dagger), wooden comb (often tucked inside their turban), specially made cotton shorts, and a *kara,* a steel bracelet worn on their wrist. In order to convert to Christianity, they had to forgo all these things, including the long hair worn piled up under the turban. Thus, before Babu Barkat could baptize them, they had to cut their hair, and the fastest way to do this was with a machete. While the would-be Christian rested his head on a flat slab of wood, Babu would unceremoniously chop off his hair with a single, well-placed whack.

Most Hindus did not convert, preferring to relocate to India rather than become Muslim or Christian. Many of them had property and houses filled with possessions, which were simply appropriated by the new refugees. Muslims moving into the suddenly vacated houses often found themselves with an unexpected bonus—all the furnishings as well.

Sadiq's new neighbors seemed quite pious, praying five times a day. Rising before sunrise for morning prayer, they prostrated themselves on the ground at specific times during the day, and prayed toward Mecca. Every morning and evening, the *mullah*, or Islamic religious teacher, stood facing Mecca, calling the faithful to prayer in haunting, resonant notes: "Allah is most great. I testify that there is no God but Allah. I testify that Muhammad is the prophet of Allah. Come to prayer. Come to salvation. Allah is most great. There is no God but Allah."

If a mosque was not handy, the Muslims simply laid down their prayer rug (if they had one), turned toward Mecca, and prayed wherever they were. Whenever possible, devout Muslims would perform ritual ablutions before praying, washing their hands three times, then rinsing their mouths, noses, faces, ears, arms, and feet. Friday was their holy day, and many people attended the mosque. During the holy month of Ramadan, the Muslims were required to fast each day from sunrise to sunset, abstaining from food, drink, smoking, and sexual relations during daylight hours.

Although not directly involved, most Christians were profoundly affected by partition. The Christians in Sadiq's village remained; they did not flee, they had no place to go. Nevertheless, Sadiq's family lost their stability, their relationships, and many friends. Some of the shops closed forever, others were taken over by the new Muslims. Mariam maintained a tenuous connection with the Muslims who remained, but things were never the same. The new residents remained mostly strangers.

"Before partition," Joseph explained, "my mother had a special relationship with all our neighbors, as well as the shopkeepers. We shared our meals and attended each other's weddings, festivals, and funerals. Whenever my mother went to Hindu or Sikh fields for vegetables or sugar cane, they were just happy that Sister Mariam had come. After partition, our Hindu and Sikh neighbors were no longer there to welcome us, their houses and property inhabited by the newly arrived Muslims, who were more circumspect. 'This is now our land and you must keep off.'

"As I grew older, I came to realize that Muslim intolerance often extended to the Christians who were frequently at the mercy of their Muslim landlords and employers. The Muslims had suffered significant oppression under the British, and apparently wanted a measure of revenge by discriminating against the Christians, presumably allies of the foreign rulers. The poor and illiterate were given to understand that the Muslims, who believed in the prophet Muhammad, were the only ones chosen by God, and that those believing in creeds like the Trinity and Jesus Christ were heretics, condemned by God and, therefore, to be shunned. This belief is the basis of the generally accepted practice of forbidding Christians to eat or drink in the same places and with the same dishes as the Muslims. In later years, whenever I was refused food or drink, I used the opportunity to explain that I was also a child of God, and equally loved in his eyes."

CHAPTER 7

The Madrassa Myth

*All men will hate you because of me, but he who stands
firm to the end will be saved.*

—Matthew 10:22

Education was highly regarded by Babu Barkat, and the family had to make many sacrifices to educate their children. Knowledge was, after all, something that no one could take away from them. Most Christian families were illiterate, so there was no real incentive to send their children to school, particularly not the girls. Schools cost money, and parents could not afford the fees—or the loss of their children's labor in the fields.

As a catechist, Babu Barkat had a bit of an edge in the education of his children. The local missionary priest was instrumental in helping the children get places in boarding school, and all of Joseph's siblings were educated through high school except the eldest. After high school, further education was achieved by their own initiative and at their own expense, and most went on to pursue advanced degrees.

Joseph's sister Mary Rose recalled one occasion when her father arrived home from the city with his salary. "After he had given Mama all he had, she said, 'Babu-ji, what is this?' He had given her the equivalent of about twenty-five US cents. 'What am I going to do for the whole month?' Papa would smile and say, 'God will provide, why are you worrying?' I had three sisters and three brothers in boarding school. Most of his salary was going to school and boarding fees."

Under British rule, education was largely restricted to the upper class. Knowledge of the English language was synonymous with learning; if you could not speak English, you were regarded as ignorant. The only option for the children of poor families—boys only—were the substandard public schools, or the Islamic religious schools *(madrassas)*, which often taught an extreme version of Islam. And too often, the mullahs at the madrassas were not themselves educated; all that was required to be a mullah was to be able to read the Quran in Arabic and conduct prayers.

After partition, Pakistan's economy, along with its educational system, was decimated. Many of the teachers were Hindus who had now left the country, and the huge influx of Muslim refugees only exacerbated the already overwhelmed schools. The Christians continued to run the hospitals, as well as many of the renowned schools established under the British, where the children of the government and military elite had been educated for decades—even though most Christians could not afford to send their own children to those schools. Pakistan may have been created as a Muslim homeland, but Christian efforts were still welcomed in the fields of scholarship and health care.

Today, there is much confusing information about the function and purpose of the madrassas. Some believe they harbor terrorists and/ or provide training to terrorists. There have been compelling arguments for and against their existence. What the madrassas do provide is a free education and often a small income for families who must manage without the labor of their children, but they generally lack the expertise and skills necessary to produce successful terrorists.

Contrary to Western beliefs, most madrassas are reasonably moderate, providing an opportunity—often the only opportunity—for the children of poor families to receive an education, albeit an extremely limited and largely inadequate one by today's standards. Unfortunately, some madrassas do misuse their power to inspire fanaticism and encourage terrorism, but they are the exception.

Many believe that madrassas teach young children to hate everything non-Islamic, and to hate enough to sacrifice their lives for the greater good, which, in their case, is pleasing God and gaining an eternity of paradise. This hostility has its basis in a number of causes, including ignorance, oppression, poverty, and lack of opportunity. Thus, they believe, it is far more meaningful to sacrifice their miserable lives for the glory of Islam and the defeat of their enemies, than to continue in a seemingly hopeless existence.

CHAPTER 8

Infidel in a Muslim School

I can do all things through him who strengthens me.

—Philippians 4:13

In April of 1948, just eight months after partition, six-year-old Sadiq was ready to take the first big step in his young life. Very early one morning, scrubbed, polished, and anxious in his freshly washed shalwar kameez, Sadiq set off on the back of Babu-ji's bicycle for the two-and-a-half mile ride to Rangilpur, the only village in the area that had a primary school. In the following weeks, he would join a group of local boys on the daily five-mile walk to and from school.

At the beginning of term, there were about twenty boys from Sunder in Sadiq's class, and no girls, of course. By the end of the term, only three remained, including Sadiq. The rest had dropped out either because they had lost interest, or were needed by their families in the fields.

Stifling during the hot months and frigid in the winter, the tiny two-room, mud-brick schoolhouse had a single door, a small courtyard, and no windows. Water pitchers with metal cups hooked over the edge sat next to a wall. There were no desks, blackboards, or textbooks, and no bathrooms.

Dressed in a tidy turban and the tunic and baggy trousers of the shalwar kameez, Master Khushi stood imperiously in front of the classroom that first day, welcoming the students. Sadiq was at first terrified, then intimidated, and finally curious. This just might be a grand adventure.

To assist him with his more than one hundred charges (in five grade levels), Master Khushi would appoint one of the smarter boys to act as classroom monitor. He would give the class a lesson and then ask the monitor to keep repeating the lesson to the children. Critical thinking and creative development were not part of the curriculum. The students learned their lessons by rote, seated side by side on a jute mat on the mud-dung plastered floor, or, weather permitting, outside in the shade of a kikar tree.

Shortly after he started school, Sadiq came to realize that he was different, and it was not just the dark skin of his Sikh/Hindu heritage or his clumsy performance in games of *gulli danda* and hide-and-seek. He was an infidel, a Christian—the only Christian—in a Muslim school. Discrimination was not new to Sadiq; he accepted it, but he did not understand it.

In school, it was expected that a Christian student would keep his distance so as to avoid any contact with the other students. Christian children were not allowed to drink water from the pitchers provided for the Muslim boys. Instead, Sadiq had to ask permission to go to the Muslim well, about half a furlong from the school.

One afternoon, hot, dusty, and thirsty—having had nothing to drink all day—Sadiq approached the well. Not allowed to draw his own water, he waited in the blistering sun, looking longingly at the promise of a cool drink. A Christian would not dare to come too close to the well, lest he touch the well and make it unclean. After about half an hour, a young Muslim woman came to fetch water. Sadiq asked politely for a drink. Cautioning him to stay away from the well, she carefully poured the water into his hands, making sure that the pail was lifted high enough so that no contact was made with the hands of the little infidel, and that any water that spilled from his hands would not fall anywhere near the well. The water was cool and wet, worth the humiliation and the wait.

This procedure would be repeated every time Sadiq wanted a drink. It was an inconvenience to be sure, but such treatment did not seriously trouble Sadiq. His family and his God cherished him, even if the Muslims didn't.

The students were taught math, reading, and writing in the Urdu language. Punjabi was the language spoken by the people of the Punjab; Urdu was the national language of Pakistan. In 1947, the newly formed government decreed that Urdu would be the national language, although only about ten percent of the population spoke it.

The first book studied in Muslim primary schools was called *Al Qaeda,* which introduced the alphabet and demonstrated how to join letters and pronounce words. (*Qaeda* is an Arabic and Urdu word with several meanings; in Urdu, it also means "the first book of alphabets.")

In school, Sadiq spoke Urdu; in the village and at home, he spoke Punjabi. His older siblings would come home from boarding school in the city speaking English, and would teach it to the younger children. Babu Barkat encouraged his children to learn English because he understood how important it would be to their future.

Once Sadiq learned to read, he became an avid reader, often devouring an entire book in a single day. By the time he was in third grade, he read well enough to be able to read the newspaper to his father. He was also very good at writing in Urdu but not so good in math. This deficiency would cause him many problems later on.

School supplies were few, practical, and usually homemade. Sadiq would scrawl the beautiful new Urdu script on his *takhti,* a writing tablet made of wood with a special white coating, a kind of plaster that, once dry, could be wiped clean and written on again. Pens were made from reeds. Babu-ji would cut a five- or six-foot length into sections about eight inches long, honing the writing point to a fine edge. Ink was made of burnt almond skins or other fruit skins worked into a paste by adding water. Students practiced their sums using chalk on a slate, coated black like a small blackboard, and sold in the village. By the time Sadiq was in fourth grade, he would finally acquire a notebook.

School started at eight o'clock in the morning and by three in the afternoon, Sadiq was home. No lunch or snacks were available. At the end of the school day, Sadiq took his takhti, slate, pen, and sometimes a reader home in a sackcloth bag tied with string. Sometimes the boys would have contests, banging each other's takhtis to see which was the strongest. The boys whose slates broke were declared to have inferior slates, and probably inferior skills as well.

Master Khushi regularly disciplined his students for failing to pay attention or not doing their homework. More than once, Sadiq was on the receiving end of his teacher's stick. On one occasion, Sadiq got a slap on his face. When his father stopped by on his way to another village, Sadiq's classmates were quick to inform, saying, "Sadiq got a beating from the teacher." Babu-ji responded with a gentle sigh, "*Bacha hai aqal ka kachha hai seekh jaiga*, he is still a child. He will learn."

There were no letter or number grades, only pass or fail, and although Sadiq was not an outstanding student, he passed each level. Math was always a problem, possibly because the teacher was not able to provide much individual attention. With only one teacher and one hundred children in five different classes, it is not hard to imagine the near impossibility of individual instruction.

During the hot months, instead of pants, Sadiq wore a dhoti tied at the waist. Young children seldom wore underwear. Twenty boys walking home barefoot in ankle-deep dust created a large dust cloud, and by the time the boys reached home, they were often unrecognizable. The heat was also a problem. In the early afternoon, the sun would be high and hot, and caps or hats were unknown. But these were clever boys. They would take off their dhotis and bind them together in a long train. One boy would hold the front end and another would hold the back end, with the remaining boys in the middle, forming a sort of tent that protected the now seminaked (but cool) boys from the blazing Pakistani sun. During the monsoon season, the roads became muddy bogs and the boys often found themselves slogging through ankle-deep puddles of muck on their way home.

One morning Sadiq arrived late to school. Master Khushi asked him why he was late and Sadiq replied that the road was very muddy and slippery and that every time he took a step forward, he slid backward two steps. Curious, Master asked him exactly how he had managed to arrive at school in this manner, to which Sadiq replied, "I walked backward."

Sadiq and his peers often encountered the "cow boys," illiterate village boys with big sticks who tended their cattle in the fields. "Come, show us the pictures in your book or we will not let you pass," they would taunt. Initially terrified, Sadiq soon realized it was a game, and after they shared the pictures, the boys always let them pass without incident, as if this had not happened the day before, and would not happen again the next.

Shoes, if they were worn at all, were locally made. Joseph remembered a particular pair of shoes that he wore when he and his family walked to Lahore, twenty miles away, for a Holy Day celebration. The shoes—his first pair—were a gift of American aid and had bright-red rubber soles. "It had rained, and as we walked along, I would deliberately splash in the puddles with my new red shoes. I never forgot those shoes."

It was not unusual to see a boy newly shod in a pair of shiny black patent leather shoes topped with frilly bows (also courtesy of American aid), the kind of fancy shoe that might have been worn by a young American girl. Girls seldom received any of this foreign footwear, since they were expected to remain at home helping their mothers while the boys ran freely about the village and, therefore, had more need for shoes.

Most people traveled barefoot and only wore their shoes when they arrived at their destination, hoping this would make the shoes last a little longer, never sure when they might get another pair.

"We had two pair of shoes, one for school and one for play," Joseph explained. "If you lost your shoes in the middle of the year, too bad. My shoes would last a long time because I didn't wear them very often. Going to school, I would carry my shoes in my hand. Before entering the school, I would dust off my feet and put the shoes back on. When I came out of school, I took the shoes off and carried them home. In the seminary, I had one pair of shoes and a pair of sandals, and they lasted me nine years."

When Sadiq was in the third grade, his cousin came to live with the family so that he could go to school. The young cousin was not really taken with the idea of education so he would often entice a very willing Sadiq to play hooky with him. On these few occasions, the boys would go off to the fields or the river to play until they thought it was safe to return home.

One day when the boys returned home, Mariam looked at the shade cast by the house and said, "You are early. It is not yet three o'clock. Why are you home?" She was not fooled, and she did not hesitate to swat her son. When Babu Barkat objected and said to her, "Why do you punish your son and not his cousin?" Mariam replied, "I am not responsible for his cousin's future, but I am accountable for Sadiq's and I will not hesitate to correct his errors in judgment."

Sadiq's final exam was held in a distant town. This would be a defining moment. If he did not pass with good marks, he would not be allowed to go to the city to continue his studies. Sadiq was understandably nervous; it was his first time to sit for an exam in such a formal setting, and this would be a three-hour test. One of his brothers composed a prayer to inspire Sadiq, and it went something like this: "Oh God, grant me wisdom and understanding so that I may pass this exam, not for my own good, but for your praise and glory." Sadiq recited the prayer over and over until he was afraid that it would be the only thing in his head during the test. Secure in the knowledge of the power of prayer, Sadiq passed his exam—and every other exam he took for the rest of his academic life.

CHAPTER 9

Message in the Wind

Do not neglect to show hospitality to strangers, for by doing that some have entertained angels without knowing it.
—Hebrews 13:2

Sunder had a mosque but no church. Holy Mass was celebrated in Sadiq's home about once a month, whenever the priest could get there. Mariam would arrange the altar while Babu prepared the people for confession and led the rosary, after which the priest would say Mass.

Mariam had built the altar herself out of mud bricks. A statue of the Sacred Heart sat on the altar, and religious pictures decorated the walls. A large picture of Our Lady hung in the center of the wall and whenever people entered, Our Lady's eyes seemed to be looking straight at them.

"Whenever the priest was coming, my mother would ask us to clean the altar, which, when not in use, became convenient storage for ribbons, baskets, whatever," Joseph's sister Maria recalls. "Sometimes we misused the altar and got a spanking, but every Sunday we had a prayer service at that altar."

There was a large kikar tree in front of the house with an iron bar hanging from a branch. Sadiq was responsible for striking the bar to announce the services; the first strike called the faithful to prepare themselves, the second strike meant "Come to our house for prayers," and the third strike announced that prayers were beginning—with or without the participants.

With about thirty Catholic families in the village, there were often as many as fifty people gathered inside the tiny one-room house. If there were visitors, the crowd spilled out into the courtyard. Most of the people knew the Psalms by heart and Babu Barkat would lead the singing with his strong tenor voice, sometimes accompanied by a *dhol* (a kind of barrel drum) or portable harmonium.

One Sunday when Sadiq was about five years old, Babu Barkat took him along to a chapel in the small village of Sultanke. Just as the congregation was about to start prayers, Babu had to leave the church for some emergency. "When my father left, " Joseph recalls, "everybody looked at me and someone said, 'Let the Junior Babu lead us in prayer.' I was suddenly paralyzed with shyness, stuck to the floor like glue. I couldn't look at anyone or think of what to say, so I started crying. I did not handle my first invitation to speak very well."

Many years later, the Holy Spirit would fill Sadiq (then Father Joseph) with the courage and inspiration to move thousands of people with his words, but he never forgot that timid little boy who was incapable of uttering even a single word in God's presence.

* * *

Sunder was the Christian center for the thirty-plus villages that comprised Babu Barkat's *ilaqa*. Babu worked hard to prepare the faithful in each village to receive the sacraments, and twice a year, all the catechists would bring their catechumens to the center of the diocese—Lahore in Sadiq's case—for a three-day retreat called "Committee." As the son of a catechist, no one had to prepare Sadiq for Committee. From the age of three, he had been preparing.

For Pakistani Catholics, Committee represented coming together in a community of the same faith, to be initiated into the church through the sacraments. In those days, Christians were quite isolated in the villages; sometimes there were only ten or twenty families in a village of five hundred Muslim families. At Committee, suddenly they were two or three hundred other Christians, and together they felt uplifted and strengthened. Their faith was their life, their strength, their "day at the beach," and the memory of the experience would last a lifetime.

The first evening of Committee, the people would meet with the Christians from the other villages and watch some sort of Christian movie or drama. The following day, the priest would test the candidates (orally, since most were illiterate). Most passed the tests. They had been prepared well; otherwise they would have been left at home. In the evening, the faithful received the first two sacraments, baptism and reconciliation (or confession). The following morning the bishop would confirm them in their new faith, and those who had prepared for their first Holy Communion would partake in the Holy Eucharist, the table of the Lord.

The center of the Catholic faith is the celebration of the Eucharist. Catholics believe the Eucharist is the true body and blood, soul and divinity of Jesus Christ, who is really and substantially present under the appearances of the bread and wine.

Sadiq was nine years old when he went for his first Committee, traveling with his father and the other sacramental candidates by bus on the two-hour trip to Lahore. Most of the children came without their parents, traveling with their catechists or other adults. The catechist was like a surrogate father, completely trusted, and no child was ever lost or misplaced.

Accommodations for the two to three hundred people who came for Committee were never a problem. People stayed at the parish house, convent, or school (if there was one), sleeping on straw mats on the floor, which had been covered with hay or rice husks. Dinner was provided, usually rice and vegetables cooked in large metal pots and served in plates on a cloth laid on the ground.

Joseph's sister Mary Rose remembers her part in the catechesis process: "Whenever my older brothers and sisters would come home from boarding school, Papa would say, 'I am so busy with my villages, I do not have time to visit all of them.' He would point and say 'You and you go to these five villages, and you and you go to these four.' My sister Justina and I were quite small, only ten and twelve years old, and he would send us too. Our job was to teach the young girls and women their prayers. The villagers treated us like little princesses."

Once, when Babu-ji was occupied elsewhere, Sadiq and his brother Benjamin were sent in his stead to help conduct a funeral on a Christmas morning. "We were hungry," says Joseph, "and we thought a lot about the rice pudding we were missing, so we were looking very sad and gloomy, and the people thought, 'Look how much they loved our brother.'"

One afternoon, three strangers, turbaned men from another village, came to Babu Barkat's house. "Mother, we have guests who need to eat so perhaps your daughters can cook something for them," Babu said to Mariam. But Mariam demurred, "You know, my poor girls are so tired, they are just home from school. What can you be thinking?"

Babu was not fooled by her protestations, gently chiding her, "Mother, do you remember what happened when the three strangers appeared at Abraham's door and he made them welcome? The visitors were really angels who had come to announce that Abraham and Sarah would have a son within the year. So, you never know who our guests might be, or when a simple act of kindness will lead to a miracle. Go and tell the girls to make some bread for our angels."

Sometimes the village girls would come to Sadiq's house during the cooler weather for spinning marathons. Each girl would bring her own spinning wheel and cotton, the string beds would be moved outside in the courtyard, and the girls—Christians, Hindus, and Muslims alike—would spin away, sometimes all night, gossiping and snacking on sweet cakes and tea. The yarn the girls made would later be weighed and sold at the market, and eventually woven into cloth.

* * *

Growing up, Joseph often heard his parents recall that, under British rule, the Christian ministers were well respected, often dispensing their authority over the police and small government departments with impunity. "Once my father was caught riding his bicycle the wrong way at the railway station in Lahore," he remembers. "There was a one-way sign written in English, but my father could not read it. The police took him into custody, where he remained most of the day. Eventually, the parish priest arrived at the station and discovered his incarcerated catechist. The priest asked the police what happened and when he realized the problem, that the sign was written in English, he told the police to 'teach him English first, then arrest him.' To my father, he said simply 'Let's go.'"

* * *

As a child, Sadiq often felt like an untouchable but it had nothing to do with caste. He wasn't an outstanding student, he wasn't very good at games, he was very shy, too sensitive, and had no particular skills. You would hardly call him handsome with his round, mahogany face etched with smallpox scars, but he had expressive eyes, an unruly mop of black hair, and a wide smile. In Punjabi, he was called *besura*, which, loosely translated, means "useless fellow, or "one who has no tune." The village kids teased him, calling him "dove" because of his gentle soul, or, a bit more harshly, *khudar*—a rough cloth like burlap. Clothes were not normally made of khudar but Sadiq's often were. There were ten children to provide for and everything, including clothes, was measured, divided, shared, and worn until it practically disappeared. Sadiq remained indifferent to his sartorial disadvantage; whatever was given to him by his mother was good enough.

The village women would call out to Mariam, "Why do you keep this ugly boy? You should sell him to us for five *paisas*"—less than a penny. "See that tree?" she would reply. "If you pile all your money to the top, he is still more precious than that."

These were ignorant women and they were only teasing, but the words cut deep. "I began to think that I really was useless, good for nothing," says Father Joseph. The two constants in his life—a loving family and a comforting, unshakable faith—had always sustained him, but his small, tidy world was changing.

One afternoon, eight-year-old Sadiq was walking home alone along the dirt road that ran past the village. Suddenly, the atmosphere became heavy, the sky blood red. Seconds later, out of nowhere, there it was—the Dust Devil—and he found himself caught in the spiraling updraft of a dusty, choking whirlwind.

Sadiq could see nothing but a haze of blowing dust. He felt the wind whipping his dhoti around his legs and his bare feet seemed to be moving outside of his body. He squeezed his eyes shut and, for the first time in his life, he cried out at the top of his voice. No one could hear him. No one, that is, but God.

"Lord, here I am, useless, clumsy, and stupid, but if you will have me, I wish to serve you. I put myself in your hands . . . I will follow wherever you lead," he cried.

Improbable as it seemed, Sadiq heard an answering voice: "Do not be afraid. I have called you and you are mine, I have loved you with an everlasting love."

It only lasted a minute, but it was terrifying—and exhilarating. As the dust washed over him, Sadiq knew instinctively that his life was changing, blessed reassurance for his small, fractured soul. God was with him. God had always been with him.

Throughout his life, Sadiq would put himself in God's hands. And each time, he would gain strength and affirmation. He never aspired to positions of power; he envisioned himself as an imperfect and humble servant of God. Alone, he had nothing to contribute, but with God, the possibilities were limitless.

The dark-eyed, sensitive young *besura* was growing up.

CHAPTER 10

Lahore

The child must know that he is a miracle, that since the beginning of the world there hasn't been, and until the end of the world there will not be, another child like him.

—Pablo Casals

Having completed his studies at primary school, it was time for eleven-year-old Sadiq to go to middle school. Early one morning in September, Babu Barkat and Sadiq, with all his possessions wrapped in a bundle on top of his head, boarded a bus for Lahore. There, he would attend Burki Middle School, where he would complete grades six and seven while living with his sister Teresa, a teacher at St. Joseph's primary school in Lahore Cantt. Later on, during holidays, Babu would take Sadiq home on his bicycle, pedaling the twenty miles each way from Lahore to Sunder and back again.

Boarding schools cost a significant amount of money, and for most Pakistani children, higher education was just a dream. For Christian children, however, the missionaries provided a small lifeline of support in both encouragement as well as financial aid. Even so, educating ten children would be a constant struggle for Babu Barkat. At the end of the month, Babu usually had no more than a few rupees remaining in his pocket, but he was still expected to pay something toward boarding and school fees. And with three or four children at a time in these schools, there never seemed to be enough rupees.

Sadiq had never been separated from his family before, nor had he ever spent more than a couple of days in a city. He had few personal possessions so he packed little in his small bundle beyond a couple of clean shalwar kameezes, a quilt, some sandals, and a thin towel, but he carried with him a wealth of dreams, something even the most insignificant of God's creatures could enjoy.

* * *

To Sadiq, Lahore seemed a magical place filled with incredible sensory delights—a teeming, energetic city full of parks, monuments, and exotic bazaars. The city's rich architectural history reflected the grandeur of the old Mughal dynasties, with its royal palaces, fragrant gardens of jasmine and frangipani, and splendid mosques with their onion domes and filigreed minarets.

Sadiq had never seen such sites, smelled such smells, or experienced such a crush of humanity. The streets bustled with life: women with huge, unwieldy bundles on their heads, bicycles carrying entire families, horse-driven tongas, bullock carts, camels, goats, and buses with people hanging out of doors and windows and piled on top of the roof until it seemed the bus would topple over.

Over the centuries, countless artists, philosophers, conquerors, and traders have been drawn by the lure of this golden city, among them Rudyard Kipling, Alexander the Great, Shah Jahan (architect of the Taj Mahal), and Akbar the Great, one of the greatest of the Mughal emperors—a compassionate leader, as well as a fierce warrior, lace maker, artist, and animal trainer.

Built in the sixteenth century, the massive Royal Fort dazzled with its white marble, stunning Hall of Mirrors, and opulent inlaid stonework. The huge Alamgiri Gate, the main entrance to the fort, was large enough to accommodate the emperor's glittering, painted elephant caravans. (The British Army occupied the fort from 1846 until it was given to the Indian Archaeological Survey in 1927.)

Opposite the Royal Fort was the Badshahi Mosque with its great marble domes and towering minarets. One of the largest mosques in the world, and certainly the largest structure Sadiq had ever seen, the ancient mosque could accommodate more than ten thousand worshippers in the prayer hall, and 100,000 in its courtyard. Gazing in eye-popping wonder at the huge building, Sadiq was quite sure his entire village, indeed several villages, would fit inside its walls. (Both the Royal Fort and Badshahi Mosque are UNESCO World Heritage sites, as is Lahore's Shalimar Gardens.)

Named after a beautiful courtesan who, according to legend, was buried alive in a wall as punishment for her illicit love affair with the emperor's son, the five-hundred-year-old Anarkali Bazaar, with its maze of narrow alleys and tiny shops, offered everything from sweets and shoes to brass, leather, and hammered gold and silver. Big wheels of paneer cheeses and sacks of roasted watermelon and pumpkin seeds were found in every alley.

Just past Anarkali was an area of wide tree-shaded avenues, stately colonial buildings, and grand houses, reminders of the city's British legacy. The old Punjab University, splendidly arched and domed, was among the most renowned educational institutions in British India, and is today the country's largest teaching institution.

On a small traffic island in front of the Municipal Museum sat a great bronze gun, Zamzama, the eighteenth-century cannon made famous by Rudyard Kipling in English literature as "Kim's gun."

A few miles east of the city were the Shalimar Gardens, the legendary "Garden of Love," with its marble pavilions, lush shade trees, brilliant peacocks and parrots, and more than four hundred fountains. Created by Emperor Shah Jahan in 1642, the gardens were a peaceful contrast to the bustling cacophony of the city.

Teresa lived in a small house inside the Catholic school compound, which also housed the school, a rectory, and quarters for the teachers, cook, gardener, and catechist. The little one-room house had a veranda across the front and an open cooking area adjacent to the house. Behind the house was an enclosed Indian-style latrine (a hole in the ground), open to the sky, pitch dark at night, and freezing in the winter.

The compound was a peaceful place, surrounded by farmland, fruit trees, and the occasional buffalo or cow. In the spring, the fields were a sea of butterflies and wild flowers. At night, fireflies would come in the hundreds; first one part of the field would twinkle and glow, then another, like a giant disco ball. The sing-song call of the *subzi wallah* (vegetable man) as he pushed along his creaky cart piled high with peppers, onions, lentils, cucumber, and tomatoes, evoked a comforting familiarity. And in the evening, the stirring strains of ancient music from the courtyards in the old city filled the streets. Although he missed his parents terribly, Sadiq thought this was a little slice of heaven.

Sadiq never tired of the haunting, melodious call of the muezzins, chanting the fourteen-hundred-year-old *adhān,* the Islamic call to prayer. Before first light, the call to prayer would echo across the city, from mosque to mosque: "Allah is most great. I testify that there is no God but Allah. I testify that Muhammad is the prophet of Allah. Come to prayer. Come to salvation. Allah is most great. There is no God but Allah."

And then there were the lights, the mysterious electric lights. At night, the city would come alive with twinkling specks of color; the windows of the houses glowing with pools of warm light and the minarets of Badshahi Mosque lit up like a Christmas tree. Sadiq was fascinated with the single light bulb in Teresa's house and how it switched off and on, its soft light illuminating his study books long after the sun slipped beneath the city.

The change from village life to city life was a sea change. For Sadiq, it was also a time of firsts; the first time to wear conventional pants, shirt, and tie, and the first time in a private school after six years in a public Muslim school. At Burki Middle School, there was less discrimination; military families were more tolerant. Sadiq sat next to both girls and boys. There were even a few Christians in the school and remarkably, this caused no anxiety or untoward problems.

Teresa frequently admonished Sadiq to maintain the crease in his new gray pants. This was apparently very important and, since he sat on the ground for many of his classes, difficult to do. Whenever he sat, the crease disappeared.

* * *

Named after General Wajid Ali Burki of the Pakistani Army, Burki was an Urdu medium school, a step up from public school, with more discipline and more organization. The headmistress was a very sweet Muslim lady who did not care much for teaching. Whenever she tired of her duties, she would dismiss the classroom teacher, bring out some playing cards (educational of course), and the whole class would join in. The only teacher who really worked hard was the math teacher, but Sadiq did not benefit much from his expertise, possibly because his previous schooling had not provided him with an adequate foundation.

At Burki, the curriculum followed the English educational system of British rule. Textbooks were in Urdu, but the students were also introduced to the English language. Coming as he did from an Urdu-speaking school, Sadiq did surprisingly well in English. Whenever the captain came around on inspection (which was often, since he was reportedly fond of the headmistress), he would always come to the English class and ask each student to read something and then explain what he or she had read. Sadiq was always the last student called upon. Once, the captain commented on Sadiq's performance, saying, "Although he has dark skin, he has a beautiful white heart." Sadiq took this as a compliment.

* * *

After completing his studies at Burki, thirteen-year-old Sadiq found a place at the prestigious St. Francis High School in Anarkali, run by the Capuchin Franciscan missionaries. For the first time, Sadiq would be attending a school of his own faith.

The task of interviewing and testing every student who applied for admission fell to the school's principal, Father Cherubim. Faith alone did not guarantee acceptance. One morning Father Cherubim, along with Brother John, came to Teresa's house to supervise Sadiq's admission test. Sadiq passed the Urdu and English tests with flying colors, but when Father Cherubim placed the math test on the table in front of him, Sadiq knew this could be a deal-breaker.

When it was time for lunch, Father Cherubim left Brother John to supervise. "My dear boy, I know you don't know the sum, and it would be cheating for me to help you pass," Brother John sighed heavily. "But I know that you must pass, there is no other option. You have to go to high school. So I will ask God to forgive me, for God knows what he has planned for you." And so the sympathetic Brother helped Sadiq complete the test, sealing the deal.

At St. Francis, Sadiq would receive a very Catholic education, which included religion classes in addition to the core curriculum, daily Mass, and a stint as an altar server. The religious atmosphere permeated all aspects of his student life and gave him much to think about. Back in public school in Rangilpur, the students were passed whether they knew the math or not. It would not be the same at St. Francis. Math would remain Sadiq's weakest subject and, while not a gifted student, he was honest and tenacious, qualities that would help him overcome his academic deficiencies. Although he had to work twice as hard as the rest of the students, he never gave up, finishing in the third (last) division of his class and graduating in 1958.

In those days, there was no particular celebration marking a school graduation. High school exam results were published in the local newspaper so Sadiq took the bus to town, purchased a paper, and looked for his "roll" number. If the number appeared, he had passed his exams. "My number appeared, I brought the paper home, and that was that."

* * *

The call to God's service was a vocation Sadiq had been preparing for all his life. But God's call would not come from a host of angels or a burning bush, but rather from a lack of scholarly aptitude. From a very early age, Sadiq believed that it was his destiny to become a priest. Later on, he took a slightly more practical approach. If he received good marks in high school, he would go to university. If he did not, the seminary might accept him. So it was a kind of fallback position, and in Sadiq's mind, exactly how God planned it.

Sadiq's brother Peter would be a major influence in his decision to become a priest. As a young man, Peter had left home to attend St. George's College in Mussoorie (now a part of India). Peter had hoped to enter the seminary after college, but during his years at St. George's, partition occurred and India was divided. "Since I was under eighteen years of age, I was not allowed to continue my studies in India," Peter recalls. "I had to return to Pakistan, and since there was no seminary in Pakistan at that time, I had to find another path, one that would enable me to support my parents as well as myself."

It was Peter who would help Sadiq write his application to the bishop for admission to the seminary. Peter was pleased that Sadiq was following in his footsteps, but he hoped that Sadiq would get further than he had. Peter eventually married and had five daughters and, finally, a son, who is today a doctor in Pakistan.

Years ago, during the whirlwind, Sadiq had had his own conversation with God. Now God was truly leading him and his life mattered, even as the sparrows were counted and known by name. And if God had his eye on every sparrow, then surely he had his eye on Sadiq, although the thought of an omnipotent and all-seeing God seemed at times a heavy responsibility.

* * *

No one comes into the world without God's plan, and in due time, Babu Barkat would lose two more children—Maria and Teresa—to God's service, just as Sadiq was getting ready to join the seminary.

"We joined the convent together, my sister Teresa and I," remembers Maria. "She was twenty-six, I was twenty. As was the custom, whenever someone left home, the father would give a big banquet, so before we left, my father prepared a feast in our honor. We raised ducks and Father killed forty of them, also some chickens. More than one hundred people came; it was a wonderful party.

"To get to our convent, we had to go first by bus to our brother Peter's house in Lahore. From there we would take the train to the convent in Sindh, and eventually to the convent in Malta for our novitiate. While Teresa and I were waiting at the bus stop, everyone was crying because we were leaving our home. Papa asked why everybody was crying. 'When Abraham sacrificed his son, he did not cry. I am giving God my two beloved daughters and I don't want you to cry.'"

In those days, foreign aid was often distributed by the priests to the catechists, and by the catechists to the poor. One day, a friend asked Babu Barkat, "Why don't you sell some of this stuff and buy a big building in the city?" Babu told the man that he could not be dishonest and take away from those whose need was so desperate. As for the building, he said, "I am going to build ten buildings, and I am working on them already. When those ten buildings are finished, the whole world will know my buildings." He was talking about his children.

CHAPTER 11

The Seminary

And I heard the voice of the Lord, saying, whom shall I send, and who will go for us? Then said I, Here am I, send me.

—Isaiah 6:8

Four months after graduating from tenth grade (the Pakistani equivalent of high school), Sadiq, now nearly seventeen, left Sunder once again, this time for St. Mary's Minor Seminary in Lahore. It was August 1959, almost twelve years since the agony of partition had torn India in two. The years ahead would challenge him, as they would his country and the church in which he would serve.

Founded in 1886, the diocese of Lahore was the oldest Catholic diocese in Pakistan. In 1951, St. Mary's Seminary had opened its doors to train Pakistan's first indigenous priests. The Catholic Church had begun to realize that the effectiveness of the foreign missionaries—who were still associated with the former British rule—was diminishing. It was increasingly evident that the Church in Pakistan would have to become more "Pakistani."

There are two types of seminaries. Both are academic institutions, offering classes toward fully accredited college degrees. The minor seminary builds the student's foundation in philosophy and theology, while the major seminary completes the training begun in the minor seminary, offering advanced degrees.

The first step to becoming a seminarian was the application form, which had to be completed, signed by both parents, and presented to the bishop of Lahore. "My father signed it right away," says Father Joseph. "He was proud that the son of the catechist was aspiring to the priesthood. It was, in a sense, a validation of his own life. My mother, however, had different concerns; she had her own plans for me. When I came to her with the form and asked her to make her thumb impression, she stalled. So my father intervened. 'Mariam, even though Sadiq is our son, he is first the son of God, a gift to us. And if he is called, who are we to say no? Just imagine,' he continued, 'if one day, Sadiq is crossing the road to collect wood and is struck by a tonga and dies, do you want to be responsible for the vocation that we did not allow? How then would you answer God?'"

Babu Barkat understood what was going through Mariam's mind; in just a few years, four of her children had left home, two sons to be married, and two daughters to join the convent. She missed her children terribly. "Do you have any idea what you're asking me to do?" she cried. "Sadiq is a child I can trust with my heart. When he is not in school, he is like a second mother to baby Shafqat, helping me all through the day and never complaining. I have already given two children to God. That's enough!"

In Babu's mind however, there was no room for equivocation. "That's not fair to Sadiq," he continued. "He should also be given the right to choose his own path."

Mariam sighed deeply, resignation and pain etched on her face. "I do trust the Lord, but the fact is, you are not well and we are not getting any younger. We will need a lot of help, and I don't want to lose him."

"We will not lose Sadiq if we give him to God," Babu persisted, "but if you refuse to sign his form, you *will* lose him. Allow Sadiq to fulfill his dreams. He will not only be an apostle to the Lord, he will also bring many souls to God."

Mariam knew in her broken heart that Babu was right. "Bring your application form and I will make my mark."

Sadly, Babu would not live to see his son ordained a priest.

In addition to the application, Sadiq also needed to undergo a per-

sonal interview (no problem) as well as meet certain academic requirements (big problem). The seminary was not especially eager to admit
Sadiq, since he had graduated in the third division of his class, but being
the son of a catechist and seeing the determination and sincerity of his
vocation, they accepted him. Sadiq would spend three years at St. Mary's
and six more at the major seminary in Karachi, preparing his mind and his
soul for God's service.

Before beginning his studies at St. Mary's, Sadiq and four other
soon-to-be seminarians would spend two months on a retreat in the hills
near Dalwal, home to one of the oldest and richest salt mines in the world.
Dalwal was also known for its hundred-year-old Mission High School run
by the Capuchin Franciscan priests. Over the years, many of Pakistan's
military and government leaders had been educated there.

During the retreat, the five students were encouraged to explore
the area, spend time in prayer and reflection, and get to know each other.
For Sadiq, it was also a time to practice his English, since the lectures were
in English (and he would be the only non-English-speaking student in the
seminary).

"We had to get up very early every morning but that was not a
problem for me," Father Joseph recalls. "I was used to rising early from
village life so I would get up before everyone else and go for a walk. The
first morning, when I returned from my walk, I noticed a strange object
on the table by my bed. Curious, I picked it up, and at that very moment it
made a loud, jarring noise. Startled, I immediately dropped it. It turned out
to be an alarm clock, something I had never seen before."

One afternoon, the seminarians went for a hike. Passing a little
swimming hole, Sadiq decided to take a closer look. Suddenly he noticed
a huge, deadly king cobra coiled at the base of a large tree. "It was spreading its hood and weaving its wicked little head in anticipation of having
me for lunch," says Father Joseph. The king cobra is the largest venomous
snake in the world, and although their venom is not the most potent, they
can inject enough in a single bite to kill an elephant.

Nearly catatonic with fear, Sadiq shouted a warning, jumped in the water, and sank like a rock. He could not swim. Luckily, another student heard him and pulled him out. Ironically, Sadiq had grown up near a river and a canal, yet never learned to swim. Mariam would not allow her children to go into the water because every year, several children drowned in the Ravi River.

In Pakistan and all over the world, the cobra is the stuff of legends, often associated with snake charmers. Traditionally a family business, the art of snake charming is passed from generation to generation, the mystique behind it a well-guarded secret. There are many theories about the practice of snake charming; some have a scientific basis, others take a more folkloric approach. Snake charmers appear to hypnotize a snake by playing a flute-like instrument—but the music is irrelevant; the cobra responds more to ground vibrations and does not hear the flute. It is the snake charmer's skillful manipulation of the snake's natural characteristics that causes it to perform, rising up and extending its hood in a normal defensive reaction. The snake thinks the swaying pipe is another snake. As the charmer moves the flute back and forth, the cobra rises up, bobbing its head and swaying to and fro, a natural reaction to the movement of the flute.

* * *

Sadiq was in awe of the place in which he found himself. The inspiring and sanctified halls of learning would fill him with spiritual fervor, and would introduce the boy from the village to the marvels of the twentieth century, among them, indoor plumbing, telephones, and hot water.

The life of a seminarian is not an easy one. The educational requirements for the priesthood are daunting—even if you do not have the handicap of language and inferior primary schooling. Although many answer the call to serve, few pass the rigorous training, and even fewer are able to sustain the lifelong commitment to their apostolic mission. But for those young men with the passion, determination, and desire to serve God, the journey becomes its own reward.

Classes at St. Mary's would be a head-full, including world history, theology, scripture, French, English, Latin, and Urdu—all taught in English. And in a country where rote learning was the system of choice, the emphasis on critical thinking would be a major change for Sadiq. In addition to coursework, seminarians also participated in daily Mass, the Liturgy of the Hours (the daily prayers every priest must say), spiritual retreats, meditation, sports, and pastoral and community service. Students were also expected to spend time reflecting on their vocation, continually evaluating their thoughts, desires, and beliefs, as well as seeking a more profound relationship with God. The cornerstone of the Catholic faith is the celebration of the Eucharist, the changing of the bread and wine into the body and blood of Christ, uniting the faithful in God's presence, a miracle that Sadiq would experience every day at St. Mary's.

Once again, the seminary was full of challenges and changes. "Even my name was changed, recalls Father Joseph. "The rector told me straight away my name was too ordinary, too common. 'You need a religious name, a saint's name.' My baptismal name was Joseph so that's what I would be called. For sixteen years, I had been Sadiq, now I would become Joseph."

Joseph also acquired a new surname. His brother Peter needed some kind of identification at the office where he worked, so he had adopted the name Nisari, which means "follower of Jesus of Nazareth." By calling himself Nisari, he was also identifying himself as a Christian.

"Growing up, some of my siblings were called by their Christian names, some were not," says Father Joseph. "My oldest brother's name was Inayat, which means 'gift from heaven.' His Christian name was Felix, but to us he was always Inayat. My second brother, Patras, became Peter. Teresa was always Teresa, Benjamin was Benjamin, Louisa became Maria after joining the convent, Sabina was always Sabina, Justina was Justina, Parveen became Mary Rose, and Paul was always Shafqat. Joseph was my father's Christian name and Christians sometimes used their Christian name as a surname, so before we became Nisaris, we were Josephs, as in Sabina Joseph, Teresa Joseph, etc. While I was in the seminary, I would be called Brother Joseph."

At St. Mary's, Brother Joseph lived in a dormitory with nine other boys. Each had his own bed with a little cupboard for his belongings. Downstairs was a kitchen, dining room and study room; upstairs was the dorm. Most of the time, the boys did their own laundry. Meals were provided, but the boys were expected to arrange the table and wash the dishes.

In public, the seminarians wore a *shervani*, a knee-length coat with long sleeves and a collar. However, none of the seminary's stash of shervanis fit Joseph, so he was excused from wearing one and instead went about in his regular pants and shirt. Even in the seminary, his sartorial situation had not improved.

There were only five students in Joseph's class, and seven professors. Joseph was the only Urdu/Punjabi-speaking seminarian, the other four students being English-speaking Cambridge graduates. This meant that their high school exams had been sent from Cambridge University, in England, in English. Brother Joseph would have to learn English quickly and well.

* * *

Early on the morning of May 1, 1960, while Brother Joseph was still at Mass at St. Mary's, a young American pilot, Francis Gary Powers, flying a Lockheed U-2A spy plane, took off from Pakistan's Peshawar Air Station on a mission to overfly the Soviet Union, photographing intercontinental ballistic missile (ICBM) sites. Powers was shot down over the Soviet Union and captured, precipitating the infamous "U-2 Incident."

Powers successfully bailed out of his aircraft, but either neglected to, or was unable to, activate the plane's self-destruct mechanism—which he should have done, according to his orders—before he parachuted to the ground, and into the custody of the KGB.

Powers was subsequently convicted of espionage and sentenced to three years in prison and seven years of hard labor. He served only twenty-one months before being exchanged, along with American student Frederic Pryor, in a spy swap for KGB Colonel Rudolf Abel.

Powers' flight was made possible by a 1957 agreement between US President Dwight Eisenhower and Pakistani Prime Minister Huseyn Shaheed Suhrawardy to establish a US intelligence facility in Pakistan. The facility became a cover for a photo-intelligence and electronic intercept operation established by the American National Security Agency (NSA). The base was closed in January 1970.

* * *

The months passed quickly and in May 1962, Joseph successfully completed his studies at St. Mary's. The following September, he would join seventy other young men at Christ the King Seminary in Karachi, eight hundred miles south of Lahore on the Arabian Sea. To Joseph, it would seem like the end of the earth.

CHAPTER 12

Karachi

But the foolish things of the world hath God chosen, that
he may confound the wise; and the weak things of the
world hath God chosen, that he may confound the strong.

—Corinthians 1:27

Very early on a steamy morning in August, Joseph and his father traveled from Sunder to Lahore by bus, hauling a large trunk (carried on Joseph's head), a bundle of bedding, and a sewing machine. In the heavy metal trunk were Joseph's books, clothes, and shoes, plus some items his two brothers, who lived in Karachi, had requested. The sewing machine was for his sister-in-law, who was a seamstress.

From Lahore, Joseph would travel by train on the twenty-hour journey to Karachi. Joseph had never been so far from home, nor had he ever been on a train.

In the early afternoon, Joseph and his father arrived at the massive, red-brick train station with its crowds of people and animals milling about in the numbing heat, swatting the ever-present flies and mosquitoes. Inside, walls of graceful arches rose tall above the vendor stalls. Coolies in their red caps and shirts struggled with the oversized loads on their heads, or pushed mountains of luggage on creaky wooden trolleys. Men slept sprawled on the concrete floor, while women tended their infants, squatting amid piles of bundles, baskets of vegetables, disturbed chickens, and the occasional goat. Vendors roamed the platform selling boiled eggs, sweet cakes, and hot tea. Families sat on the floor eating their meals, the few Catholics among them crossing themselves before eating.

The train Joseph would take to Karachi was not the train popular-
ized in *National Geographic's* early photographs of India, with peasant
bodies covering every square inch of the train, crouched on the roof, and
hanging out of windows and doors. Those were the local trains, the ones
that traveled shorter distances, and wherever people could put a foot or
grab onto something, they did. The funny thing about trains in Pakistan
was that they would sell tickets to ride on any surface—roof, floor, wherever. It really didn't seem to matter.

Joseph's train was the Karachi Express, "the fast current," and
although not crowded in the extreme, it was fully occupied. The train had
about seventy *boggies* (cars). First-class passengers rode in the first car,
followed by the second-class cars, then the economy class. Nobody had
thought (or knew) to make reservations, so Joseph immediately set out,
going from car to car, searching for an empty seat. There were none.

When the screech of the whistle and bursts of steam signaled the
train's imminent departure, Joseph still had no seat. Finally, Babu pushed
him through the door and shuffled the trunk through a window. The bedding also came through the window, landing on Joseph's head. The trunk
quickly disappeared among the jumble of bodies and possessions.

Meant to hold about fifty people, nearly one hundred had crammed
themselves into the stifling compartment, sitting or standing wherever
they could find a scrap of space, on the floor, on the hard, wooden seats, on
trunks, bedrolls, even in the luggage racks. As Joseph stood there, sweat
streaming from every pore, bedding on his head, and sewing machine in
hand, the aged olive-green train lurched into motion, clacking down the
track past the barren, late-summer landscape.

Babu stood in the fading light of the station platform and waved
forlornly. It would be a year before Joseph saw his family again.

Thirty miles out of Lahore the stuffy, airless train made its first
stop and several people got off with their baskets and bundles. Suddenly
Joseph spotted his trunk. Someone was sitting on it. He didn't have the
courage to tell him to get off, but at least now he could put the sewing

machine and bedding on the floor.

Hour after hour, the train rolled south across the Punjab, toward the deserts of Sindh. Still Joseph stood. The train made a few more stops and each time, a few more people got off. Now a spot on the floor was available, and Joseph settled down with his feet stretched out in front of him. Finally, around midnight, a berth opened up. Joseph grabbed it and was instantly asleep.

When the train pulled into the last stop, Joseph was still sleeping. One of the porters came along and shook him. "Young man, where are you going?" he asked. When Joseph told him, he shook his head. "Your stop has long passed. You will have to go back." But the coolie had a kind heart as well as a solution. "You seem to be new, so give me three rupees and I'll get you a return ticket," he said. "There's a local train leaving in ten minutes." In a few minutes, the porter had secured a ticket and was helping Joseph transfer his luggage to the other train. This time, he got off at the right stop.

Although Joseph had finally arrived in Karachi, he had no idea where to go. He knew only the name of the street where his brother lived, and that it was the last house on the lane. His mother had told him that much. The station was hot, dark, and weirdly quiet. A few coolies were about, even at this early hour, in their red shirts and red turbans, a roll of cloth on top of their heads to cushion the loads. Joseph approached one and explained his dilemma. The little, wiry, brown man squatted down while Joseph put the trunk on his head and the bedding on top of the trunk. Joseph took the sewing machine and off they went through the humid, starless night, to find his brother's house. It was four o'clock in the morning when they finally knocked on Felix's door. The next day, Joseph went to the seminary. He took a taxi.

* * *

Surrounded by hundreds of miles of desert, Karachi—in 1962, the capital of Pakistan—was a huge, sprawling port city, a cultural melting pot, and an architectural mix of British colonialism and the exotic style of ancient dynasties. The narrow, winding alleys of the old city ran alongside wide boulevards lined with contemporary buildings. Camels, donkey carts, and three-wheeled rickshaws creaked along beside modern cars and buses. Along a mile-long stretch of the Layari River, people still washed their clothes as they had for centuries at the *Dhobi Ghat*, the city's largest public laundry.

To Joseph, Karachi was another world, a cosmopolitan oasis in the middle of the desert. Steeples and minarets dotted the skyline, and on Sundays, the bells from St. Patrick's blended with the Islamic call to prayer floating from the city's mosques. Near the city center, the National Mausoleum—the tomb of Pakistan's founder, Muhammad Ali Jinnah—dominated the landscape with its graceful Moorish arches and white marble dome. A four-tier crystal chandelier hung in the cool, tranquil interior, a gift from the People's Republic of China.

Joseph had never seen the ocean before. He recalled the first time he went to the beach. "I just stood there looking at the endlessness and immensity of it. You could even go for camel rides along the beach. Later on, we seminarians would go fishing at Clifton Beach and, lo and behold, I was the one who caught the most fish. Me, who had never fished before or even seen an ocean."

* * *

Christ the King was a new seminary, having opened just five years earlier with only four students, among them Lawrence Saldanha, who later became Archbishop of Lahore. Other alumni included Bishop John Joseph of Faisalabad, who would fatally shoot himself in 1998 to protest the death sentence handed down to a Catholic convicted of blasphemy under the infamous Blasphemy Law.

Although much of Karachi was barren, sandy, and dry, the seminary compound was located in an area called the green zone, with lush tropical plants, palm trees, and a pleasant little stream flowing through the grounds. The compound included several stately old buildings, one housing classrooms, seminarians, and the rector, the other housing the vice rector, spiritual director, and additional classrooms.

St. Patrick's Cathedral, the seat of the Archdiocese of Karachi, was about eight miles away. Opened in 1881, the massive brick church could seat 1,500 worshippers. In front of the cathedral, a magnificent, larger-than-life marble monument commemorated the Jesuit mission in Sindh, and was dedicated to Christ the King, inscribed with the words, "Thou art Peter, and upon this rock, I will build my church." The cathedral was adjacent to St. Patrick's High School for boys and the Convent of Jesus & Mary (CJM) school for girls. Pakistan's ruling classes had been educated at St. Patrick's since the nineteenth century, and CJM had been among Pakistan's most renowned girls' educational establishments for decades, counting among its graduates Benazir Bhutto, a two-time prime minister of Pakistan and the first woman elected to lead a Muslim state. (Bhutto was assassinated December 27, 2007, two weeks before the Pakistani general election, in which she was a leading opposition candidate.)

The curriculum at Christ the King concentrated on academic as well as spiritual training, with courses in philosophy, theology, history, comparative religion, liturgy, and canon law. Students prepared for their future missions in a variety of hands-on environments, including schools, hospitals, and local parishes. Practical learning, such as preaching, celebrating Mass, and pastoral counseling, was also included. Seminarians in their third year and above wore white cassocks with a blue sash. And this time, Joseph would find one that fit.

Once again, Joseph was the only non-English-speaking student. Although his English was much improved, a considerable amount of his class work would be lost in translation.

Seminary life was rigorous and regimented. Students rose in the morning at five thirty, attended Mass at seven o'clock, and ate breakfast at seven thirty. For breakfast, there would be omelets, perhaps *paratha* or porridge. Lunch was usually rice with curry or vegetables; supper was chapatis, lentils, and other vegetables. Tea was offered every afternoon at three o'clock, and if there was a feast day or special occasion, there might be snacks with the tea. Students studied from three thirty to four thirty, followed by sports (hockey, basketball, or volleyball) from five to six o'clock. Supper was at seven thirty, after which the students studied again until nine thirty, followed by prayers and lights-out at ten.

At Christ the King. Joseph would have his first encounter with a modern indoor toilet—a toilet that *flushed,* if one could imagine. It seemed like pure magic. At St. Mary's, the seminarians had used only the ubiquitous Indian-style latrines.

* * *

When Joseph's sister Sabina was sixteen years old, she joined the Franciscan Sisters of Christ the King in Karachi, a local congregation started in India. Unknown to Sabina, Joseph was, at the same time, in his first year at Christ the King Seminary, also in Karachi. Communication being what it was in those days, Sabina had no idea that Joseph was in Karachi, nor was Joseph aware of his sister's presence in the same city.

Some time after Sabina arrived, she began to feel homesick. "I was not allowed to communicate with my family and I didn't know anyone," she remembers. "One month passed and there was nobody to speak to—everything was in English. We were not allowed to speak Punjabi or Urdu, and I didn't know English.

"After the second month, I still could not communicate with the other nuns. One day, our confessor came to the convent to hear confessions. Father Louis knew that I was Joseph's sister and, after listening to my litany of frustrations, he said simply, 'Go to Joseph.' I did not understand what he meant. Who was this Joseph? I went to my novice mistress and told her what Father Louis had said. What could this possibly mean, I asked her. She told me to go and pray.

"Some time later, I was kneeling in the chapel and Father came to me again. 'Did you go to see Joseph?' he asked. I said no. Then I went again to my novice mistress. By now, she was also concerned and went to see Father Louis. 'Why are you telling Sister Sabina to go to Joseph? She has no idea what you are talking about.' Father replied, 'I told her to go to her brother, Joseph, who is a student at the seminary.' When the novice mistress told me that my brother was right there in Karachi, in the seminary, I was ecstatic. I, of course, had no idea that my brother's name was now Joseph, which is why 'go to Joseph' had no meaning for me."

Sabina recalls the moment when Joseph came to the convent to see her. "I was summoned to the parlor and Joseph was hiding behind the door. When he saw me, he said 'Boo!' and hugged me. Immediately I started crying. I was so happy."

Sabina told Joseph of her frustrations. "I explained that my biggest problem was, quite simply, I couldn't speak English. Prayers were said in English, everything was spoken in English, and I could not follow. I was very frustrated."

"Don't worry, you'll catch on," Joseph consoled his sister. "Meanwhile, just speak broken English. You'll make them laugh, and in a couple of months, you will be fine."

Before she joined the convent, Sabina had studied the saints and read many books about their lives to her father. "I remembered reading about their sacrifices and that there was a lot of penance involved. Coming from a warmer part of Pakistan, I did not have the proper clothes for cold weather, and during the winter, I was always cold. I would not ask for more blankets because the saints did not ask. Instead, I prayed to God for strength, and like some of the saints, I even kept some stones under my mattress. I would offer up my discomfort in the name of Christ. I slept on those stones every night. One day, my novice mistress asked me to put my bedding in the sun and she saw the stones. 'Why are you doing this mad thing?' she asked. By then, I knew she liked me."

* * *

In the summer of 1964, nearly blind and suffering from emphysema, Babu-ji was nearing the end of his life. Joseph was in his second year at Christ the King Seminary.

As a catechist, Babu-ji had spent his life visiting and ministering to people. One of the most significant characteristics of his interaction with his flock, and an important cultural connection, happened when all the men would come together in a circle, sitting on charpoys either inside or outside, and smoking the hookah, which had been a social mainstay for centuries. According to the village men, they digested their food better when they smoked the hookah.

Although still in use in many cultures, cigarettes eventually replaced the hookah. But enjoying the camaraderie of the hookah all his life probably played a part in Babu-ji's eventual demise. Women did not smoke often, and never in public, but when Babu-ji came home, he expected his hookah to be lit and ready to puff. It was Mariam's job to prepare the hookah and keep it going until her husband came home, but in order to keep it going, she would have to puff a little now and then. One day when Mariam had to be gone for a little while, she asked Sadiq, then about ten years old (and not yet called Joseph) to prepare the hookah while she was away. To keep it going he had to take a few puffs, so he puffed away. By the time Mariam returned, the hookah was still going—but Sadiq was not.

The summer that Babu-ji died, Joseph was home from the seminary but remained at the disposal of his church, and of his parish priest and family friend, Father Fidentian. "Sometimes I would go with him on his rounds on his motorbike," says Joseph. "I admired this man who could ride a motorbike that was spitting fire while the sky was scorching, the road sizzling, and the tar melting. For me, a young Pakistani, the heat was hard to take, but he was a Belgian in his late fifties, so his endurance was all the more amazing.

"We would start in the morning from Lahore and travel to Shahdara, and from there to Pattoki thirty miles away, then another ten miles to Chunian, blessing, praying, and officiating at weddings and funerals. Then we would head back home again—an eighty-mile round trip—arriving around nine o'clock in the evening. To myself I thought, Wow, this is really hard work."

His health failing, Babu-ji had moved in with Joseph's brother Peter and his family. In those days, emphysema was thought to be infectious, so family members were not allowed to come close to him, nor could friends visit him. All his life, he had been a man of the people and the imposed isolation was the cause of great frustration.

As his condition worsened, Father Fidentian took Babu-ji to the Mayo Hospital, one of the oldest and largest hospitals in Lahore, named after the then viceroy of the subcontinent, the Earl of Mayo. While his father was in the hospital, Joseph would visit him whenever he could. After a few days, Babu-ji was taken back home, his emphysema so bad they could do nothing more.

In those days, health care for the poor was (and still is) extremely inadequate. There were many committed and excellent doctors, but their success was severely hampered by the lack of modern equipment, sophisticated medicines, and adequate salaries. In most hospitals, patients had to have a family member with them to provide even simple care and, since no meals were served, they also had to supply the patient's food.

On Joseph's last visit, his father no longer recognized him. A fog had fallen upon him; his mind as well as eyes had gone dark. The next day was Sunday, and Joseph went by bus to Lahore to attend Mass. Afterward, Father Fidentian approached him and said, "Babu-ji is dead, he has gone to his God."

Babu-ji was far too young—sixty-five years old—to have been taken from this earth, Joseph thought, but God is the gardener, and he had plucked one of his finest fruits.

It was the custom to bury the dead on the same day, so those family members who lived further away in Karachi missed the funeral, arriving the day after. There was a funeral Mass and afterward Babu-ji was buried, without a coffin, covered by a simple sheet. Typically, only the men attended the burial service, but this time custom would not prevent Babu-ji's wife and daughters from saying goodbye to their beloved husband and father.

Saddened at the loss of the man he loved most in the world, Joseph was concerned for his mother. "What are you going to do now?" he asked her.

"I will be fine," she replied. "God will look after me."

* * *

During his fourth year in the seminary, Joseph was appointed head beadle. The position was an honor of sorts, and his new duties included mentoring, representing the students to the rector, and representing the rector to the students. Joseph had gained the trust and good will of the rector, but when the other seminarians began to call him "God Almighty," he felt perhaps he might have been a little too zealous in his beadleship.

At every step along the way, the seminarians were continually testing their constancy, evaluating their vocation, and renewing their commitment. After his fifth year, Joseph was ordained a transitional deacon— one step away from the priesthood. As he had always done, Joseph worked hard to overcome his academic deficiencies. Night after night, month after month, he pondered theology and philosophy (in English) and slowly came to know the power and love of his God.

People often wonder how priests "learn" to celebrate Mass. "It starts during your last year in the seminary," Father Joseph explained, "after your ordination date is set. The rector or spiritual director guides you through the steps, and when you use the Mass book, there are rubrics written in red in the text: 'At this prayer, raise your hands,' 'At this prayer, join your hands,' 'Now lift up the chalice,' and so forth. The celebration of Holy Mass was a daily event in the seminary, and when you observe something every day for many years, it eventually becomes a part of you. Learning to preach, however, is something else. My classmate delivered his first sermon to the seminarians, but he was so nervous he couldn't stand because his knees were shaking so badly. We brought him a chair to hold on to. Now he is Archbishop Everest Pinto of the Karachi diocese."

During the last six months of study, Brother Joseph embarked on his pastoral training at Issa Nagri, a small village near the seminary with a large Christian population. Because he spoke the language of the people, Joseph achieved some degree of success, conducting Bible services and frequently assisting the priest at Mass. The liturgy at the time was said in Urdu and since most of the local people still spoke Punjabi, Joseph had the advantage of fluency in both. In time, he would become a popular and much sought-after preacher in Urdu and Punjabi. But he still struggled with English. The rector cleverly avoided giving him assignments at the English-speaking churches in the area that served the Anglo-Christian population.

"With English, I still struggled to express myself. The fluency was not there, and I found it frustrating to think, translate, and preach, all at the same time. But I never used a prepared paper. I relied completely on the Holy Spirit, and although it was quite a lot to ask, he never disappointed me. Every day, I felt that God was working through me, even though I was not a very sharp instrument."

On June 11, 1968, Joseph attended the last day of his last retreat in the seminary. "I still remember Monsignor Jack's words: 'So far we have only opened your eyes. Your training and education does not stop here, it begins here, and you will never stop learning.' He also told us what to expect in our parish ministries and how we should relate to people. 'The elderly in your flock will be as your fathers and mothers, those close to your own age will be your brothers and sisters, the younger ones will be your children in spirit of the Lord.'"

After a grueling nine years of study, the long journey drew to a close and Joseph passed his final examinations. The shy little *besura* from the dusty plains of the Punjab was about to become an ordained priest. Profoundly grateful to God for his vocation, he thought not only of what had passed, but what was yet to come. *"Am I worthy? Will I be able to lead people to God?"*

CHAPTER 13

Ordination

*Going therefore, teach ye all nations; baptizing them in
the name of the Father, and of the Son, and of the Holy
Ghost. Teaching them to observe all things whatsoever I
have commanded you: and behold I am with you all days,
even to the consummation of the world.*

—Matthew 28: 19, 20

At ten o'clock in the morning of January 6, 1968, Brother Joseph
was ordained Father Joseph Nisari at the historic Sacred Heart
Cathedral, in his own diocese of Lahore. He was twenty-five
years old.

Joseph had been preparing for this day all his life, yet he felt anxious, exhilarated, and totally unqualified for the enormous task ahead. After morning prayers and meditation, Joseph walked in procession with the
bishop from the Bishop's house to the cathedral. This would be Bishop
Alphonse Raeymaeckers' first ordination, Joseph the first seminarian to be
ordained by his hand.

Rich in history and symbolism, the ordination ceremony is a sort
of spiritual alchemy, transforming an ordinary man into something extraordinary. It is the sacred rite in which a man becomes a priest, enabling
him to minister in Christ's name, forgive sins, baptize the faithful, prepare
the dying, and most notably, to transform bread and wine into the body
and blood of Christ.

Most of the liturgy in the two-and-a-half-hour ceremony would be
sung in Latin, still the formal language of the church at the time. For the
benefit of the congregation, a priest would provide an on-going explanation of the ritual in the Urdu language.

As the sacred music resonated through the church, Joseph entered the house of God, accompanied by more than fifty priests and seminarians. The bishop then called upon Almighty God to receive his servant. Offering public testimony to his worthiness, Joseph presented himself before his God, the church, and the community, prostrating himself on the marble floor in a sign of humility and submission.

Laying his hands on Joseph's head, the bishop then ordained him, calling upon the Holy Spirit to bless and guide the new priest. Each member of the assembled clergy then passed before the newly ordained priest and laid their hands upon his head. He was, at that moment, officially a priest of God. The faith that had been passed down through the centuries from Jesus himself would continue now in Father Joseph.

After the bishop recited the Prayer of Ordination, Joseph removed his deacon's stole and received the presbyteral stole and chasuble, the symbols of his new office. Moments later, he received the chalice and paten, signifying the importance of the Eucharist, the cornerstone of the priesthood. "Accept from the holy people of God the gifts to be offered to him," the bishop intoned. "Know what you are doing, and imitate the mystery you celebrate: model your life on the mystery of the Lord's cross." Then Joseph joined the bishop and his fellow priests on the altar to concelebrate the Mass.

The Mass concluded with the kiss of peace and the solemn blessing. The clergy welcomed the new priest with embraces, and Bishop Raeymaeckers knelt before Joseph to receive his first blessing. Then Joseph turned to his mother, brothers, and sisters seated on the first row, to bestow his second blessing. A proud Mariam wiped away tears, "He worked so hard for this. He will be a good priest."

When Joseph went to bed that night, he felt completely at peace, yet profoundly changed.

The next day, his white cassock and white sash replacing the old seminarian blue, Joseph began his first day on his new job, full of grace, apprehension, and more than a little apostolic zeal.

The following Sunday, the newly-minted priest celebrated his first Mass at St. Joseph's, where he had spent so much of his time while at Burki Middle School, and where his brother lived and his sister and sister-in-law taught at the Catholic school.

"Many years later, I heard from a priest who, as a teenager, had been present at my first Mass," Joseph says. "He told me he was delighted to hear me celebrating the Mass in Urdu with such fluency. He was used to the Belgian priests, foreigners who could hardly speak our language. This pleased me enormously, and still pleases me today."

The Sunday after that, Joseph went back to Sunder to celebrate Mass in the little village of his childhood. There was still no church, but it was a bright, sunny January day and an altar had been set up outside. This would be the first Mass to be celebrated in the village with the celebrant facing the people, in accordance with the changes from Vatican II.

"My aunt, who was in her eighties, arrived at the service late," Joseph recalls. "She probably had no idea what was going on, and since I was facing the people, she may have thought I was blessing them, but I was actually in the middle of celebrating Mass. After a few minutes, Auntie Jivan toddled slowly toward the altar, leaning heavily on her walking stick. Pausing, she looked up at me with proud, gentle eyes and, placing her hands on my head, bestowed a traditional expression of love and blessing. I had to stop for a minute and collect myself before I could continue the Mass. I don't know how much of the Mass she understood. The catechists tried to explain these things to the people, but only God knew how much they really understood."

In 1962, Pope John XXIII had convened the Second Vatican Council (Vatican II), which would have profound implications for Catholics, introducing far-reaching changes in freedom of choice and democracy in the political arena, and bringing the church into the twentieth century. For the first time, priests would celebrate Mass with the people rather than for them, facing the people rather than facing the altar. The faithful would no longer be required to endure incomprehensible Latin Masses; the liturgy would now be said in the local language.

Perhaps most surprising for those raised in pre-Vatican II Catholicism was the new teaching that even non-Christian religions could offer salvation.

Standing as he was, between the old and the new, Joseph was one of first native priests after one hundred years of foreign missionaries. He was among the first to introduce the villages to the changes of Vatican II, and he was involved early on in changing the economics of the church in Pakistan. Accustomed to receiving aid from foreign countries, it was obvious that the church had to become more self-supporting, changing its position from one of receiving to one of giving. He would also be among the first to break the color barrier: in Pakistan he was a dark-skinned native priest in a land dominated by white-skinned foreign clergy; later in the US, he would be a dark-skinned foreign priest in a land of white-skinned native clergy.

Joseph was warm, engaging, and approachable—and he spoke the native language. The people adored him; many had never heard the gospel spoken in their own language. Ultimately, Joseph would gain significant celebrity preaching throughout Pakistan at Masses, missions, and conventions, and for the next ten years, he would delight in his ministry.

Joseph was given a week in Lahore after his ordination, and then he went back to Karachi, where he would remain in the seminary for six more months. As an ordained priest, Father Joseph would have his own bedroom—for the first time in his life. Newly ordained priests were assigned separate bedrooms so they could spend time reflecting and celebrating Mass on their own.

New priests typically spend the first six months after ordination gaining practical, hands-on experience in a parish setting. Joseph was assigned to Issa Nagri, the little community where he had worked while in the seminary. Going back as an ordained priest was thrilling, both for Joseph and for the people. "Our Brother Joseph is now Father Joseph," the people said. Joseph affectionately remembers their ordination gift to him, a fat Urdu dictionary with a beautiful inscription that read, "From the people of Issa Nagri, with heartfelt gratitude and blessings of God on your ministry."

CHAPTER 14

The Biker Priest

The Spirit of the Lord God is upon me; because the Lord has anointed me to preach good news to the poor. He has sent me to bind up the brokenhearted, to proclaim freedom for the captives and release from darkness for the prisoners.

—Isaiah 61:1

After completing his pastoral year at the seminary, Joseph was assigned to Immaculate Heart of Mary (IHM) Church in Anarkali, Lahore. The Reverend Lawrence (Larry) Saldanha, the first ordained priest from the local seminary, was pastor at IHM; he would later become Archbishop of Lahore. Joseph would be responsible for 150 villages, while Father Saldanha would handle the urban communities. The assignment would be temporary because Joseph was filling in for a Belgian priest who had gone home on vacation. This was, altogether, not a bad first assignment considering that one of the most common difficulties in a priest's life is the isolation. In Pakistan at the time, as in many other countries and rural communities, the priest was often isolated by his education from the largely illiterate people in his parish community. Having someone with whom to share and communicate on the same level would be a bonus.

At IHM, Joseph was reunited with the motorcycle that had been in his head since he was a small boy. The motorcycle would become both a passion and a practical instrument in his ministry. With the realization that the power of God was at work within him, Joseph began to consider himself rather invincible, moved by the Spirit beyond normal human limitation (and often it seemed into the realm of plain stupidity).

Joseph found the motorcycle in the garage, a big, red, ten-year-old, 460-pound British-made Ariel 350. Every morning, Joseph went to the garage to look at the bike. One day, the catechist who lived next door said, "Father-ji, every day I see you coming to the garage to look at the motorbike. You will need to use it to visit the villages, so why don't you take it for a spin?"

"I don't know how to ride it," Joseph replied.

"Not a problem. I will help you. The first thing to remember is to keep the handles straight. Otherwise, it's like riding a bicycle."

Well, not exactly.

There was a kind of sloping road that ran from the church down to the playground. "Just sit on it and I'll give you a little push, and you can take it to the playground and make a couple of circles. You'll be fine," the catechist said encouragingly.

Gingerly, Joseph sat on the motorbike, the catechist pushed, and he coasted warily down to playground. Now what to do? A flock of children immediately gathered around. "Are you going to start the motorbike?" they asked.

Fortunately, the kids knew a great deal more about motorbikes than Joseph. One pointed out the clutch handle, another showed him the kick-start. A skinny little fellow with eyes full of mischief leaned in and showed him how to use the kick-start (jump up and down). Another said no, you must open the throttle first. Joseph opened the throttle and kicked. Nothing. He kicked again. And again. Suddenly the bike roared to life, and everyone cheered.

"Now let the clutch out slowly," one of the children directed. Joseph popped it too quickly. The bike stopped.

"Push your clutch handle back, put it in neutral, and kick again."

He kicked again and the bike started up. Slowly, he went around in a shaky first-gear circle. He was getting the hang of this.

"Why don't you put it in second gear?"

"Where is this second gear?" Joseph asked.

"You push the lever up."

Cautiously, he pushed the metal lever forward, picking up more speed. Twenty minutes later, sitting ramrod stiff so as not to disturb his second-gear momentum, Joseph arrived proudly at his brother Peter's house, five miles away. He had come through real (and terrifying) traffic. Never had a person learned so little about a motorcycle so quickly.

It was almost three in the afternoon, the hottest part of the day, when Joseph drove into the compound, sweat streaming from every pore. The bike was also hot from running five miles in second gear. Peter sent his daughter to tell Joseph it was time for dinner, so he parked the bike and went to wash up at the pump, holding his hot hands under the soothing water until they ached and began to stiffen. Suddenly, his hands became frozen, completely immobile, unable even to form a fist.

Meanwhile, an annoyed Father Saldanha was wondering what had happened to his priest. Suspecting he might find him at his brother's house, he took off on his bicycle. (Telephones at this time were still mostly the purview of the elite and well connected.)

"I thought I might find you here," an exasperated Father Saldanha said upon his arrival. "What happened?"

Joseph explained his predicament.

Looking like he wanted to kill Joseph, Father Saldanha took off on his bicycle with Joseph on the back, in search of some hot wax to treat his injured hands. Dipping hands or joints in hot paraffin was a common treatment for the relief of pain and stiff joints, a therapy that had been in use since the time of the Roman Empire.

It would be two days before Joseph's hands were well enough to drive the bike home.

Joseph's euphoria at having managed to tame the bike was short-lived. What happened next was clearly not his fault, at least not entirely.

Joseph's first out-of-city trip on the motorcycle was to visit one of his catechists in Dhokemandi, a village thirty miles from Lahore. Traveling along the narrow road at a good clip (having now added third gear to his repertoire), cheeks rippling in the wind, Joseph saw a bus coming toward him on the opposite side of the road. In front of him was a bicyclist with a large bundle of bedding on his carrier. Joseph honked, but the cyclist was too afraid to abandon the relatively smooth road for the gravel shoulder. Joseph pulled out to pass the bicycle, but soon realized there was not enough room for him and the bus to both pass, so he desperately applied his handbrakes, one of which struck the bundle on the back of the bicycle as he collided with it. Both riders went flying.

The catechist's house was not far away, and an astute villager quickly reported to him: "Your priest is wrecked down the road." The catechist came immediately and found Joseph, his pride bruised, but otherwise unhurt, sitting on the side of the road in a very dirty cassock. The catechist helped Joseph back to his house, but since the bike chain had been broken in the accident, Joseph had no way of returning home on the bike. The poor catechist had to go by bus to Lahore, which was thirty miles away, find a mechanic and a new chain, and then return by bus with the mechanic and chain.

Motorbikes were rare in the villages, and Joseph created a sensation wherever he traveled, dressed nattily in a black leather jacket over his white cassock; later on, he would add a helmet. Most animals ignored the bike and for the most part, gave no challenge. The dogs however, were attracted to the strange, noisy machine, a fact that would create trouble later on.

* * *

On a sweltering August morning, Joseph packed his Mass box, straddled his motorbike, and set out on the thirty-mile trip to Gazi Kakka. It was the first day of his first *daura*, or tour of the villages, as an ordained priest, and he really had no idea exactly where he was going, having no map and only the most ambiguous of directions. But first, Joseph had to make a slight detour.

Justina, Joseph's younger sister, had applied for teacher training at St. Joseph's school and needed a "domicile"—a document similar to a birth certificate—from Pajian, the village in which she was born. And she needed Joseph's help to get this document. So before he headed for Gazi Kakka, he would first have to drive to Pajian, hoping to see the *numbardar,* the village chief, and the only one who could provide this document. The document would then have to be delivered to the school in Lahore before Joseph could continue on his way to Gazi Kakka.

Arriving in Pajian about nine o'clock, Joseph discovered that the village chief had just left for a neighboring village. So off he went to the next village, only to find that the chief had just left for Lahore, where he apparently had another office. Off Joseph went again to track down the elusive numbardar.

Stopping at a traffic light, he suddenly noticed that his gear lever had gone missing. This presented a bit of a dilemma since, although the bike was running, it was in third gear. If he turned off the engine, he would not be able to start it up again. As he sat there pondering his predicament, a young man approached and asked what had happened.

"I've lost my gear lever and I have no idea how to start up the bike in third gear," said Joseph.

"No problem," said the young man.

Fortunately, Joseph's new friend had a wrench and helped him wrangle the bike into second gear. "There's a mechanic down the road who might be able to help you."

Joseph started off, traveling slowly in second gear. After the mechanic heard his story, he said simply, "Don't stop, just keep going," and hopped on the back of Joseph's bike. Down the road, they found a junkyard and managed to locate a gear lever on an old Triumph motorcycle.

"This is close, but if it doesn't fit, we can weld it," the mechanic said confidently. Back to the shop they went. It didn't fit, so he welded it.

With the newly welded, oversized gear lever in place, Joseph set out again, eventually securing the domicile for his sister and delivering it to the school. By then it was after two o'clock, and Joseph still had to get to Gazi Kakka, still thirty miles away. After a quick bite of rice pudding at the parish house, he headed off again, finally on his way to his regular job.

Traveling on daura often meant negotiating miles of unmarked roads, barely discernable ox-cart tracks, muddy canal banks, and unfriendly livestock. Most priests could only manage a daura a few times a year, so the villagers were accustomed to attending Mass only a couple of times a year.

When Joseph traveled on daura, he typically wore pants, an undershirt, and a white cassock, tucking the cassock up to keep it from getting caught in a wheel. In summer, he wore sandals; in winter, shoes. At home, he still wore the traditional shalwar kameez. He carried his vestments in his Mass box along with the chalice, communion wafers, candles, and wine. Communion wafers would be consecrated during the Mass, and any leftovers would be consumed by Joseph after the Mass. In a country where alcohol was prohibited, wine was the one thing the police would check whenever he traveled near the border. He was stopped frequently, and the questions were always the same. "Where are you going? Where are you coming from? What is in the box?" And they would open it and see the wine. "What's this?" they would ask.

"We use it for our celebration of the Mass," Joseph would reply. They did not understand the significance of the sacramental wine, but they always let him go, sometimes with a warning, sometimes with a quick nip for validation. Even though he was not crossing the border, he was in a sensitive and heavily guarded area, and police and border security inspected everyone, especially those on motorcycles who could obviously travel greater distances.

Joseph had been traveling for about an hour when he reached the village of Muridke. According to his directions, he was supposed to turn right after he crossed the stream, but the bridge was out. How could he get across? He decided to push his bike across the shallow part of the stream. A gentleman waiting on the other side asked if he could catch ride to his village a few miles away. Good idea, Joseph thought. Two heads would be better than one and besides, the man would at least know the way to his village.

When his hitchhiker hopped off at the next village, he gave Joseph a few more clues: "Go about two miles to the railroad track, cross over the track, then go down a little dirt road." Having gone only a short distance, Joseph suddenly found himself stuck in deep, powdery sand. The bike refused to move through the sand, so Joseph got off, left the engine running, and pulled the bike along, eventually arriving at the railroad crossing. On the other side of the crossing, Joseph was astonished to find himself suddenly knee-deep in water. He wondered if he was being tested. Was this "sea" going to part?

The water was coming from the canal that formed the border between Pakistan and India. Broken in several places, it had overflowed its banks after recent rains and now covered the roadway, all the way, it seemed, to the next village, about five miles away. By now, the bike was covered in mud, so Joseph tucked up his cassock, took off his sandals, rolled up his pants, and pushed and pulled the still-running bike through the water, until he found a semi-dry spot where he could put the kickstand down and go for help.

By now, twilight was fading and nightfall approaching. Whatever he did, he would have to do it soon. Hearing voices in the distance, he called out. Nobody answered. Finally he decided he would have to walk to the village, a risky undertaking since he was a total stranger in the middle of nowhere and would have to trust the safety of his motorcycle and Mass box to the Lord. With shoes in hand, Joseph took off wading through the night toward what he hoped was the village of Lahorian.

Walking soundlessly, Joseph could hear everything around him, water lapping, frogs croaking, crickets buzzing, bats winging, insects zinging, his heart thumping. After about half a mile, he noticed some rice paddies, barely visible in the dark. If he hadn't touched the ground, he would not have known what kind of crop it was. Arriving at a clearing near the edge of the village, he heard female voices and guessed the women had finished serving dinner and were now visiting the open-air latrines, a regular evening ritual. Often, when the moon was full and the night bright, the women would dance and sing after they finished their business, a kind of social hour or coffee klatch without the coffee. Joseph called out, "Dear sisters, I am a stranger here, looking for some Christians. Are there any here?"

"Dear brother," a woman replied out of the dark, "go to your right and you will find a little path through the paddy. You will come to a well and you might find some Christians there." Joseph thanked her and followed the little path to the well. Someone in the distance had a lantern and in the dim light, Joseph could make out several women and a few small children. Sweaty and covered in mud, he greeted them and asked for a drink of water, having had nothing since early afternoon. A woman gave him a cooling cup and he drank his fill.

"I am Father Joseph from Lahore, on my way to Gazi Kakka, but my motorcycle is stuck near the railroad crossing. Is there a numbardar whom I might ask for help?" One of the women replied that the numbardar would be arriving shortly.

About ten minutes later, the gentleman arrived and Joseph made his request again. "Come with me," the numbardar said, and they set off for his house where he grabbed a lantern and a big stick and, with Joseph in tow, proceeded to several other houses where he recruited three more men, some carrying swords, some rifles. Joseph asked why they carried guns and swords. "It is very dangerous now. This is a paddy crop and it is harvest time and wild boars are everywhere. If one sees you, it will attack, maybe even kill you." Joseph explained that he had traveled from the railroad crossing, alone and in the dark, and hadn't seen any. "Man of God is why," they reasoned. The villagers' concern was real. Wild boars were known to charge a man and slice him open like a watermelon.

Walking cautiously, ever on the alert for wild things, the men led the way back to the motorbike, where they took off their shoes and together pushed the bike through the water and back to the village. Then the numbardar asked his wife if she had made any food, to which she replied, "How could I? You took the lantern and I could not light the fire."

By this point, Joseph was no longer interested in food and asked only for a bed. It was now too late to continue his journey. "You cannot go to Gazi Kakka anyway. The hour is late and the border police will surely catch you," his host explained. "You can sleep here, and tomorrow morning you will have no problem." Joseph thanked him for his kindness and went immediately to sleep. Never had a simple charpoy felt so good. It was the end of Day One of his first daura, and Joseph had yet to find his first village.

Sometime around four o'clock in the morning, Joseph woke to the sound of bells, a sound he had heard every morning in the seminary. Dawn was just breaking as he looked out and saw two oxen shaking their heads, the bells ringing around their necks as they headed to the fields to plow. Everyone was still sleeping, so Joseph decided it was a good time to leave. Not knowing how to thank these kind people and not wanting to disturb them, Joseph rolled his motorcycle silently out to the road, started it, and took off along the bank of the canal, accompanied by a cheery morning symphony of crowing roosters, cawing crows, and barking dogs.

Around four in the afternoon, Joseph finally arrived at Gazi Kakka. His catechist, a gentle man called Brother Paul, was standing by the road, pacing up and down, visibly upset. When he saw Joseph, unable to contain himself, he blurted out, "What happened to you? We waited for you the whole night and were very worried . . . the direction from which you were coming is very dangerous. Hardly anyone has slept."

Joseph told him his story and the agitated man calmed a bit. "OK, you are here and you are safe, we still have time."

Brother Paul had two arms, but only one worked; the other hung limp and useless by his side. He wore a dhoti tied at the waist. Pakistani men did not wear underwear, and on one memorable occasion, Paul was riding on the back of Joseph's motorcycle when his dhoti became entangled in the wheel. Joseph heard some noise and when he turned around,

Brother Paul was lying on the sand, naked, his shredded dhoti still in the wheel of the bike. The people in the village provided him with another but he was greatly embarrassed.

Right away, Brother Paul went around calling to the villagers. "The priest is here, wash up and get ready, we will have Mass at so-and-so's house." There were about thirty families in the village, and this would be the first time the people would be introduced to the new Vatican II style of celebrating the Mass in Punjabi (instead of Latin), and facing the people instead of the altar.

For eight years, no priest had visited this tiny village. The priests who had previously served the area were foreigners, and since this was a border area, they were no longer allowed. Joseph explained the changes created by the Vatican Council in the simplest words possible because the people of Gazi Kakka were illiterate to a man.

Joseph began the Mass, which included forty baptisms, from tiny babies and toddlers to teenagers and a few adults. After Mass, Joseph finally sat down to eat. He had not eaten since his bit of rice pudding the day before and the simple meal they placed before him—eggs and tea with *paratha* (fried bread stuffed with vegetables)—looked like a wedding feast.

Joseph was the first Pakistani priest to visit the area, following a string of Belgian missionaries, who had established their own protocol regarding how breakfast was done for the priests. The Belgian priests loved boiled eggs, so Joseph got boiled eggs. "One day I had fourteen eggs from five different villages. Every village had prepared the same thing."

The visiting priest always attracted some curious non-Christian kids and a few adults. When Mass was celebrated in someone's house, the Muslim onlookers would gather outside, some climbing up on the wall for a better view. Ever aware that they were listening, Joseph's message was also for the benefit of the Muslim groupies. "Let whoever wants to listen, listen. I am only an instrument of God," he would say.

The next day, Joseph headed back to Lahore. One of the young men from the village had some business in Lahore and asked if he could catch a ride with Joseph. They took off, traveling on the left side of the road with the traffic—a British influence. Suddenly Joseph spotted a tonga coming toward him at full gallop. At the same time, a taxi was trying to overtake the tonga. The driver had little control of his horse, and suddenly the wheel of the tonga grazed the motorcycle, tossing both men into the air. The tonga driver had anticipated what was going to happen and jumped. He seemed none the worse for his unscheduled flight, but Joseph had fallen hard and had scratches and lacerations on his arms and legs. His passenger was unscathed and took him to a nearby dispensary where they patched him up.

When Joseph finally arrived back at the parish house, Father Saldanha was waiting. He was not happy. "What happened this time?" he sighed in exasperation. Aside from his penchant for skinning himself alive, Joseph felt that he had done nothing to cause any concern, and most certainly was not at fault. Father Larry always expected a story of Joseph's adventures, and Joseph never disappointed.

Joseph's brother Peter, like Father Larry, was not fond of the motorcycle. "Joseph was well known for making accidents with his motorcycle," Peter recalls. "Thank God, he survived to continue his work, despite his sheer negligence in driving that thing."

The following week, Joseph arranged another daura with another catechist. As soon as he arrived at the first village, he had a flat tire. Joseph— of course—had no idea how to fix it or even where to get it fixed; it was a small wonder that the tire had lasted this long. It took some time to get the tire repaired and Joseph was unable to return to Lahore that night. When he finally got back to the parish house the next day, the long-suffering Father Saldanha was waiting, as if on cue. "Always the motorbike," he sighed. "Perhaps it is an instrument of the devil rather than the Holy Spirit?"

Some time later, Joseph arranged to meet another priest at Gujranwala. About fifteen miles into the thirty-mile trip back to Lahore, the motorbike began to slow down and make strange noises. Finally it stopped cold. Perplexed, Joseph kick-started it, and the bike struggled on for about half of a mile. Then it slowed again, made more strange noises, and stopped. This time it refused to start back up. Joseph pushed the crippled bike fourteen miles back to Lahore in 110-degree heat, stopping at the first place that had a mechanic. "Please, water," Joseph gasped. He was too parched to talk.

"It's a good thing you stopped, your oil is almost paste," observed the mechanic with a toothless smile.

After an oil change, the bike started with the first kick and Joseph was on his way again, back to face Father Saldanha. He still had much to learn about this motorcycle.

* * *

During daura, Joseph maintained an exhausting schedule, typically visiting five villages a day, arriving at the last village after dark. Mass was usually celebrated in someone's home, often with as many as one hundred people crowded in and around a tiny airless house. During summer, an open door and some ventilation in the roof were the only relief from the oppressive heat. There were no windows and no lights—no electricity at all—but people managed well enough with candles and lanterns, which only added to the heat. Dressed in all his priestly vestments, Joseph would sweat profusely.

In every village, the routine was the same: hear confessions, review family cards, say Mass, conduct baptisms. The people were always thrilled to have the priest visit their village and would prepare elaborate songs for their special guest. The music was stirring, uplifting, and full of enthusiasm; they had, after all, been preparing for months. Unfortunately, Joseph often fell asleep before the concert was finished, snoring away to the sound of their beatific voices.

Slowly, Joseph made small changes in the traditional customs of the daura. Early on, he decided he would not submit to the customary washing of the feet. Because of the heat and dust of the region, whenever the priest arrived in a village, the villagers who greeted him would first receive his blessing, then bring a basin with water, soap, and towels, and wash his feet. But this was not Joseph's way. They were his people and they would not wash his feet. Joseph also rejected the custom of having the catechist give his monthly report to the priest while standing humbly before him, head bowed. Joseph's catechists would sit in a chair across from him. They were his assistants and would be honored and respected. There were always extra chairs in his office so that they didn't have to go looking for a place to sit.

"I was only a young priest; some of the catechists had thirty or more years of experience," Joseph remembers. "Whenever an older catechist would tell me 'I enjoyed your sermon,' it was high praise indeed. For the catechists, it was a big change from foreign to local priests; some probably didn't even think I was very knowledgeable because we had grown up believing that knowledge was the purview of the white people."

* * *

Joseph's next posting was at St. Luke's in Shahdara, and when he arrived, it was a troubled parish. The little community, once a prosperous entry to Lahore from Kabul and Kashmir and now a poor, dusty suburb, had planned to build a church and even had a site all staked out. As the story goes, the priest was supposed to supply the funds for the construction of the church. But, as Joseph soon discovered, in the neighboring community of Shadra Busti, there were also plans to build a church. The people of the two communities were divided on where the new church should be and who should support it, and were refusing to talk to each other.

Joseph realized some kind of compromise or reconciliation would be necessary to make peace so he gathered the two groups together in the middle of the village and sat down on the ground between them. Several people urged him to take a chair, but Joseph told them he would remain on the floor until they resolved their issues. Only then would he accept a chair. It took several hours to unravel things, but finally a compromise was struck. Everyone hugged everyone, and Joseph accepted a chair. Then Joseph declared, "In order to bind this unity—and this community—we need a project. Let us organize a *Mela* [gathering] in honor of the Assumption of the Blessed Virgin Mary," which was celebrated worldwide on August fifteenth.

Mela festivals were the community celebrations of the poor. For a Pakistani peasant, a Mela was like a country carnival or a day at Disney World. The Protestants had their religious conventions with famous imported speakers and entire evenings of prayer and celebration, and the Muslims had their own celebrations, but there had never been a Catholic Mela.

The parish collected funds and bought whatever was needed. Friends, relatives, and strangers were invited, and the result was a beautiful coming together of the community in feast and celebration. The bishop even came to celebrate Mass. The tradition of that very first Mela in honor of Mary, begun by Joseph so long ago, continues in Shahdara to this day.

CHAPTER 15

Sialkot

Christianity can never be a merely personal matter. It has
public consequences, and we must make public choices.
                              —Archbishop Desmond Tutu

In September 1968, Joseph began his ministry in Sialkot Cantt with a funeral. People commented that this was a good omen, but he would have preferred a happier occasion.

Located in northern Pakistan near the Kashmir-Jamun border, Sialkot would be Joseph's first permanent assignment, and he would spend the next year as a parish priest at St. James Church. Sialkot would also be Joseph's proverbial baptism of fire.

Sialkot is probably best known in Pakistan as the birthplace of the national poet and philosopher Sir Muhammad (Allama) Iqbal, whose vision of a sovereign state for the Muslims of British India would inspire the creation of Pakistan. It is also known internationally for the manufacture of sporting goods and surgical instruments.

The Catholic church in Sialkot was more than 120 years old, and many historians believe that Christianity began in the area. At the time, Sialkot had about twenty thousand Catholic families, three Catholic churches, three Catholic schools, and the well-known Convent of Jesus and Mary, established in 1865 as the first Catholic mission school in Punjab. Sialkot was also home to the renowned Murray College, founded by Scottish missionaries in 1889. In 1972, the Pakistani government would nationalize the college and dismiss the missionaries who had worked so hard—mostly without compensation—to educate the people of another country.

St. James was one of the oldest churches in Sialkot, celebrating its 150th birthday in 2006. Joseph would be the first Pakistani priest assigned to St. James, and would be responsible for the convent, one school, six catechists, and more than one hundred villages. It would be an enormous challenge, but one that Joseph welcomed.

Every October, the community celebrated the feast of St. Francis with a special Mass followed by a drama and a celebratory meal. To accommodate the large crowds, a stage had been erected outside the church, where Mass would be celebrated. This would be Joseph's first homily in his new community and he had prepared well. Full of zeal and enthusiasm, Joseph tucked up his sleeves in preparation for his usual animated oratory. But before he could utter the first word, there was a whisper from behind the stage curtain: "Just keep it short." At first startled, then mystified, Joseph could not believe his ears. He choked back a response and proceeded with his sermon—his very short sermon. Later, he said to the fellow behind the curtain, "You're lucky I am a priest."

Christmas had always been one of Joseph's favorite celebrations and he wanted his first Christmas at St. James to be something special for the congregation. He came upon the idea of writing down the Christmas story, in his own words, to be narrated during the Christmas Mass. In his mind, the story would begin with the creation, continuing with the promise of Mary and Jesus, the prophets, the angel appearing to Mary, her betrothal to Joseph, the holy family's trip to Bethlehem, the birth of Jesus, and the choir of angels—pretty much a large chunk of the Bible. Joseph also decided that he wanted his parishioners to act out his narration.

He began thinking about his pageant in November, but by the beginning of December, things were not going well. The creative juices weren't flowing; perhaps he should reduce the scope of the production, he thought. One morning, he got up around two o'clock, and the inspiration was there. He dashed off the first sixteen pages of his "screenplay," complete with action, dialogue, and set design, the scenes separated by light and darkness. He was inspired by the Bible verse that said, "Before Christ, the light of the world, everything was in darkness . . . "

At midnight on Christmas Eve, Joseph stood nervously behind a pillar, the spot from which he would deliver his narration. All the actors were in place, dressed in their colorful costumes. At the appointed moment, they began to move slowly across the stage, alternating at the appropriate moments between soft light and dark shadows. The narration continued in the background, increasing in emotion and intensity as the scenes morphed into the Christmas story. The audience sat mesmerized in the dark church, so quiet you could hear a pin drop. People were holding their breath so as not to miss a single word. And then . . . Christ was born, the angels came, the shepherds gathered, the bells rang, the lights came up, and the choir gave forth with the beautiful sounds of Christmas, the music of the angels.

The people of St. James Church in Sialkot would never forget that Christmas. Nor would Joseph.

Finding himself with the responsibilities of a parish priest for the first time, Joseph initially found his assignment in Sialkot very challenging. "I had to kind of test my wings and follow my instincts. Being both young and inexperienced made it difficult to establish tradition where there was none, or to follow traditions where they existed, especially since I didn't know the program. I'm sure I made mistakes, but fortunately, I never heard about them."

The more Joseph worked with his parishioners, the more familiar and comfortable he became, and they slowly adjusted to each other. He went frequently on daura by bicycle, following the same general routine he had before. The bicycle worked well, especially in areas where there were few roads. When roads were crossed by streams, which happened often, it was relatively easy to lift a bicycle—rather than a heavy motorcycle—and carry it across. If he was traveling a greater distance, he would put the bike on the train and get off at the station closest to the catechist's village. When the week was over, the catechist would return to his center, and Joseph would take the train home.

When the people in the villages were informed that the priest was coming, they would sweep the roads and hang welcoming palm branches. When Joseph arrived, they would gather at the chapel (if there was one) or at someone's home, and he would hear confessions while the catechist led the rosary. After confessions, Joseph celebrated Mass and baptized the children and any new converts.

On one occasion, the catechist went around to all the houses where the Catholic families lived telling the people "Father is here." Then he invited all the children to come and greet Father-ji, the new priest. Meanwhile, Joseph was waiting inside the house, dressed in his white cassock and seated on a charpoy covered with a bed sheet. The children filed in, looked around, and then went back outside, asking, "Where is the Father?" Then another group was invited to come and greet the new priest. Same thing. "Where is the Father?" Finally, the catechist brought all the children together inside the house. "There is Father Joseph," he said, pointing directly at the dark man in the white cassock on the charpoy. The children were used to seeing the white faces of the European priests. "Is this really a Father?" they would ask. Even for the older folks, Joseph was a great surprise. It was the first time they had ever seen a Punjabi priest.

Joseph came to know the names of every Catholic family in each village, as well as the names of all the children. As he traveled around the villages, he would often have dozens of barefoot, toffee-colored children hanging off him in every direction. Christian, Muslim, whatever, Joseph loved them all.

* * *

Bishop Raeymaeckers had given Joseph some good advice. "When you go to a new parish," he had said, "spend some time observing. Look around, spend time with the people, get to know them, baptize their children, bury their dead, and only then should you start planning what you can accomplish. Spend the first year in observation and during the second year, or whenever the time is right, you can start something constructive."

While still in the "observation phase" in Sialkot, Joseph was transferred to St. Mary's in Jamke Cheema, another parish in the same district, where he replaced an ailing priest. It was a much smaller, much younger parish, with about 1,200 families and 110 villages. There was also a boarding school for boys, and it was there that Joseph began his lifelong mission to educate children. Whenever he preached, whenever he visited the villages, he encouraged children to get an education. Over and over, he pleaded with the parents to send their children to school, believing with all his heart that education was the answer to poverty, ignorance, and oppression.

Every year, the Belgian missionaries would return to their country for vacation. While there, they would also do a little fundraising, which is how they acquired the bikes and motorcycles (and sometimes jeeps) they used in their missions, as well as the funds used to help many of the children with their school fees. Families were asked to contribute what they could, but Catholic schools were, at that time, largely subsidized by the church. Joseph, being a Pakistani priest, lacked that kind of financial support, but he remained enthusiastic about educating children. After Mass, those catechists who had trained their people well would announce, "The Mass is over, but if anyone wants to say *salaam* to the priest, please . . ." That also meant "Bring your money." People would give whatever they could, a few rupees or perhaps a chicken, some vegetables, or fruit.

As more native priests were ordained, the bishops began to focus on changing the church's dependence from foreign money to local contributions. Increasingly, people were being made aware that they were the church and they were expected to support it, to become a church that was extending its hands in giving, rather than in receiving.

The diocese called in experts in church finances to help the local churches become more self-supporting. They started a "card" system; catechists would distribute cards to the families, and whatever they contributed would be written down, making their gift a matter of record. But these were still desperately poor people, and it was slow going.

Most of the time, the people continued to bring wheat or other crops to the catechist. He would keep what he needed for himself and deduct the value of what he took from his salary. It would take some time—years, in fact—to effect any significant changes. Eventually, as more native priests appeared on the scene, the people began to feel that the priests were their children, their own young men, and that they must support them.

Very early one morning, Joseph arrived at a village along with two catechists, all on their bicycles. The people received them joyfully. One old woman, however, used to the pomp of the foreign missionaries who had visited before, remarked disappointedly, "Oh, this is sad. The other priests used to come in their jeeps and everyone would know that our priests were here. Now you come only on bikes, a very poor showing indeed."

Joseph replied that those priests that used to come in their jeeps came in their impressive vehicles because their brothers and sisters bought those cars for them. "When *you* buy us jeeps, we will come in them," Joseph responded jokingly. "I don't think she got the joke."

* * *

As the Christians of Pakistan began taking their first small steps toward supporting their church, 238,857 miles up in space, the American Neil Armstrong became the first man to walk on the Moon, uttering the immortal words: "That's one small step for man, one giant leap for mankind." The astronauts left behind an American flag and a silicon disk containing statements from Presidents Eisenhower, Kennedy, Johnson, and Nixon, as well as greetings from the leaders of seventy-three countries. The disk also included a message from Pope Paul VI, quoting from the Eighth Psalm, a hymn to the Creator:

O Lord, our Lord, how great your name throughout the earth, above the heavens is your majesty chanted.

By the mouths of children, babes in arms, you set your stronghold firm against your foes to subdue enemies and rebels. I look up at your heavens, made by your fingers, at the moon and stars you set in place.

Ah, what is man that you should spare a thought for him? Or the son of man that you should care for him?

You have made him a little less than an angel, you have crowned him with glory and splendor, and you have made him lord over the work of your hand.

You set all things under his feet, sheep and oxen all these, yes, wild animals too, birds in the air, fish in the sea traveling the paths of the ocean.

O Lord, our Lord, how great your name throughout the earth!

To the glory of the name of God who gives such power to men, we ardently pray for this wonderful beginning.

Right: The Nisari family at
Joseph's ordination (1968).
Back row (l to r): Peter, Teresa,
Father Joseph, Justina,
Benjamin. Middle: Sister Maria,
Mariam (Joseph's mother),
Felix, Sister Sabina. Front:
Mary Rose, Paul.

Left: Father Joseph and
friends on his beloved
Ariel 350.

Right: Joseph
visits the Holy
Father, Pope
John Paul II.

Right: Father Joseph with Mother Teresa during one of her visits to Pakistan.

Below: Father Joseph's niece Sonia and her husband, Younas.

Below: Joseph's mother, Mariam.

Above: Joseph's father, Babu-ji, suffered from bad eyesight in his later years, and wore sunglasses for protection.

Right: Reception at Shahdara honoring Father Joseph. The special turban worn by Joseph symbolizes the transfer of authority to a new priest. Also pictured: Father Joseph's sister Teresa and her husband.

Above: Father Joseph is honored on the 40th anniversary of his priesthood.
L to R: Younas and Sonia (Father Joseph's niece); Bishop Gregory Aymond; Father Joseph; Msgr. Michael Mulvey; Joseph's sisters Sabina, Mary Rose, and Maria; and niece Angelina.

Above: Father Joseph celebrates his 65th birthday.

Left: Bishop Gregory Aymond (now Archbishop of New Orleans) at the fortieth anniversary of Joseph's priesthood.

On this page "Missionaries of Hope" schools

Left: Father Joseph welcomes guests and students at official opening of Jesus, Mary & Joseph School in Pajian.

Right: Young scholars at Holy Family School, Bhaiperu.

Left: Jesus, Mary & Joseph School, village of Pajian.

Right: Father Joseph and his kids.

Left: Archways, Badshahi Mosque, Lahore (16th century).

Below: Sacred Heart Cathedral, Lahore, where Joseph was ordained.

Left: Young camel tender and his charges.

Above: Picturesque mountains of Northern Pakistan.

Left: Alamgiri Gate, Lahore Fort.

CHAPTER 16

Narowal

The Spirit of the Lord is upon me, because he has anoint-
ed me to preach the gospel to the poor. He has sent me to
proclaim release to the captives, and recovery of sight to
the blind, to set free those who are oppressed.

—Luke 4:18

As tensions between India and Pakistan escalated, foreign priests
were no longer allowed to serve in the sensitive border areas of
Pakistan. Since Narowal was only a few miles from the Indian
border, the Belgian priests who were living there were ordered to move
inland, and Pakistani priests were sent to take their place. In January of
1970, Joseph was transferred to St. Francis Xavier in Narowal, where he
would remain for the next five years.

In Narowal, Joseph's ministry would flourish. He survived the
parish observation period, continued through the planning period, and was
finally able to achieve something constructive in his parish ministry. His
old friend Father Saldanha joined him in Narowal. Father Peter Joseph,
an exchange priest from another diocese, was also part of the team at St.
Xavier's. The parish's large ilaqa was divided up between the three priests.
Father Saldanha served the city district as well as some of the local Catholic enclaves, managing his area with four catechists. Father Peter Joseph
had five catechists, and Joseph had seven, because he had the most villages: 150 to Father Peter's one hundred.

Acutely aware of the compromised position of most Christians
when it came to equitable employment—or any employment at all—Joseph decided to establish a branch of the St. Vincent de Paul Society at St.

Xavier's. The Society had been founded in 1833 under the patronage of St. Vincent de Paul (the Father of Charity) to help the poor, provide aid to the suffering, and promote human dignity. Joseph believed the mission and purpose of the Society was a perfect fit for the needs of his new congregation.

The first function of the nascent Society was to start a small business for the desperately poor people. The Society bought several machines that the men could use to make rope, as well as some sewing machines that could be used by the women to make clothing. These efforts resulted in a number of small but profitable entrepreneurships; in a town where the people had no specialized skills, this was a welcome innovation. The Society also provided health care as well as emergency assistance and adult literacy programs, and over time, even funded several Catholic primary schools, which continue to function today, almost forty years later.

* * *

The Protestants in Pakistan had been hosting Christian conventions for years. Similar to old-fashioned mission evangelism, the events would last several days. But the idea of a Catholic convention was new; something Father Joseph felt would give Catholics in the isolated villages a chance to come together in community and faith. Where there might be only ten or twenty Catholic families in a village of five hundred, a convention could provide an opportunity for unity as well as camaraderie.

First, the parish organized the speakers, inviting renowned preachers from other areas, even as far away as Europe. They also provided translators. Choirs were located and preparations for food and entertainment began. The catechists spread the word about the convention in their villages and the people, eager for any opportunity to socialize, responded by the hundreds.

The first night, the guests were expected to provide their own food. A light lunch and an evening meal were provided the second day, and on the third day, a brunch was served. Lectures and entertainment programs were offered in the evenings, and Mass was celebrated on the last day.

The first convention at St. Xavier's attracted more than two thousand people. Eventually, the event became an annual tradition, and continues to be a source of faith-building and social support for Christians separated by circumstances and physical distance.

Some weeks after the convention, Joseph was returning from daura on the motorbike, making good time on a dirt road along the canal bank. As he approached a village, he slowed, always on the lookout for stray children or animals. Suddenly, a large, ragged and very determined dog bolted out from under a bush, charging toward him, ears flying, aiming for Joseph's feet. Another dog scrambled after the front tire. Seconds later, the bike went over and Joseph somersaulted, landing hard on the ground.

After a quick inspection, Joseph found that his arms and legs were still functioning, his hat was still on his head, and his glasses intact, but his cassock was shredded, the Mass box broken, gear lever smashed, brake bent into the body of the bike, headlight gone, and the first dog dead. The second dog had disappeared.

Upon closer examination, Joseph discovered that his arms were slashed, peeled from hand to elbow like the skin from an onion. It was getting dark and he was still thirty miles from Narowal, so he pulled the gear lever back to where it would function and pushed the brake off the chassis. With the headlight missing, it would be slow going, but the bike started on the first kick.

About an hour later, Joseph sputtered into the church compound, dirty, tired, sore, and unbelievably stiff. His cassock was stuck to his arms, his pants to his knees. The cook and gardener came quickly to his aid, helping him remove his pants and cassock, inch by painful inch, careful not to remove any skin.

"Sister Doctor" came right away with her ointment and iodine—she was not a doctor, but a bit more than a nurse—cleaning his wounds and ordering a tonga to transport him to the dispensary. Unable to lower his arms, Joseph had to keep them raised over his head in a kind of dancing position for several days. "I'm sure this was a learning experience, but apparently I did not learn anything," Joseph says.

* * *

While Joseph was at St. Xavier's, he came to know an extraordinary man. In his mid-fifties, Emmanuel Ruhi was distinguished and charismatic. He had been a mufti, an Islamic scholar, very well educated and deeply imbued with the Islamic faith. Some years earlier, for reasons lost to history, Ruhi had abandoned his Islamic faith and was baptized a Christian by an Anglican priest. When he met Joseph, he was living with a Christian family in Narowal. When Ruhi heard about the Catholic Church, he came to see Joseph.

"I was delighted to meet him as well as a bit apprehensive," Joseph recalls. "I was happy that he had already converted because, even in those days, I was aware that for a Muslim to convert was a risky thing—both for the convert and for the converter. Any Muslim who left the Islamic fold—an act regarded as treasonous at the time—was effectively signing his own death warrant.

"Since he was already baptized, I felt humbled and honored to prepare him for his first Holy Communion and the sacraments of confession and confirmation," Joseph recalls. "He would call me 'his lord,' and although I explained that there is only one lord, Jesus Christ, and that that was not me, he insisted that since I had brought him to the Lord, I was his lord."

Ruhi became a popular evangelist, teaching and preaching as a witness for Christ, always on crutches, since he had only one leg. When his family found out he was going to convert to Christianity, they tried to kill him for having disgraced the family. While he was traveling from Karachi to Lahore by train, some of his male relatives followed. At a junction where the train slowed, they pushed him off and left him for dead. By amazing luck, he survived, but the train had severed one of his legs.

"In those days, things were different, people were more tolerant," says Joseph. "Terrorism was not as ubiquitous as it is today and there were fewer fanatical acts. What did surprise me was that this man became a Catholic. Most of the time, Muslim conversions involved transitioning into the Protestant faith where they became preachers and ministers; some even starting their own churches. But Emmanuel Ruhi wanted to become a Catholic and serve as a layman in whatever capacity he could."

Ruhi spent many years traveling around Pakistan, preaching the gospel, holding Bible services, and strengthening the Christian communities, always without possessions, depending on the mercies of others for food and shelter. In spite of his many Muslim enemies, he never felt threatened or afraid. Joseph deeply admired Ruhi and as long as he remained in Pakistan, they stayed in touch.

* * *

Ever since Pakistan became a nation in 1947, relations between the country's two parts, East Pakistan and West Pakistan, had been tenuous. Although the two areas shared a common religion, they shared little else, divided by economics, language, culture, and one thousand miles of "enemy" territory. Home to the nation's capital, West Pakistan had the added advantage of a larger geographical area, better roads, the bulk of political power, and nearly total control of the military forces.

In March 1971, West Pakistan launched a military operation to suppress East Pakistan's bid for autonomy, forcing millions of East Pakistanis to seek safety in India, whose allegiance lay with East Pakistan's resistance efforts.

By December, full-scale hostilities had developed, and West Pakistan launched multiple attacks against Indian airfields. Indian air raids against Karachi and Lahore followed, and on the night of December 4, 1971, Indian missile boats attacked Pakistan's navy, striking a destroyer and a minesweeper in the port of Karachi.

On December 16, the East Pakistani army surrendered, more than ninety thousand soldiers, civilians, and military personnel became prisoners of war, and East Pakistan became the independent state of Bangladesh.

Despite the wartime conditions, Joseph and his mother set out for Karachi in early December to witness the perpetual vows of his sister Sabina, who, having overcome her initial misgivings, was being admitted to the Franciscan Sisters of Christ the King.

Even under normal circumstances, traveling by train in Pakistan in 1971 could not be described as a pleasant experience. The war only exacerbated an already tortuous trip, traveling as they were at an excruciatingly slow speed under brownout conditions.

It was slow going, traveling with no lights at a reduced speed, and instead of the normal twenty hours it would take almost three days to reach Karachi.

Several hundred miles from Karachi, the train slowed and the lights suddenly went dark. The port of Karachi was under attack. From the train window, Joseph could see flares streaking across the night sky, as well as the gaping holes of a bombed-out train lying in the moonlight like a beached whale on the tracks next to them. The conductor told Joseph that the Indians had been targeting a train filled with armaments, but missed it and hit a train filled with bananas instead.

Three unescorted Muslim women, probably in their fifties or sixties, were traveling in the same train car and began chatting with Mariam and Joseph. The women quickly recognized that Joseph and Mariam were Christians (possibly because many Christians had darker complexions than most Muslims), but they had no concept of a Catholic priest. When Mariam called Joseph "Father," the Muslims incorrectly heard it as the name "Fazal." He did not correct them.

Mariam had prepared a meal with some sweet tea and chapatis, which they shared with the women. Muslims typically did not accept food or water from Christians, but these were fearful times, the dining car was no longer serving, and the train was no longer stopping at stations along the way.

The women explained that they were going to the far side of Karachi, past the main city, to visit family, and for whatever reason, they had made no arrangements beyond the train trip, so they asked Mariam where she was going. She explained that she and Joseph were getting off early, at the Drigh Road station, where Joseph's two brothers lived. Terrified to be traveling alone and in wartime, the ladies asked Mariam if she would allow Joseph to accompany them to their final destination. "Perhaps your son, Fazal, could go with us?"

Mariam decided at once that she could get to her son's house in Karachi by herself. She had been there before and knew how to go. "These ladies are very afraid, so you must accompany them," she told Joseph. There would be no further discussion. But as soon as the train stopped at Drigh Road, Joseph found a coolie and asked him to take his mother to his brother's house. He gave him a few rupees for his services. "Although coolies were very trusted men, there was a war going on and in my heart I knew I was sending my mother off with only a coolie to protect her. I would have to trust the Lord.

"When we got off the train," Joseph said, "it was past midnight and there were no taxis to be found, nor were there any city lights of any kind. I decided to take the ladies to St. Patrick's Cathedral because that was the only place I knew where somebody would recognize me and give us shelter.

"We were stopped a few times by security, who told us not to walk on the road, to stay in the shadows, and to hide our bright clothes. The women were wearing white silk kameezes, which shone like beacons in the moonlight.

"When we arrived at the bishop's house, one of the local priests answered the door. 'Joseph, what are you doing here at this hour?' he asked. I explained that I was on a mission. 'These ladies are not Christians, and I am escorting them to their relatives' house as soon as there are taxis available. So if you can put us up for a few hours, I would be grateful.' The priest showed us to the living room and asked the ladies to sit down.

There was a large statue of St. Anthony in the parlor and, forgetting for a moment that these were Muslim women, the priest advised them to 'pray to St. Anthony, he will protect you and be glad for the company.'

"Upstairs, the priest found me a small room with a wooden bed and a blanket. It was a warm night and if I covered myself, I would be too warm, and if I left my feet or face uncovered, the mosquitoes would attack. In Karachi, the mosquitoes were always mean and many. Around four in the morning, I went downstairs. About an hour later, the sun came up and I went to look for a taxi. By six in the morning, we were at the relatives' house. They invited me to stay for breakfast, but they did not know what was in my heart. I was worried about my mother, so I declined. The ladies wanted to pay me, but I refused and left immediately for the train station and Drigh Road. My mother was, of course, OK."

The next day, Mariam, Joseph, and his brother Felix attended the celebration of Sister Sabina's Perpetual Vows. Joseph concelebrated the Mass with Archbishop Joseph Cordeiro (who would become the first Pakistani cardinal in 1973) and five other priests, and afterwards, there was a reception and dinner at the convent.

Shortly thereafter, Joseph learned from the priest at the Drigh Road church that Father Peter Joseph had quite suddenly left the rectory in Narowal, and that there was no one minding the shop, so to speak. Joseph would have to return to Narowal as quickly as possible. Since train service had now been suspended altogether, Joseph and Mariam had to travel to Narowal by bus. Mariam secured a seat on the inside of the overcrowded bus, while Joseph perched on the roof with the other men. It took five days to get back to Narowal.

Back in Narowal, only a few miles from the border, Joseph found more than half of the city deserted. Many had fled to the villages to be with relatives. The church compound was empty and even Joseph's cook had fled. "The first couple of days I finished all the food in the refrigerator," Joseph said. "Then one morning I went out and some security rangers recognized me. 'What are you doing here?' they asked. I replied that this was my place."

As it turned out, most of the city's cows and buffalos had not been milked since their owners abandoned the city. Several of the rangers recognized the situation and took it upon themselves to resolve it. They now had abundant quantities of milk, and were inviting everyone they saw to take as much as they wanted.

Joseph knew immediately what to do with the milk. "I ate rice pudding for a week."

* * *

On a clear spring day, St. Xavier's invited two newly ordained priests for a visit. It was the custom to welcome new priests with a grand reception. It was also an opportunity for them to become acquainted with the area and the people. Friends and relatives were invited from all around; some came on foot, others by tonga or bullock cart.

Mass was held in the morning, followed by lunch. Afterward, the sisters invited the staff, the new priests, and Joseph to the convent for tea, which of course meant more tasty fare.

Late in the afternoon, the guests took their leave, Joseph carrying one of the new priests on the back of his bike. When they arrived at the railroad tracks, he noticed the train was stopped and a crowd had gathered. "There's been a terrible accident," someone said.

Seven adults and a twelve-year-old boy had been on their way home from the church celebration in a tonga. When they came to the railroad crossing, the horse stopped—right in the middle of the tracks. Nothing could budge the intractable animal, not the anxious shouts of the driver or the sting of the whip. When the train came around the bend, the driver did not see the cart sitting immobile on the tracks. The tonga driver, seeing the train approaching, dived off the cart into the dirt. The train plowed into the cart, shattering it and all but two of its passengers into so many pieces of wood, unraveled turbans, sandals, and body parts. The young boy was thrown clear, suffering only a broken leg. A man who at first appeared to be unharmed on the outside was terribly injured on the inside and died later at the hospital.

Joseph told his passenger to take the motorcycle and continue on home; he would stay and do what he could. They spent the next few hours collecting all the body parts, returning six bags of human flesh — legs, hands, feet, a head — to the church where they had been celebrating only hours earlier. The bags were laid on six charpoys, now funeral biers covered with white sheets.

A messenger was sent to the village to notify the families, and shortly after midnight they began to arrive, shocked and horrified. "Where is my father, where is my brother, my husband?" they cried. No one knew exactly, other than in the bags under the sheets. Joseph attempted to comfort the distraught families. The awfulness of the tragedy was numbing, and although he was a priest of God, he had no answers. God's way was not always easy to understand. He found comfort in a familiar Bible verse: "I am the resurrection and the life. He who believes in me will live, even though he dies" (John 11:25).

The bodies had to be buried before sunrise, but no one was prepared to go to the cemetery and dig, so Joseph grabbed a shovel and a few men followed.

About four o'clock in the morning, news came that the graves were ready. As the men lifted the six charpoys onto their shoulders, the women began to wail in a mournful cacophony. A full moon shone eerily on the white sheets as each man was laid to eternal rest in the freshly dug graves. Afterward, Joseph walked to the convent about a mile away and had his cassock washed.

Later in the morning, Joseph said the funeral Mass, reading from the Gospel of St. John: "Lord, Martha said to Jesus, if you had been here, my brother would not have died." He had been there, yet still they died.

After Mass, Joseph set out to join the bishop at the blessing of three new chapels. It was time to move from the valley of the shadow of death to joy and celebration. Such is the life of the priest.

* * *

One afternoon in late summer, Joseph and his sister Sabina were traveling home to their village. About halfway between Lahore and Pajian, Joseph and Sabina had to change buses. The two were tired and thirsty, so while they waited for the next bus, they bought two bottles of Miranda—the drink also known as Fanta—from a small roadside kiosk. Joseph asked the proprietor for two glasses and a jug half filled with water. "We would add the two bottles of Miranda to the jug of water, mix it up, and voilà, we would have three glasses of Miranda," says Joseph.

Afterward, they returned the glasses and jug to the kiosk and settled down to wait for their bus. Suddenly, a dark-eyed, big-haired boy came toward them, holding the two glasses and the jug. Staring at his feet, he mumbled, "You must pay for these." Joseph asked why, but he knew the answer.

"Because we can't use it anymore," the boy replied, all the while staring at his toes. Again Joseph asked why. The young boy was unwilling to continue the conversation. "Is it because I am a Christian?" Joseph pressed, suddenly overcome with righteous indignation. "Why do you think that being Muslim makes you better than me? Your own holy book, the Quran, commands you to respect other people, including Christians, the people of the book."

Meanwhile, a crowd had gathered and Sister Sabina became very nervous, pleading with Joseph to stop. Moments later, the owner of the shop came and led the young boy away. Someone brought a small table and someone else found two chairs so Joseph and Sabina could continue to wait for their bus in comfort.

"Whenever I was refused food or drink, or forced to use separate utensils, I always used the opportunity to explain that I, as a Christian, was also a child of God, and equally loved in his eyes," Joseph explained.

"But if I were to talk that way to a Muslim today, I would immediately be arrested and probably beaten—or worse—for blasphemy."

* * *

St. Xavier's maintained a boarding house and high school (St. Paul's) for boys, which was located in town, and a girls' boarding house and high school about two miles away, in the Sisters' compound. There were about forty girls in the girls' school, along with a mother superior and a full teaching staff. Some of the teachers lived in the compound and helped out with the boarding house; others were local and lived in town.

In 1972, all of Pakistan's private educational institutions—including those endowed and run by Christians—would be nationalized, without compensation, under the government of Zulfikar Ali Bhutto, a proponent of Islamic socialism. This resulted in some obvious changes at St. Paul's: the school was now under government administration with a Muslim headmistress and teaching staff, religious education was restricted, and all crosses, pictures, and other references to Christianity were removed.

"As the result of nationalization, St. Paul's inherited a very forceful, and quite prejudiced, young Muslim principal; the nun who had been principal was now her subordinate," says Joseph. "Straight away she changed the identity of the school, writing on the front, in large block script, the Kalimah, the Islamic profession of faith: 'There is no god but Allah, Muhammad is the Messenger of Allah.'"

Twenty years after the nationalization of private schools, the Supreme Court of Pakistan overturned the ruling, declaring it unconstitutional. Almost immediately, private school owners began the process of reclaiming their institutions, an action many government-employed administrators and teachers refused to accept, fearing the loss of their jobs. In 2001, the parish priest of Renala Khurd would be murdered as he assisted the Dominican Sisters in regaining their school.

After the private schools were nationalized, non-Muslims were admitted to the Muslim schools by means of a quota system—if any seats were available. This had the obvious effect of limiting the education of minorities so that they would remain marginalized, laboring in the most menial of positions, for which education was not a requirement.

CHAPTER 17

A Hostile Arrangement

We shall steer safely through every storm, so long as our heart is right, our intention fervent, our courage stead- fast, and our trust fixed on God.

—St. Francis De Sales

Joseph was posted next to Kasur, a border town in eastern Punjab province about fifty kilometers from Lahore. One of the oldest cities in Pakistan, Kasur was only thirty miles from Changa Manga, a renowned man-made forest planted during the time of the British Raj to provide lumber for the Indian railroads.

Six months after his arrival in Kasur, Joseph was sent to the Philippines for a course on human development. In the bishop's mind, the Philippines was a relatively benign country in terms of morality, while Europe was a corrupt place, full of temptation, vice, and decadence.

Joseph was thrilled. It would be his first plane trip, as well as his first trip out of Pakistan, his first time in a predominately Catholic country, his first opportunity to experience a new culture, and, if he played his cards right, his first vacation ever.

Normally unflappable, Joseph was surprised to find himself anxious about boarding the plane. Planes, he reasoned, could be tricky. What if the baggage weighed too much and the plane couldn't take off? What if the engine quit or the wings dropped off? Joseph's fears soon evaporated as the plane rose into the sky through a sea of puffy, sun-struck clouds.

When the plane landed in Manila, Joseph noticed right away that the women were dressed in the American and European style, with modern skirts, short dresses, and even hats. He did not see any dupattas, chadors, or shalwar kameezes. And there was music in the air, like a celebration. He was immediately mesmerized by this strange, enchanted place.

Manila was a huge city, a vibrant, cosmopolitan mix of cultures and flavors. There was also appalling poverty, choking smog, and horrific traffic. Once thought to be one of the most beautiful cities in Asia, World War II had decimated the city. Filipino (derived from Tagalog) was the national language, but most spoke English well.

In the taxi, Joseph noticed a little altar on the dashboard with dangling rosaries and pictures of St. Francis, St. Anthony, and Our Lady. Looking out the window, he saw churches on *both* sides of the streets. He did not see any mosques—or any mud-brick houses.

Joseph would stay at Holy Cross Church with the Divine Word fathers, who were Americans, and who would introduce him to yet another culture. The human development course would be taught in a nearby cultural center. He was relieved to discover that he could make himself understood in his imperfect English.

There was a movie theater in the area and Joseph's colleagues thought the films would be good for his English, since the movies were in English with no subtitles. "In Lahore and most major Pakistani cities at that time," remembers Joseph, "many of the people were educated and could speak a little English but oddly enough, most of them went to the movies for the action, especially movies like *The Ten Commandments* and *Ben-Hur,* movies that have since been banned in Pakistan."

Whenever he was needed, Joseph helped out with the Sunday Masses, discovering, to his great pleasure, that his preaching—for the first time in English—was understood and even appreciated by the local people. "You speak about the scriptures and God's word, while the Philippino priests preach about Marcos and politics," the people of the congregation told him.

When the course was finished, Joseph asked permission to remain in the Philippines a little longer to learn about a new Christian movement known as Basic Christian Communities (BCC), and to meet the man who had started the group in the Philippines, Father Bart Pastor from Tacloban, a half-hour flight from Manila.

BCC was a concept that evolved from the early Christians, who were part of a community that, having experienced the Pentecost, were obliged to go forth, witness, and form a community. The first community was formed in Jerusalem; the people lived together, ate together, and celebrated the Eucharist together, and, according to Joseph, "Nobody considered their property their own; it belonged to everyone. It was about living as one family and caring for one another."

The resurrected movement in the Philippines served as a way of returning to a more personal experience with God, a coming together in community to share the word of God and join in fellowship as a Eucharistic community.

A predominantly Roman Catholic country, the Philippine nation is comprised of more than six thousand islands. BCC was one attempt to bring together those small, isolated communities so they could practice their faith as a committed, witnessing community. Joseph believed that, for the Christians of Pakistan, who were a very small minority in a large majority of more than one hundred and fifty million Muslims, BCC could provide a unique opportunity for their splintered communities to come together as one faith in unity and strength.

In Tacloban, the rectory had a Philippino priest who loved Philippino food, of which Joseph had decided early on he was not very fond. Every morning he was served some rice with a big fish, baked or dried, complete with head and eyes. This he had no affection for, but the menu seldom varied. Occasionally he would be served a special treat, rice pudding cooked in coconut milk.

"I had been told that the most beautiful time to be in the Philippines was December," Joseph says. "There was a considerable Spanish influence in the culture, with very unique Christmas traditions, so I decided to use my free time to do some sightseeing. There was also an

Independence Day celebration in Lete, and a friend invited me to attend the parade. And there she was—Imelda Marcos herself, First Lady of the Philippines, dressed in colorful traditional costume, smiling and greeting everyone. She was tall and very impressive. Someone introduced us and we shook hands."

* * *

A few days after his return, Joseph met with the bishop and other members of the local clergy to brief them on the Basic Christian Community program he had studied in the Philippines. Joseph believed this new program was ideal for Pakistan's small Catholic enclaves, and was, in fact, so impressed with the program that he asked the bishop if it could be implemented in the Lahore diocese. After some discussion, the bishop decided to allow those priests who thought it feasible and appropriate to adapt it in their own parishes. Father Joseph started a program at St. Anthony's in Lahore, but over time, it died out. In the end, the success of the program would require dedication and long-term commitment, which, at the time, were in short supply in the Lahore diocese.

A week later, Joseph returned to Kasur, where Father Simon had been holding down the fort during his absence. When he entered the church compound, he was surprised to find it filled with people. He went in search of his catechist, asking, "What has happened, why are these people here?"

The catechist explained that the fourteen families gathered in the courtyard had been evicted from their homes by the village *chowdhrys* (headmen). The people were farm laborers who lived in houses on land owned by their Muslim landlords who, having discovered they were seeking employment elsewhere, had expelled them. The evicted men claimed that they were being paid such meager wages they could no longer afford their situation. Every year, the landlords promised them a little more, but nothing ever happened. If a family incurred a big expense such as illness or a wedding, they were forced to borrow money from the landlord, which would then indenture them for life. Thus, they had decided to seek work elsewhere, hoping to improve their lot by laboring for daily wages on the roadways or in the brick kilns.

When the choudhrys discovered the Christians were no longer working for them, they simply locked up their houses and threw them out. "This land is ours, and since you are not working for us any longer, go and find your own," they told them. They had a point, perhaps, but there had to be a better way. Unfortunately, in those times, the landowners were often the only law, and they needed no court for indictment or enforcement.

Joseph took this all in, quickly deciding that he might need more than divine guidance to resolve the situation. He would need a miracle, perhaps even some loaves and fishes. He asked his catechist to find some food for the people and went in search of Father Simon. "Put on your cassock Father," he told him. "We're going to pay a visit to the police inspector." Then he directed the people to follow him, walking two by two, down the narrow dirt road in a long procession.

As the piteous group proceeded down the road, Joseph invited everyone who greeted them to join their procession. By the time they had gone the mile and a half to the police inspector's office, the group numbered more than three hundred.

The people settled down in the shade of some old kikar trees, unsure of what to expect, while Joseph and Father Simon went off to find the inspector, locating instead an orderly who told them the inspector was sleeping. He asked Joseph if they could all come back later.

"Young man," Joseph sighed, "look at all these weary people. Ask them if they will come back later in the evening and, if they agree, then we will come back."

The orderly immediately disappeared inside, and five minutes later, the inspector appeared, chewing on a kikar twig, not at all happy to have been disturbed. Joseph knew him slightly because his children attended the Catholic school. The inspector asked for three chairs, sat down, and asked what he could do for them.

"Inspector sir," Joseph began, "these people have been shut out of their homes, forced to leave with nothing but the clothes on their backs, and they have no place to go. What will happen to them? If we cannot find a solution, I am prepared to take this problem elsewhere . . . "

It was a bold move, one that could have impinged mightily on the inspector's reputation. Nor would it look good for a police inspector to be outmaneuvered by a simple priest from Kasur. Joseph knew he had little chance of helping these people without a trump card; justice in the villages seldom involved fairness or humane treatment.

The inspector listened intently, realizing that Joseph had no intention of going away peacefully. "You don't have to do this," he said. "We will find a solution." After an uncomfortable silence, the inspector continued, "We will go to the police station in their district and see what action they will take. I will send my deputy inspector with you and I will follow."

Joseph did not feel at all optimistic about this turn of events. Police stations in Pakistan were not known for their fair and impartial justice. Joseph told the people to return to the church compound; they would have a solution by the next day. The deputy inspector got in his jeep along with Joseph and Father Simon, and they began the twenty-mile ride to the police station.

At the police station, their report was received with snorts of surprise. The police chief huffed and sighed heavily, "We need to speak to the headmen in the village where this has happened and in another hour it will be dark. Since there is no road from here to their village, we will have to go on horses, and since this is the time of the rice planting, the fields will be wet and travel treacherous. *Inshallah* [God willing], perhaps we can meet here again tomorrow morning?"

Joseph and Father Simon returned to the church compound in Kasur, and by eight thirty the next morning, Joseph was back at the police station. The headmen from the village in question were also there. As Joseph entered the gate, an old man with a dirty turban and a slight limp approached him nervously. He was a Muslim laborer from the same village, and appeared to be extremely agitated. "Are you the priest who reported this problem?" he asked. Joseph said that he was. "You have done a very bad thing. These are dangerous men. If somebody points a finger at them, they will cut off that finger. Calling them to come here is a big insult. This cannot have a happy ending."

This sounded ominous, and ominous was not what Joseph had hoped for. He knew that in his country, Muslims rarely lost face, and never an argument. "Come with me and we'll see what happens," was all he said. The constable told Joseph that everyone was ready. "Can I talk to them before you come in?" Joseph asked. The constable looked at Joseph like he was mad, and nodded yes.

The village headmen were seated on charpoys arranged in a semi-circle, definitely not happy to be there. It was a subdued group, but tension simmered, eyes glared, and turbaned heads stared, their enmity palpable as they fingered their swords. Joseph suddenly recalled the words of St. Matthew: "But when they deliver you up, be not anxious how or what ye shall speak: for it shall be given you in that hour what ye shall speak" (Matthew 10:19).

God had promised to guide him in all things; it was time to test his guidance system.

Joseph stood before the assembled group, feeling like he was facing the proverbial lions, only these lions had knives and turbans. He felt no fear—only the tiniest bit of terror.

"*Assalamu alaikum*, peace be to you," he began. No one responded.

"I am Father Joseph, and I am most distressed at the situation that brings us here today. Surely you are no longer choudhrys, now that your brothers and sisters, who are Christians, have been thrown out of their homes. You are not even honorable Muslims because, according to the Quran, you are supposed to respect and acknowledge the people of the book. Nor are you respected Pakistanis, since you do not recognize fellow citizens who have also fought for this country. And you are not even civilized human beings, because you do not acknowledge fellow humans who come from the same God."

Then he was finished. There was no sound except the air being sucked into lungs. His anger spent, Joseph looked at the men. They did not return his gaze; their eyes remained cast down and their heads bowed. One of the men, perhaps their leader, stood up and joined his hands together. "We have been insulted and disgraced enough. I speak for all my brothers here when I ask your pardon. We are illiterate, ignorant people who know nothing of what you speak, but perhaps what we did was not a good thing. Please ask our Christian brothers and sisters to come back to their houses and we will prepare a meal to welcome them." This was the ultimate gesture of Pakistani hospitality.

When the man finished speaking, it was the constable's turn. In his own rough language, he continued where Joseph had left off, even borrowing his argument: "How could you throw fellow human beings, your own people, out of their homes, out of the village where they have lived all their lives?"

Later, Joseph would recall that moment. "I did not think about what I was saying, and any impulse toward gentility that I might have had was quickly replaced by my anger at the injustice. These were proud men who had great difficulty acknowledging their transgression, but in the end, they resolved the problem in a beautiful way, with words instead of swords. But this could not have happened in Pakistan today. I would have been immediately convicted of blasphemy—or worse."

About a month later, a similar incident occurred in another village sixty miles from Kasur. One evening shortly after dark, two middle-aged men entered the church compound, their faces covered. They were very nervous. "Father," they said, "something very bad has happened in our village. The Muslims are refusing to have any dealings with the Christians. They have closed all their shops to them and the Christians are not allowed to come out of their houses or take their animals to the fields."

There is a phrase in Punjabi, *"hookah pani"* (the hookah is a water pipe used for smoking tobacco, and *pani* means "water"), which refers to the traditional method of socializing among Pakistani men. When you refuse hookah pani with someone, it means you will have nothing to do with that person. That is basically what had happened in the village; the Muslim majority was having nothing to do with the Christian minority.

Joseph told the men to return to their village by bus and that he would follow on his motorcycle, but first he would make a stop at the police station. It was nearly eight o'clock in the evening when Joseph arrived at Chunian, the town with the closest police station. For the second time in less than a month, he asked to speak to the police inspector. As he was speaking, a jeep drove up carrying the police inspector, who dashed into his house. A few minutes later, one of his servants came out. "We told the inspector you are here and he said to make yourself comfortable and as soon as he says his evening prayers, he will come."

"A praying man," Joseph thought. "I can talk to a man who prays." After about fifteen minutes, the inspector came out and sat down. Choosing his words carefully, Joseph explained the situation, getting right to the point. "This is unacceptable; we must find a solution. This is the second day these people have been under house arrest." The inspector paused for a long moment, then said, "I will go and see what the problem is. You go ahead and I will follow."

An hour later, Joseph arrived at the village. All was eerily quiet. There was no noise, no activity, nothing but darkness. In this village of five hundred families, there were about fifty Catholic families. Immediately Joseph went to the Christian enclave and started knocking on doors and calling out, "I am Father Joseph. Do not despair; we will find a solution to your situation. Eat your supper, then come to the catechist's house where we will have prayers."

Joseph could hear some murmuring, then a little noise, and then some children appeared. He could feel the life coming back into the homes. A little later, the people began arriving at the catechist's house. They were soon interrupted by the rumbling of two big trucks filled with police, followed by the inspector's jeep. The police went from street to street, house to house, asking every Muslim man to come to the community center. When the policeman arrived at the house where the Christians were praying, he called out, "I am sorry to disturb you but the police inspector is asking for you." Joseph replied that they would come as soon as prayers were finished.

When Joseph and his little band of Christians arrived at the center, several hundred Muslim men were already there, sitting on the ground. The Christians sat down on one side, the Muslims with their mullah on the other. The inspector sat in the middle, with Joseph on his right. Next to Joseph was his catechist.

It turned out that the Christians had been hoping to build a church and a school in the village, and in a Muslim village, this was unacceptable. The Muslims felt that once a Christian church and school were established, their own children might begin to attend the school. To the Muslims, this seemed a blatant propagation of the Christian faith and an insult to Islam. There was, of course, no concept of religious tolerance or equal rights in their minds, and certainly not in their community.

As he had in the previous situation, Joseph asked if he could address the gathering.

"*Assalamu alaikum*, peace be to you," he said. "I am Father Joseph, and I have come to ask you why you are barricading your Christian brothers and sisters in their houses? These people are your neighbors, with whom you have lived in peace for many years. If you accept that they are also fellow Pakistanis and citizens of the same country for which you have all fought, then they do not deserve such treatment."

It was the same song, a different village.

Then it was the inspector's turn. When he was through speaking, he said, "Now I want to know how all this got started." Searching for some excuse to justify their behavior, the Muslims looked at each other with accusatory faces. Then the mullah rose to his feet, rubbed his hands together, cast a long, unhappy look at Joseph, and explained that the Christians had not consulted the Muslims about their building project. "And so, without our knowledge, they were going to do this." Then the headman spoke: "They also desecrated our mosque when their young men played the drums and sang songs while passing in front of it."

The police inspector, whose patience with the "he said, they said" argument was beginning to wear thin, uncharacteristically threatened the errant Muslims with unspoken consequences if they did not address the Christians' grievances and make amends. After a few tense moments, the headman stood before the gathering, sputtered a bit, and offered a sort of apology for the Muslims' actions and alleged error in judgment. He also reminded everyone that the land that was set aside for the church and school had been donated by one of their Muslim brothers.

To the Christians, he said, "We will let you build your church and your school, and perhaps you will provide some wisdom, and maybe our children will be able to learn and won't be wandering around in the streets." In light of this magnanimous admission, the inspector declined to pursue the matter any further. And once again, the conflict was settled, peace restored, and a grand meal was shared by all. A feast was always a most satisfactory gesture.

In his zeal, Joseph had hoped only to make the people aware of who they were and what their relationship with God and country should be. He was more than satisfied.

"In Pakistan, it is politics as much as religion that has severed the traditional bonds of relationships," says Joseph. "For centuries, village loyalties were aligned with family and neighbors, rather than political affiliations. The real problem today is ignorance and a kind of mob mentality. Educated people generally have a different approach to conflict than illiterate people. When I spoke with the villagers, I may have touched a nerve, but I was respectful. They realized that I was not the enemy."

CHAPTER 18

Turning Point

Have patience with all things, but chiefly have patience
with yourself. Do not lose courage in considering your
own imperfections, but instantly set about remedying
them; every day begin the task anew.

—St. Francis de Sales

In 1977, after two years in Kasur, Joseph was transferred back to Lahore, to St Anthony's parish. An elegant, old, red brick church, St.
Anthony's was also known as the Railroad Church because a large
contingent of its early parishioners had been employees of the state-run
Pakistan Railways.

One afternoon, Joseph called his catechist, Babu Augustine.
"Since this is St. Anthony's Church, and St. Anthony is known for his
powerful intercession, why don't we start a devotion to him?"

For more than eight centuries, St. Anthony has been a part of
Catholic life and the refuge of those who have lost things, whether temporal and spiritual. Around the world, on any given Tuesday, the faithful
gather in their churches for Holy Mass and a special devotion to honor this
beloved saint so often called upon for the recovery of things lost.

Joseph asked Augustine to visit St. Anthony's Church in Karachi,
which had a popular service dedicated to the saint. The next week, Augustine met with the priest in Karachi to learn about their program. The
following weekend, Joseph announced that St. Anthony's Church would
begin a special service to the saint on the following Tuesday. On Tuesday,
about thirteen people showed up. Two weeks later, the church began to
fill up, and within a month, the church was full every Tuesday night. Six

months later, St. Anthony's had to offer two Masses on Tuesday nights.

Over time, word got around, and soon other area churches began to offer a devotion to St. Anthony. The next to start a devotion was St. Joseph's in Lahore Cantt. They had no statue, but a picture of St Anthony worked just as well. Soon Sacred Heart Cathedral started a service, then Immaculate Heart of Mary in Anarkali. Five years later, the devotion to St Anthony had traveled far beyond Lahore into the villages and catechist centers, and is still going strong today.

"I remember one old man who used to come to the St. Anthony service, arriving late and always drunk," recalls Joseph. "He would stagger around the statue of St. Anthony, pleading, 'St. Anthony, don't you remember that I asked you to grant me a favor? Well, you forgot and I'm here again, asking that you grant my favor.' One Tuesday, he arrived in quite an angry state. 'Look, St. Anthony,' he said, 'I've been coming to you for many months and you still haven't granted my favor. Now you look out because the next time I come, if you haven't granted my favor, I'm going to break your head.' I immediately called Babu Augustine and told him the man was going to come back and break the statue. We didn't have another one, but Babu Augustine had a small statue at home, so the following Tuesday he removed the big one and put the small one in its place. Sure enough, on Tuesday, the old man returned, drunk as always, and began shouting from the back of the church. As he walked forward, he stopped suddenly in front of the statue. 'Hey Junior,' he said, 'where is your father?'"

* * *

Toward the end of the school term, Joseph took some of the younger girls from the sewing center at St. Anthony's on a field trip to see some of the historical sites in Sheikhupura. In the evening, as they were returning to St. Anthony's, the group stopped at Minar-e-Pakistan, a popular monument commemorating the Pakistan Resolution.

The girls went off to buy some snacks, and Joseph told them to return to the bus in an hour. The snacks were served on small ceramic plates,
and when it was time to pay, the proprietor told the girls, "Since you are
Christians, we can't use these plates again. You will have to pay for them."

The girls went running straight to Joseph. "Father, what shall we
do? We don't have the money to pay for these plates!" This got Joseph's
attention. He immediately went over to the shop and sought out the owner.

"Why do the children have to pay for the plates?" he asked. "Is it
because we are Christians?" Then he took all the plates—about fifteen of
them—and broke them into pieces on the road. Then he told the girls to
get on the bus.

"Come to my office at St. Anthony's and I will pay you for your
plates," Joseph told the astonished man, who had probably never encountered anyone who had refused outright to pay his charges, much less break
his plates. He never did come to St. Anthony's to get the price of his plates.
That would have been admitting discrimination, which was not "officially"
condoned. The law may not have been enforced, but it was understood.

"Had anyone asked, I would have explained that you cannot bully
someone just because they are Christian, but I believe the gentleman got
my message," says Joseph. "I am, first, last, and always, a priest of God
representing my people, and I feel the power of God in all things—although I may have misunderstood any directive involving plates."

* * *

One Sunday, a Japanese couple came to Joseph and asked if he would of-
ficiate at their marriage. He agreed, and after the ceremony, as they were
leaving for Japan on their honeymoon, they asked Joseph what he would
like them to bring him. "What about a television set?" the couple suggested. "Wow," Joseph thought, "I never imagined having a TV."

They sent it by mail, and some time later, Joseph got a notice from
the post office that he had a package. He guessed it was the television and

could hardly contain his excitement. He picked it up, brought it home, and plugged it in. Immediately he was transported to the amazing world of Western television. And then he made an interesting discovery. He had noticed the local children singing odd lullabies and using strange words he did not recognize, and had wondered where the words were coming from. The very first time he turned on the television, he had tuned in to a daytime children's program. He understood immediately where the children's odd lullabies were coming from.

A few weeks after Joseph obtained his television set, he acquired another possession that would give him much joy, and much more sorrow. He bought his first car, a Ford, an old clunker that needed a lot of repairs. He bought it very cheap, about one thousand rupees (or fifty US dollars). His cousin, the bishop's driver, taught him how to drive.

Joseph's first trip in his new fifty-dollar car was from Lahore to Pajian. His mother Mariam, sister Rosemary, nephew Andrew, and niece Parveen went along. Mariam sat in front with Joseph, the others sat in the back, and the trip to Pajian went smoothly enough. When it was time to return to Lahore, everyone piled into the car except Mariam, who remained behind with relatives. By now it was late in the day, and Andrew was in a hurry to get back in time for some big television program. As the kilometers rolled by, Andrew grew more anxious about missing his show. The road had speed breakers, as they were called, and Joseph was probably driving too fast. Suddenly, they were on one.

"We hit it hard and the car overturned," Joseph recalls. "The front and back windshields popped out but did not break. Everyone was OK except Rosemary, who sustained two broken fingernails. Some villagers helped us get the car back on its wheels, but it was not drivable, so we hitched a ride back to Lahore. The next day, I had to find someone to tow the car back to Lahore. That was the end of the fifty-dollar Ford."

Joseph's second car was an old Toyota. A classmate from St Francis High School was having some financial problems and needed to sell his car, so Joseph bought it. It didn't last long either. After the Toyota met its demise, Father Mani sold Joseph his old Renault.

"That car was possessed," says Joseph. "I had just had it repaired for the fourth time when the bewitched vehicle died again. It continued to live and die for about six more months. That's when I made a resolution: I would never buy another old car."

His first "new" car was purchased for him by the diocese, and as such, belonged to the diocese. Four-wheel-drive vehicles had recently made their appearance in Pakistan, very practical cars for the unforgiving terrain over which the priests traveled. Foreign priests had been importing them from Belgium and Holland, and the local Pakistani priests had begun looking longingly at them. At the time, there was an understanding in the diocese that priests were not eligible for a diocesan vehicle until they had ridden a motorcycle or bicycle for at least ten years. Joseph had driven his motorcycle for at least that long, and he had driven several dilapidated old cars beyond that. It was time for a *new* car.

One of the first minivan models to arrive in Pakistan was a four-wheel-drive Suzuki, and Joseph was designated to receive one. It was an amazing car, and Joseph could not quite believe his luck. Like most cars in Pakistan at the time, it had no air-conditioning, but the vehicle was such an improvement over his previous possession, he did not mind.

* * *

As Joseph's methods of transportation were changing, his country's government was also changing—in ways that would have far reaching effects. In July 1977, a particularly zealous Muslim general, Muhammad Zia ul-Haq, became president of Pakistan after successfully overthrowing Zulfikar Ali Bhutto. Zia's government wasted no time initiating a hardline Islamization program to bring Pakistan's political and legal system in line with Islamic principles. The shift to Islamic law—sharia—was a monumental change from the country's British-influenced, largely Anglo-Saxon law, seemingly reverting back hundreds of years to the time when stoning adulteresses and whacking off the hands of thieves were common punishments.

Two years later, in 1979, Zia would enact several significant and particularly abhorrent laws, including the Hudood Ordinances. Under these laws, the punishment for theft was amputation of the right hand; the penalty for robbery was amputation of the right hand and the left foot. In reality, it proved problematic to carry out these sentences since most of the doctors had been educated in the West and found it difficult to rationalize the surgery.

The Zina laws, also a part of the Hudood Ordinances, made adultery or any "unlawful" sex (including rape) punishable by flogging, prison, or stoning to death. Under this ordinance, extramarital as well as premarital sex was criminalized; making consensual sex between two people not married to each other a crime against the state.

In 2006, President Pervez Musharraf passed the Women's Protection Bill, which amended, but did not overturn, the ordinance. Under the new bill, rape cases would be tried under the Pakistan Penal Code, which is based on civil law, rather than Islamic law, enabling convictions to be established by forensic and circumstantial evidence. Non-marital consensual sex, while still considered a crime, would be subject to lesser sentences than under the original law.

* * *

It is said that, for a priest, the first ten years of ministry are the "honeymoon" and Joseph's was coming to an end. He found himself increasingly frustrated with the fact that he had not been allowed the opportunity to advance his catechesis training, especially since he was still involved with the catechists' monthly training seminars.

Deeply influenced by his father, who had been an inspired and committed catechist, Joseph was continually searching for more effective and faith-affirming methods of evangelization, believing that ignorance and poverty were the major obstacles to any real change in the quality of life for his people. Joseph believed that each catechist shaped the community in which he served, according to his own special skills and knowledge. If he were a holy man and well informed, so also would be the community. The education of his catechists would become Joseph's passion, fueling his mission throughout his years in Pakistan.

"My people may have been low caste and desperately poor, but they were Christians nevertheless, and therefore, children of God," says Joseph. As Christians, Joseph believed his people had already attainted a relatively lofty position, at least spiritually; it was their life on earth he worried about. Children needed to go to school. Education was the way out, the way to achieve, to inspire, to shine so that they could be more effective human beings and children of God.

During his first assignment, Joseph had realized how woefully unprepared his catechists were, many of whom did not even know the simple prayer for the sick. He felt that the catechists were hopelessly cast in a role that was subservient to the priest. "I would look at my father as he stood before the priest, hands joined and head bowed. I wanted to change that. A catechist was not a servant; he was the one in the field, in the trenches, with the people."

Minimal training was offered to Pakistan's catechists at a training center in Sialkot, but it was very basic: Bible interpretation, delivery of sermons, keeping of family records. Catechists were literate but not highly educated, generally only through the fifth grade. (Later, it would become obligatory that catechists have a high school education.)

Since 1969, Joseph had been a member of the diocesan catechetical team, responsible for conducting annual refresher courses and monthly seminars designed to teach the catechists how to improve their ministries. Joseph could see the change these efforts made; the catechists were hungry for knowledge and new information, but it was not enough. He believed that it was especially important for catechists living in an Islamic country to be firmly grounded in their faith and to be able to have an informed dialogue with their Muslim neighbors.

Every year, the foreign missionaries would return to their home countries on holiday, and every year when they returned to Pakistan, they brought back new theological teachings and new methods for enhancing their ministries. Joseph observed all this, which only enhanced his feelings of inadequacy. He had no new ideas or information to impart. "I desperately wanted more training, so I kept asking the bishop for an opportunity."

For whatever reason, the bishop continued to ignore his requests. Perhaps the bishop believed Joseph was not academic material. He had, after all, not been a stellar student in the seminary, albeit partly due to his lack of fluency in English. He was an exceptionally talented preacher, but a scholar he was not. But what Joseph lacked in academic prowess, he made up for in determination and perseverance. Some might have called him stubborn.

Nevertheless, Joseph and his bishop continued to lock horns. Appointed Bishop of Lahore in 1975, Armando Trindade was an Anglo Indian, a Portuguese from Goa, with excellent credentials and two master's degrees in education. He had been a school principal in Karachi and many felt that he treated his priests as if they were his students. Proud of his Goan heritage, Trindade appeared to have little affection for the Punjabi priests of the Lahore diocese. Joseph chafed at the perceived injustice, his pride getting in the way of his purpose.

Dispirited and frustrated, Joseph felt that he was losing his edge. He was still one of the best preachers in the country, but new priests were coming along. He began to take a back seat, trying to be more pastoral and spend more time with his people.

In the spring of 1978, Joseph decided he needed a vacation, his first in more than three years. Maybe he would find new perspective, something to recharge his spiritual batteries. He would use his meager savings to travel to Europe, home of the foreign missionaries of his youth.

Joseph went first to London, where the Franciscan Sisters of the

Sacred Heart of Jesus had a convent at which he could stay; two of his sisters were members of the order. From there he traveled by train to Brussels, where he knew a Belgian priest that had served with him in Pakistan. They had been good friends, and Joseph decided to look him up.

Arriving at the rectory in Brussels, Joseph was given a room, but no particular welcome. There were three priests in residence, and they took their meals at a local hotel. During Joseph's short visit, there was little communication and no apparent interest in a visiting Pakistani priest. The next day, Joseph went to visit his friend, Father Lawrence, who was the chaplain at a local prison. At the gate, Joseph rang the bell and a disembodied voice drifted down over the intercom asking his name and with whom he wished to speak. "I wish to speak to Father Lawrence," Joseph responded in English. The voice at the other end replied in Flemish. Neither one comprehended the other. After about ten minutes, Joseph gave up and left.

From there, Joseph decided to make a pilgrimage to the National Shrine at Lourdes in France, as revered by Catholics as Mecca is by the Muslims (in fact, Lourdes has the second largest number of hotels in France).

The distance was not great, and there was a tour bus leaving Brussels the next day. It was a silent trip. No one spoke to the dark-skinned priest from Pakistan. When the bus stopped for a meal, no one but Joseph prayed over his food. How odd, Joseph thought, that I am the only one making the sign of the cross and praying among this group of Belgian Catholics. This was, after all, the country that had helped bring Christianity and brotherhood to Pakistan.

The faithful have been coming to Lourdes ever since 1859 seeking a cure for the incurable. In 1858, the Virgin Mary is said to have appeared to a fourteen-year-old peasant girl, Bernadette Soubirous, asking that a chapel be built on the site. Mary also directed Bernadette to drink from the spring in the grotto—but there was no spring there. When Bernadette dug at the chosen spot, water began to flow and continues to flow to this day. The water from this spring has demonstrated remarkable healing power, although it has no curative properties that modern science can identify.

While many claim to have experienced miraculous cures at this sacred site, the Catholic Church has declared only sixty-eight healings as scientifically and medically inexplicable.

When Joseph arrived at the shrine, he went first to the Grotte de Massabielle (Cave of Apparitions), where the Virgin Mary is said to have appeared to the young Bernadette eighteen times. Profoundly inspirational and overwhelmingly serene, the grotto did not disappoint Joseph. Discarded crutches and canes were visible everywhere, silent testimony to thousands of cured cripples and the power of the Blessed Mother's intercession.

At the huge, life-sized bronze statues of the Stations of the Cross, the people made their way slowly over a rocky path, from station to station, lost in prayer and contemplation, some on their knees, some on bare feet. "I saw a young couple, the man with his little girl on his shoulders," Joseph remembers. "He had his pants tucked up, exposing his knees, and at every station, he would get down on his knees and pray. He had a hard time getting up with his daughter on his shoulders, so his wife would help him up and wipe the perspiration from his face."

Back on the bus, Joseph was full of questions. "Again I was sitting by myself. I attempted to start a conversation with the gentleman in front of me, but his wife stopped him. Suddenly I was acutely aware that I was the foreigner, and I did not enjoy it. Having known many of the Belgian missionaries as spiritual leaders in Pakistan, and having met some of the Belgian people, I found the two to be very different."

Back in Lahore, Joseph found himself assigned to St. Mary's Seminary where, twenty years earlier he had been a student. Now he would be a professor of history and Urdu. Joseph, the struggling student, would now be the teacher.

While challenging, the new post did not replace his desire to make a difference in the life of his catechists. He taught at the seminary for one year, and in 1980 the bishop sent him to Mariamabad, home of the National Shrine of Our Lady.

CHAPTER 19

Mariamabad

Two criminals were crucified with Christ. One was saved;
do not despair. One was not; do not presume.

—St. Augustine

Mariamabad has existed for more than a century and was perhaps the oldest Catholic village in the diocese of Lahore. Established by Capuchin Franciscan priests who felt that the Christians in the area were being denied the basic employment necessary to survive, the priests set out to create an independent, self-sufficient community for their impoverished faithful, one that would give them a sense of community and solidarity, and—on a more practical level—survival. The Catholic diocese purchased a plot of land, selected families from each of the area villages, and relocated them to the new village they called Mariamabad, or "Village of Mary." The newly conscripted families built homes, worked the land, and received compensation for their labors from their landlord, the Catholic diocese.

Eventually, Mariamabad built a school and a boarding house for boys and girls through fifth grade. The girls would continue their education at Mariamabad through high school, while the boys would go on to matriculate at St. Francis High School in Lahore. The diocese also benefited from the agricultural bounty. The crops, mostly rice and wheat, helped to supply the boarding house as well as the boys' school in Lahore.

Every year during the first week of September, a three-day festival is held in Mariamabad in honor of the Virgin Mary, mother of the oppressed. The pilgrimage to Mary's village first began in 1949, when Father Frank, a Belgian Capuchin who was later martyred, built a grotto and a church, a replica of Lourdes, which became Pakistan's National Marian Shrine.

According to popular legend, a Muslim woman from a neighboring village actually built the first shrine to our Blessed Mother in Mariamabad. She had borne no children in her marriage, and one day, on her way to visit her parents, she passed the church at Mariamabad and saw the Holy Mother's statue. "Oh Mother of Jesus," she prayed, "I hear that you have great powers and I am asking you, woman to woman, to pray for me that I may have a child. And if I am successful, I promise to build a shrine in your honor." It happened that a year later she gave birth to a son, and true to her promise, she built a shrine to honor Mary. There is no evidence to support this story, but it is perhaps more unique than the original.

The shrine is legendary among Pakistani Christians for its seemingly miraculous powers. Women who have prayed before the statue for sons have delivered sons, the jobless have found employment, and the sick have been healed. The faithful who come to honor Mary spend hours waiting in long lines to touch the holy statue, leaving her offerings of flowers, scarves, gold and silver crowns, and money—even goats, lambs, and chickens.

In 2007, the government added electronic gates and deployed more than one thousand policemen to safeguard the shrine and pilgrims. In 2008, the fifty-ninth annual Marian pilgrimage attracted nearly one million pilgrims from all religions, including Catholics, Muslims, Hindus, and Sikhs.

Mariamabad was not new to Joseph. For the past ten years, he had served as the general secretary of the annual pilgrimage. Every September, Joseph would travel to Mariamabad to meet with the committees to arrange the schedules, select the speakers, and coordinate the various services necessary to accommodate the thousands of pilgrims. During the event, Joseph also served as moderator and narrator, gaining a credible reputation as a speaker, his clear voice and inspiring message resonating where previously there had been only foreign accents.

Mariamabad would be a plum assignment for Joseph. He would remain there for one year.

* * *

Easter, the celebration of the risen Lord, is the most important day in the Christian calendar, and Joseph's first Easter in Mariamabad would be one he would remember for a very long time, and not because of any spiritual epiphany.

After Mass on Easter Sunday, Joseph set out to visit a family who had asked him to bless their house. After sharing a cup of tea with them, Joseph started back across the village to the rectory. As he passed the convent, he came upon two boys, probably nine or ten years old, locked in mortal combat, fighting fiercely, seemingly intent on killing each other. Joseph grabbed the boys and pulled them apart, but the bigger one wrestled himself free and began pummeling the smaller boy all over again in a murderous rage. Joseph, the man of peace, acted instinctively.

"The larger boy was stronger and more aggressive, and seemingly unaware of his strength," Joseph recalls. "He also had no interest in ending the fight, so I grabbed him and struck him smartly on the side of his head. That was enough. Then I sent them home, first one, then the other."

Later, back at the rectory, Joseph was in his office when he heard a commotion outside. He went to the door and saw several nuns running towards him calling, "Go back, don't come any closer!" Then Joseph saw him, a tall, thin man wearing no shoes and a ragged turban running towards him with murder in his eyes and bricks in his hands. "I was pretty sure he was not planning to make me a gift of the bricks."

Joseph grabbed the man's hands, stopping him in his tracks. Dropping the bricks, the would-be attacker stood there glaring at Joseph, his eyes crackling with anger. By then a group had gathered and several men led the assailant away.

The boy that had been anointed by Joseph's hand happened to be the son of a catechist, and the man who came after Joseph was the boy's uncle. His family would be held responsible for the attack of a priest, as would the entire village, since the man's actions were perceived as a reflection on the village.

It was most unusual for a villager to seek revenge on a man of God just because of a young boy's complaint. Boys routinely received much worse than Joseph's slap at the hand of a parent or elder. There was, of course, more to the story. The diocese happened to be involved in a legal proceeding against the catechist because of some irregularities. The catechist had been asked to leave the mission house, which belonged to the church, but he had not cooperated. "As the parish priest, I was, by default, also involved," says Joseph, "but the poor man did not improve his situation by sending his brother after me."

The news spread quickly to Lahore. Priests came from all over the diocese to speak to the people of Mariamabad. "This act is a desecration of a priest and an excommunication for the man who attacked Father Joseph," they said.

About a week later, the bishop removed Joseph from the rectory in Mariamabad, and although he remained in charge, Joseph would live at the mission center of Sangla Hill, a thirty-minute drive from Mariamabad, until the village made their peace with the bishop and with Joseph.

Several months later, the village arranged a day of reconciliation. When Joseph arrived at the designated spot, the same spot where he had broken up the boys' fight, the entire village was gathered to greet him. Amid much joyful singing, the people presented Joseph with small gifts, hung huge garlands around his neck, and placed a *pagari,* a special turban, on his head.

As Joseph looked down, he saw two strips of sugar cane making a cross on the ground. *This is the life of the cross,* Joseph thought to himself, *and although I am being honored today, my cross will continue.*

Some years later, Joseph met his would-be assailant again at the seminary in Lahore. The man was ill and had sustained some incredibly bad luck; two daughters had been born blind and mute.

The moment he saw Joseph, he prostrated himself at his feet, begging for forgiveness and mercy for him and his family. Joseph told him that he had forgiven him many years ago, at the moment of his transgression. "I have nothing to forgive you for," he told him. "You are already forgiven."

The desperate man pleaded, "Help me please, there is something very bad troubling my family, and I know it is because God is punishing me."

Joseph blessed him and told him to go in peace. He would pray for him.

"I saw him again a couple of times back in Mariamabad," says Joseph, "and on one occasion, he invited me to his house. I had a meal with his family and met his daughters, two girls about ten and eleven, both blind and dumb. Over the years, I have observed that whenever a priest is disrespected or insulted, the assailants seem to suffer some calamity in their lives. I don't know if you can draw any kind of conclusion from this, but I have seen it happen more than once."

* * *

Joseph continued to plead his case for more advanced studies with the bishop. Finally, in August **of** 1981, he received the news he had dreamed of for so many years. The bishop was sending him to Dublin, Ireland, where a special program in catechesis was being offered. Joseph was ecstatic and made plans immediately to leave Mariamabad as soon as the annual pilgrimage was completed on September tenth. He would travel first to Lahore then on to Karachi, where he would depart for Ireland on the eleventh.

But Joseph never got to Ireland. He would end up in Rome instead, in a sudden (and ironic) turn of events.

It happened that a priest from another diocese had a discussion with the bishop. The priest had said, "Why don't you send Joseph to Rome for his training? The course in Ireland is very expensive, and if you send him to Rome, it will cost very little. The Pontifical University is free, and Joseph can live there at very little cost."

The bishop had then replied that Joseph would go to Rome for his studies.

Joseph was devastated about the change in plans. He tried to explain himself to the bishop: "If I am going to Rome, I should know Italian, which I don't. In Ireland, at least the course would be taught in English."

But the bishop could not even offer Joseph any guarantee that Rome would offer the coveted catechesis training, the specialized teaching of Christian doctrine that would help Joseph expand and enhance his ministry.

"Rome is an international city and the center of the Catholic faith," he said. "You will learn a lot of things."

So that was that. Joseph had never been to Rome, and it was most certainly an extraordinary opportunity, a dream of a different stripe perhaps. He would make the best of it.

And so at six thirty in the evening on September 12, 1981, Joseph boarded the plane for Rome.

CHAPTER 20

Rome

*Therefore I prayed, and understanding was given me; I
called upon God, and the spirit of wisdom came to me.*

—Wisdom 7:7

Joseph landed at Leonardo da Vinci airport at eight thirty in the morning and took a bus to Stazione di Roma Termini, Rome's massive and elegant train station, a small city unto itself and the main hub for public transportation around Rome. There were no chariots in Rome.

The ancient, eternal city—splendid and seductive with the magnificence of the Vatican, the ageless Forum, the awe-inspiring ruins of the Coliseum, and more than thirty centuries of turbulent history—was heady stuff to the simple priest from the Punjab plains. Joseph was intoxicated by the tantalizing aromas of the city: savory Sicilian spices, pungent sausages, Italian espresso, old leather, ripe garbage, and everywhere the exhaust fumes. Traffic in Rome was legendary and chaotic, with fast drivers, more vehicles than roadways, and a very cavalier attitude toward road signs, pedestrians, and traffic laws.

From the train station, Joseph hailed a cab to Vatican City, arriving about ten o'clock in the morning at Collegio San Pietro, the Vatican residence where he would live for the next two years. The Collegio was a popular haven for priests coming from the mission territories, and Joseph would find himself part of an exotic blend of diverse cultures, traditions, and languages. The vice-rector showed Joseph to his room in another building a short distance away, where he was greeted by the rector. "What happened to you?" the rector asked. "You look like someone has beaten you up."

"I have not slept for three nights," Joseph replied.

When he opened the door to his room, all Joseph saw was the bed. He slept—like a stone—the rest of that day, through that night, and into the next day. When he finally woke up, disoriented and having no idea where he was, he opened his back door and saw at once the glorious, iconic dome of St. Peter's. *Dear God, am I really in Rome?* Joseph wondered. He had seen St. Peter's in pictures, but there it was, right in front of him, only a twenty-minute walk away. It was three o'clock in the afternoon.

Until recently the largest church in the world, with a capacity of more than sixty thousand people, St. Peter's Basilica was constructed on the site where Peter the Apostle, the first bishop of Rome, was crucified—upside-down by his own request—and buried. Construction on the basilica began in 1506 and was completed more than one hundred years later in 1626.

Written in Latin along the base of the inside of the dome, in letters more than six feet tall, is the inscription of Matthew 16:18-19: "TV ES PETRVS ET SVPER HANC PETRAM AEDIFICABO ECCLESIAM MEAM. TIBI DABO CLAVES REGNI CAELORVM" ("You are Peter, and on this rock I will build my church . . . I will give you the keys of the kingdom of heaven").

The courses Joseph would take would indeed be taught in Italian, so the following week, he began Italian classes at the Collegio, a short walk from the Pontifical Urbaniana University. Joseph's initiation to the Italian language included twenty classes, at the end of which he went to register for his courses at the Pontifical University, an institution largely dedicated to the training of priests, religious brothers and sisters, and lay people for service as missionaries.

At the University, Joseph first encountered a secretary who asked him lots of questions in Italian. Joseph understood little—so much for the Italian classes. The secretary found a translator and the questions began again. "What type of training are you looking for?" she asked. Joseph responded with his well-rehearsed litany about specializing in catechesis. Through the interpreter, Joseph came to understand that the only classes being offered in catechesis were very basic, primarily for lay missionaries and religious sisters and brothers, not for ordained priests.

"You will be wasting your time because your seminary training has already taught you most of the information covered in these classes," the secretary told him.

Joseph took a deep breath. He could not believe what he was hearing, his long-awaited opportunity seemingly slipping away. After all the years of waiting and hoping, he had come so close. "Catechesis training is the only reason I am here," he insisted. The secretary suggested an alternative program called Missiology, which was offered for missionary priests. The Missiology course was basically an update on theology, cannon law, and the practical side of evangelization in the missions. Most of the material Joseph had already been taught in the seminary, and he did not believe the course would significantly enhance his ability to help the catechists in his diocese in Pakistan. Nevertheless, he had no time to debate his situation. He had to make a quick decision; behind him were lines of other priests waiting to register. For just a tiny speck of an instant, he considered going back to Pakistan—but that would be admitting defeat, and losing a valuable opportunity to take advantage of the gift of Rome. He was disappointed, but he was not stupid.

"Maybe it's not what I want to do, but it is God's will," Joseph reasoned. "Since I am here, let me use my time well." It was God's plan and, it appeared, God favored Italian.

Sitting through hours of Italian lectures every day was daunting, but after a couple of weeks it became easier, the words more familiar. Conjugating verbs in Italian every evening, out loud, to the walls of his small room seemed to help.

* * *

Born Karol Józef Wojtyła, Pope John Paul II served as the 264th pope of the Roman Catholic Church from October 1978 until his death nearly twenty-seven years later. John Paul was the only Polish pope the Catholic Church had ever known, and the first non-Italian pope since 1520. A gentle, charismatic figure with a beatific smile, John Paul was reportedly fluent in at least eight languages, including Greek, English, French, German, Italian, Latin, Russian, and his native Polish. He would become a popular international figure and a tireless moral voice in an increasingly secular world, a true servant of the servants of God.

"I had met His Holiness on his previous visit to Pakistan in 1981," Joseph recalls. "It was a large impersonal gathering at a national stadium, but powerful and overwhelming nonetheless. My meeting with him in Rome was very different, very special, very personal. I concelebrated Holy Mass with the Pope, along with sixteen other priests, in his private chapel in the Apostolic Palace. He celebrated the Mass facing the wall, the old style. During the Mass I had a chance to observe him very closely. He seemed far removed from this world, lost in God."

After the Mass, the priests were all invited into the Pope's private library, a spacious room with high paneled ceilings, comfortable furniture, and two large windows overlooking St. Peter's Square. They were divided into several groups—Italian, French, German, Spanish, and English-speaking. There was no Punjabi group, so Joseph joined the English-speaking group. The Holy Father spoke to each group in their own language, shaking hands individually and speaking a couple of personal sentences to each of them.

"Before I left Rome, I met the Holy Father once again, this time in an open visit in St. Peter's Square," recalls Joseph. "The crowds, as always, were tremendous, and everybody wanted to get close to him, to touch him. They had put up barricades but I was lucky to be right in front with another priest from Pakistan. We were able to shake his hand. He was especially wonderful with the children. Two little boys in particular were hollering at the top of their voices, but when the Holy Father approached, they fell suddenly silent. He spoke to them, picked each one up, blessed them, and after he moved on, they continued to tag along behind him for some distance, inside the barricades, until their frantic mothers grabbed them."

* * *

Despite Joseph's initial disappointment with his coursework, Rome offered fascination and wonderment in abundance. It was indeed a transcendent city, and he reveled in its history, architecture, and churches.

In April, something happened that would make Joseph's visit to Rome beyond memorable. After class one day, Professor Angelo announced that the entire Missiology class would be making a pilgrimage to Israel during Spring Break, providing everyone managed to get the requisite visas and plane tickets (paid for with Joseph's Mass stipends). For Joseph, Israel had always been a dream, an ancient land full of sacred history for Jews, Christians, and Muslims alike. And now that it was actually a possibility, Joseph could hardly contain himself.

"Padre Angelo's announcement immediately resurrected a lifelong, seemingly unattainable dream of mine to see the sites, smell the air, and touch the land where Our Lord Jesus Christ, King of Kings and Lord of Lords, his blessed mother Mary, Joseph, and the apostles had lived. The dream, however, had long since been buried since I knew of no possibility within my means to make such a trip."

The following week, Joseph went to the Israeli embassy to obtain a visa. After being thoroughly searched, Joseph presented his Pakistan passport and was immediately told he could not travel to Israel.

Stunned, and without waiting to draw breath, he launched into every argument he could think of, the words sputtering from his mouth without thought. "If the Muslims can go to Mecca for Hajj and the Jews to Jerusalem for their annual celebration, and if other religions can encourage their followers to make a pilgrimage to their holy places, then why can't the Pakistani Christians go to Israel to see their holy places?"

A very sympathetic embassy clerk explained that Israel had no objection to Joseph's visit, but that the government of Pakistan would have a problem since Pakistan did not recognize the nation of Israel.

Crestfallen, Joseph watched his trip to the Holy Land crumble into a thousand pieces, each more heartbreaking than the other. Unable to sleep that night, Joseph dragged himself to class the next morning with a heavy heart. Nearly in tears, he told Padre Angelo about his discouraging and deeply disappointing trip to the Israeli embassy. The priest smiled and patted Joseph's shoulder. "Never mind, Guiseppe," he said. "Don't be sad, I will take you to Israel. We will apply for a *laissez-passer*, a special travel document issued by the Vatican to those holding a passport not valid in a particular country, in this case, Israel (and accepted by many countries without the need for a visa)."

Suddenly his despair evaporated. "The colors around me brightened, the air seemed fresher, and the voices of my classmates sounded like a heavenly choir," Joseph recalls. "Among the entire group of pilgrims—twenty-five priests, nuns, and lay people—I was perhaps the most excited."

When the plane landed at Ben Gurion International Airport in Tel Aviv, Joseph wanted to go down on his knees and kiss the Holy Land, the land of Yahweh and his beloved Son, Jesus Christ. But he restrained himself on the advice of his professor.

Padre Angelo would be the guide for the twelve-day tour. A Franciscan friar born and raised in Rome, Angelo seemed to know more about Israel and its holy places than he did about Rome. Every day, Padre Angelo offered splendid insights into the magnificent, historical sites, but his explanation was in Italian, his mother tongue. Joseph had begun to understand and even speak a little Italian, but Angelo's classical accent and fast delivery made it difficult for him to understand his narratives.

One day, the group went out on a boat in the Sea of Galilee, an area where many of Jesus' miracles are said to have occurred, including his walking on water and calming a storm (Mark 4:38-41). A few hundred feet from shore, the captain made anchor and silenced the engine while the guide described their surroundings over a loudspeaker.

"On the right is Galilee, the place of Peter, Andrew, James, and John. And the lake in which we are floating is the same lake where Peter—at the command of Jesus—caught so many fish after toiling the whole night and catching nothing. To your left," the guide continued, "is the Mount of Beatitudes, and in the center is perhaps the same spot where Jesus fed more than five thousand people with only two fishes and five loaves of bread."

Afterward, the group visited the house of Peter and Andrew, and then it was time to celebrate Mass. Each day, Padre Angelo selected a different place to celebrate Mass and each time, a different priest was asked to be the main celebrant. This time, it was Joseph's turn, and this time, Mass would be said in the open, in an area where the Apostles had walked more than two thousand years before.

Surrounded by the history and glory of the life of Jesus, and in his broken Italian, Joseph addressed the group. "Let us close our eyes for a moment and, with the eyes of our mind, imagine Jesus surrounded by His disciples and the throngs of people—the sick, the crippled, the blind, the hungry. This ground on which we stand has been touched by the divine feet of the Son of God. The air still resounds with the words that carried his message of hope and mercy. Some of these trees have witnessed the presence of the Lord, and this lake has borne the boat that carried Our Lord and supported him on its waters. Let us become a part of this living history and carry with us the special blessings this place offers, for the Lord is not of the past but lives in and through us."

In Nazareth, the pilgrims visited the house where Jesus, Mary, and Joseph had once lived. "Since my last name is Nisari, which means follower of the Nazarene, I felt a special connection to Nazareth," says Joseph.

The group traveled to Masada, the ancient rock plateau where the Jews were besieged by the Roman army and, after seven days, chose death rather than surrender. As the story goes, since Judaism rejects suicide, the defenders chose lots and killed each other—one by one—leaving only the last man to actually take his own life.

In the heart of the old city of Jerusalem, Joseph visited the Temple Mount—one of the most historic sites in the world—on which stands the Al-Aqsa Mosque and the Dome of the Rock, the oldest Islamic building in the world. Sacred to Jews, Muslims, and Christians alike, Temple Mount was originally the site of the early temples of Jerusalem. The Western Wall, one of the holiest of Jewish shrines, is part of the original retaining wall that enclosed the Second Temple. The wall is also known as the Wailing Wall because for centuries, Jews have come here to mourn the loss of their temple and to slip prayers between the cracks in the stones of the old wall.

Just outside of Jerusalem, the group toured Calvary, stopping to pray at the Stations of the Cross as they followed the route that Jesus took to his crucifixion. They prayed by the tomb from which Jesus rose on Easter Sunday, and in the Garden of Gethsemane, where Jesus and his disciples prayed the night before his death. The olive trees in the garden date back to the time of Jesus and two thousand years later, still bear fruit.

At the house of St. Elizabeth, mother of John the Baptist, Our Lady's song—the magnificent Magnificat—was written on the wall surrounding the house, in all the major languages of the world.

"The high points of the pilgrimage," Joseph remembers, "were visiting the room believed to be the site of Our Lord's last supper, and Mount Tabor, where Christ was transfigured as the glorified Lord."

For Joseph, it was indeed the experience of a lifetime, and he had to pinch himself regularly to ensure that it was not a dream. "Celebrating Mass at all those holy places gave us an almost mystical sense of the Lord's presence," says Joseph. "For me, it was a life-changing pilgrimage."

CHAPTER 21

Coming to America

The Lord said to Abraham: "Leave your country, your people and your father's household and go to the land I will show you."

—Genesis 12:1

During the summer, the Vatican colleges closed and the student priests had to find their own summer assignments or vacation "opportunities." Catholic parishes in other countries often needed priests to fill in for their vacationing clergy, and frequently asked the Vatican students to help out, which also provided the students with a unique opportunity to experience other cultures.

Since Joseph could not afford the price of a ticket to Pakistan, and since the only foreign language he could manage with any fluency was English, he would have to look for something in a place where English was spoken.

All his life he had heard about America, dreamed about America, never believed he would ever go to America. Now he had an opportunity to visit this fabled place. It was a propitious decision, one that would change Joseph's life in ways he could never have imagined.

Someone from the Collegio put Joseph in touch with Father Tom Kelly in Hancock, a small village in upstate New York. Father Kelly was pastor of St. Paul the Apostle Church, and he was going to Ireland for two months, exactly the amount of time Joseph had free.

A plane ticket to the United States was expensive for a priest living on a small stipend and Mass Intentions (donations), so Joseph set about finding the cheapest flight available. He booked a ticket on Japan Airlines, on a route that would take him from Rome to the US, with an overnight stop at an obscure town in Russia. I was full of apprehension," he remembers. "I wondered what America would be like, if I could adapt. It turned out to be unlike anything I had ever imagined."

By bus and by plane, Joseph traveled two days, arriving at JFK International Airport in New York City on June 14, 1982. He was traveling with a friend, an Indian priest. The two men were dressed in traditional attire, shalwar kameez for Joseph, and a *kurta* (long shirt) and baggy pants for his Indian friend.

Once inside the terminal, Joseph queued nervously in the customs line, finally presenting his immigration form to the agent, a humorless, middle-aged African American lady who couldn't be bothered by a simple civil greeting. "This form is incorrect, you've missed a line," she snapped. "Get another one and come back."

Joseph searched for another form, but all he saw were forms in Japanese, Chinese, and other foreign languages. Finally he found one in English, filled it out, and returned to the customs window. This time, a young man checked the form and his passport. "Welcome to the US," he said, smiling.

Father Kelly was waiting in the reception area, searching anxiously for a Pakistani priest he had never seen. If Father Kelly was looking for a Catholic priest in a traditional Roman collar, he did not find one. But he did find Joseph, who was not easy to miss with his dark skin, odd clothes, foreign accent, and Indian friend.

Father Kelly introduced himself. "OK then, I am here for you," Joseph replied. The two men shook hands and hustled the luggage out to a waiting car. As the car pulled out of the airport, Joseph got his first look at America. "I thought I was dreaming," he says. "So many cars. So many *big* cars."

Joseph was mesmerized by the Statue of Liberty and the unimaginably tall buildings, the twin towers of the World Trade Center visible for miles. They stopped at a restaurant and Father Kelly handed Joseph a menu. "What is barbeque?" Joseph asked. "I did not recognize a single item." Finally, he told Father Kelly he would have the same as the priest from Hancock, a hamburger and a 7 Up.

After lunch, the two priests headed upstate toward Hancock, two hours away. As Joseph watched the scenery fly by, he reflected on this astonishing new place. "Everything was so big, so beautiful, so majestic." Rome had also been majestic, but on a different scale. Rome was ancient, vibrant, thrilling, challenging. New York, at least this part of it, seemed full of wide spaces, tall trees, and panoramic views as the wide four-lane highway melted into the green hills and valleys. "Everyone seemed to be driving on the wrong side of the road," he remembers. "In Pakistan, we drove on the left side."

The cars especially impressed him. Later, in Hancock, whenever he saw all the cars parked in the driveways and on the streets, he would look at them and marvel. "I would measure them by stepping off their length, one step, two steps, seven steps, oh my, this is a very big car."

Foreign priests arriving in the United States were no different from other immigrants, often experiencing culture shock in addition to isolation and the loss of family, friends, and the familiar support systems of their native dioceses. In addition to adapting to the culture of a new country, they also had to adjust to the unique ecclesial culture of the Catholic Church in the US. Not only did Joseph have to learn a new liturgy, he also had to learn currency conversions, where to catch a train, how to use a phone, do laundry, order food, light a stove—a whole list of simple day-to-day functions necessary for survival in this new country. Even the door locks, plumbing, and light switches were unlike anything he had ever seen.

In time, Joseph would adjust to this strange new country of immense wealth, material excesses, vast spaces, and natural beauty. He would eventually come to embrace America, but not before encountering some life-changing experiences.

"The America of my dreams was a very great, very rich country,

with streets paved in gold and populated with generous and special people," Joseph reflected. "Part of this perception came from the American
aid I remembered receiving as a child in Pakistan. However, the longer I
stayed, the more I realized that America was indeed a land of plenty, but
it also had its problems and its share of imperfect people. Nevertheless, it
was still the world gold standard for freedom, democracy, and opportunity,
and I enjoyed two wonderful months in Hancock, surrounded by beautiful
people and wondrous things."

Joseph would be spending his summer in a most delightful place.
Nestled in the foothills of the Catskill Mountains, the little hamlet of Hancock was pleasant, quaint, leafy, and serene. The Delaware River, along
with the many streams and lakes that surrounded Hancock, were full of
fish, providing a fisherman's haven and what many described as "the best
fishing in the United States." The world-famous Louisville Slugger baseball bats were made from Hancock lumber for over eight-five years, and
the wood from Babe Ruth's bat came from a Hancock tree.

Joseph was amazed that Father Kelly played golf, a sport Joseph
associated with the elite, the wealthy, kings, and bishops. "Regular" people did not play golf where he came from. The morning after Joseph arrived in Hancock, Father Kelly left for Ireland and Joseph was left to sink
or swim. He would not sink but he would have some trouble keeping his
head above water.

Early on, Joseph made the astonishing—to him anyway—discovery that he was expected to cook his own meals. "In Pakistan, I was used
to pastoral visits where we would eat with the people in their homes. In
the rectory in Pakistan we had a cook, so I wasn't really prepared for this
cooking thing."

A few days after Father Kelly left, Joseph announced from the
pulpit, "I don't know how to cook or how to shop for groceries. If you
want me to be alive when Father Kelly comes back, you will have to in-
vite me to your homes for a meal." The parishioners of St. Paul's needed
no prompting. They were eager to spend time with the priest from Paki-

stan, and invitations poured in. In fact, when Father Kelly returned, there were still about fifteen families whose hospitality Joseph would not have a chance to accept before he returned to Rome.

In America, Joseph was always looking for cuisine that resembled the Pakistani food he was used to, but it was hard to find. "I discovered that I liked Italian and Mexican food, but I never got used to hamburgers, and I don't really care for steak, even though it is a big treat for Americans. This is likely due to the fact that I never ate much meat in Pakistan."

But what surprised Joseph the most was the quantity of food and the size of the servings, not to mention the fact that people trimmed the fat from the meat, and left meat on the bones and food on their plates, then tossed the leftovers into the garbage. "In Pakistan, we could have fed several families with just the leftovers."

Early on his second morning in Hancock, Joseph was in the kitchen looking for matches so that he could light the stove and make tea. It was a gas stove, but it was automatic; all you had to do was turn a handle. When the cleaning lady arrived just before noon, she asked Joseph if he had had his breakfast. "I had some fruit but I couldn't get the stove to work," he replied. "Do you have some matches?"

The cleaning lady started laughing. "We don't use matches here. Come, I will show you."

"Wow," was all Joseph could say.

With his dark skin and foreign clothes, Joseph was a novelty in Hancock, although his neighbors seemed as exotic to him as he did to them. Most of Hancock's citizens had never even heard of Pakistan. He might as well have been from the Moon, but most people actually thought he was from Africa.

About that time, Joseph met Dan Rizzo, an Italian who had a local restaurant. La Salette was within walking distance of the rectory, so Joseph ate quite a few meals there.

"My English was still not so good but I managed," Joseph recalls. "One of the best homilies I ever preached in Hancock was after Dan Rizzo got me drunk.

"Being Italian, Dan naturally spoke the language very well. I knew that if I could improve my Italian as well as my English, things might go easier for me when I returned to Rome, so I asked Dan if he had any free time to practice Italian with me. He came to the rectory right away and picked me up. The first place we went to was a bar owned by some friends of his. Right away, Dan ordered two drinks, manhattans I think, which he convinced me were all part of American hospitality. 'Please, you can't refuse, it would be rude,' he said. He introduced me around as the priest from Pakistan, which amazed everyone, since they thought there were no Christians there.

"Then we went to another place and again they filled our glasses and said 'Welcome, make yourself at home.' There was some chit-chat and then another glass appeared. At the fourth bar, I said, 'Dan, I think I'm getting a little unsteady and I have to preach tonight.' He said, 'Well, you know you can't refuse American hospitality, so just take a little bit and put the rest in my glass.'

"We got home about four o'clock in the afternoon, and I quickly washed my face and drank some water, hoping to regain my composure, but it did not help. Being basically a non-drinker—alcohol was hard to come by in Pakistan—I should have been quite liberally intoxicated, but I wasn't. Apparently there was something important God wanted me to say that day.

"With my head spinning, I started Mass, hoping I would not spill the wine—or worse—and that my words would come out right. After Mass as I greeted the people at the door, someone said, 'Father Joseph, that was a great sermon.' To myself, I said, 'What did I say?'

One morning about two weeks into Joseph's stay in Hancock, Caroline Molinsky, a lovely parishioner who was married to Richard, a charming Polish gentleman, arrived at the rectory. "Today we are going to Binghamton," she announced. "You need a clergy suit." Off they went to the mall in Binghamton. After years of wearing cassocks and kameezes in

Pakistan, Joseph now had his first Western clergy suit.

Through his ministry in pastoral counseling, Joseph came to know a family who was going through some difficulties. The man was rather introverted and, believing that he did not need any guidance, did not benefit from Joseph's efforts. The wife, however, seemed glad for a sympathetic ear. At the time, she was about eight months pregnant, and one afternoon, she asked her husband to take her to the hospital for her regular checkup. "I cannot take you," her husband told her. "Ask Father Joe to take you, he seems like a nice man."

At the appointed time, the pregnant parishioner arrived at the rectory along with her two-year-old son. She felt too uncomfortable to drive, so she asked Joseph if he would mind. "I had never driven in the US and since we drive on the left side in Pakistan, this was a bit of a problem, but I managed. Of course, it wasn't long before the news spread—all the way back to Pakistan—that 'Father Joseph was married and had a couple of children.' If I hadn't heard about it personally, I wouldn't have believed it, but it gave me a good laugh," says Joseph.

In August, the parish had a combination birthday party and farewell celebration for the priest from Pakistan, and Joseph experienced his first American potluck supper. Everyone brought his or her special foods to share, and there was even a big, beautifully decorated birthday cake. "Every family wanted their picture taken with me—I was a novelty, the first Pakistani priest most of them had ever seen."

CHAPTER 22

Long Day's Journey

The gift of grace increases as the struggles increase.

—St. Rose of Lima

After his summer service in Hancock, Joseph had to return to Rome. He would travel first to London to visit Pakistani friends who had two daughters, one a few months old, the other about two. The family wanted Joseph to baptize the girls at their local parish church, at a Mass celebrated in the Urdu language.

When Joseph arrived at Victoria Station in London, the first thing he spotted was a hefty Englishman begging for alms. In a sudden flash of irony, Joseph thought, "These were the people who ruled our country, they were the kings, we their subjects and servants. And now this unfortunate British gentleman is asking for my help." He gave him all the coins he had.

Joseph's friend Salim was at the station to meet him. Joseph had known Salim's wife back in Narowal when she was at the boarding school. Joseph stayed with the family for several days and then headed for Rome by train, via Paris and Lyon.

At Lyon, Joseph had to change trains but he had no idea which platform the train to Rome would be departing from. He held out his ticket and showed it to some of the other travelers, hoping someone would have a clue. "They would look at me expecting me to speak French, but my French was not up to the task." Then Joseph used his fractured French to ask people if they spoke English. None did. Eventually Joseph found a

French National Railways employee who pointed in the direction of the train to Rome—which began moving as he was speaking. "What do I do now?" Joseph asked.

"Tomorrow at this time the same train will come and you can take it," the man replied.

Joseph now had about twenty-four hours to kill, and the railway station seemed like the best option, since he didn't have much money, didn't speak much French, and was already there. He found a trolley for his two bags—one containing his clothes and the new clergy suit, the other filled with gifts—hung his shoulder bag over his shoulder, found a place to sit, and settled in for a nap.

About eleven o'clock that night, everyone was asked to step outside so the station could be cleaned. After several hours of standing in the cold, everyone was invited back inside the station, where at least it was warm. Joseph put his shoulder bag on the trolley with the other two bags and looked around for a place where he could lie down and get some sleep.

Suddenly, out of nowhere, a man streaked past Joseph, snatched his shoulder bag from the top of the trolley, and disappeared. Joseph gave chase and then, realizing his other bags were unattended, gave up. Slowly he began to realize what had been in the stolen bag, what was now all gone—his precious mementos, his passport, train ticket, money, breviary, his entire identity. And it occurred to him that he was now stranded in a train station in a foreign country with no passport, no money, and no identification.

The thief was reportedly a young Turkish man, and Joseph would later learn that Turkish boys were especially adept at this sort of crime, stealing the passports of foreigners, which they could then sell for thousands of dollars because they were already stamped and in use.

Joseph asked around in his broken French about reporting his stolen bag. He was advised to go to the police station, a short distance away. He could not take the luggage trolley, so he dragged his remaining two bags with him to the police station, where he told his story. There, they wrote a report, gave Joseph a copy, and advised him to go to his embassy, get a new passport, and then go to the Italian Embassy and apply for a visa to return to Rome. And since he had no money, they gave him two tokens for the subway and directions to the embassy.

Realizing that it would be difficult to take his luggage with him, Joseph cleverly looked for a corner where he might hide his bags, at least for the time being. Then he struck out for the embassy, knowing his bags would at least be safe in the police station.

It was now about eight o'clock in the morning and the embassy was just opening for the day. He could see a small crowd of Pakistanis gathered outside, and the embassy clerks were shouting, "Half of these guys have sold their passports and are now coming to tell us they have lost them!" And here comes Joseph with his equally suspect story. Once inside the embassy, he showed them the police report, explaining that he was a citizen of Pakistan, that his last passport had been renewed in Rome, and that he was now in need of a new passport. The words tumbled out in a desperate attempt to establish some sort of credibility. Unbelievably, they accepted his new application, but they could not tell him when he should return for his new passport. He had their telephone number and, for the moment, it was enough. Now all he needed was a place to stay, but he had no idea for how long.

For the next several hours, Joseph walked around the surrounding neighborhoods looking for a church. Any church. Whenever he found one, he would repeat his story, "I am a Catholic priest from Pakistan and I have lost my bag and identification and I need a place to stay for a few days."

The answer was always the same: "Sorry, but without any identification, we cannot let you stay here."

By three in the afternoon, Joseph was getting worried. He had had nothing to eat in many hours, nor any access to a bathroom—he would have to pay to use one—and it would be dark in a few hours. He started asking everyone he saw, including the receptionist at the Catholic cathedral office, if they knew where he might find a place that hosted foreign priests. No one knew of any such place.

Around five o'clock, he came upon a Polish church and asked to see the person who was in charge. Speaking in broken bits of Italian and French, Joseph made the man understand that he was a Pakistani priest and needed a place to stay. The priest spoke only Polish and Italian, but he understood something; he gave Joseph the address of a hostel for international missionaries. "This is the place you should go," he said.

Exhausted, hungry, and more miserable by the minute, Joseph thanked him and left. Down the block he saw a furniture shop, and for some unknown reason, he went inside and asked if anyone spoke English. "A little bit," the gray-haired, mustachioed proprietor replied. Joseph repeated his miserable story. The gentleman was so moved by Joseph's situation that he gave him fourteen francs—about three US dollars. It seemed a princely sum.

With his newfound wealth, Joseph was inspired to take the subway back to the police station to retrieve his bags. The night staff had replaced the day shift so they did not remember him, and suggested he check the lost-and-found department in the basement. By now it was six o'clock and the clerk was hurrying to close up and go home.

Joseph produced the police report, described his bags, and *voilà,* it was done. Outside, he hailed a cab and gave the driver the address of the hostel for foreign priests. As they drove along, Joseph kept an eagle eye on the meter, and when it reached fourteen francs, yelled "Stop!" When the driver asked why, Joseph replied, "That's all the money I have." Being a cab driver, Joseph hoped he understood, but the man continued driving until he reached the address. The fare was now twenty-one francs, and Joseph repeated that he didn't have any more money. The cabbie was not pleased. He tossed Joseph's bags out and drove off in a grand French huff, squealing his French tires as he departed. But, by the grace of God and one short and very annoyed French cab driver, he had arrived . . . at a place to stay.

Joseph dragged his bags into the office and repeated his story. "Wait here. The monsignor is coming and he has been to Pakistan," the receptionist told him. Joseph felt his luck changing.

Once the monsignor arrived, Joseph said, "I am Father Joseph Nisari from the Lahore diocese . . . "

"Oh, and Monsignor Trindade is your bishop," he said with a smile. "We have an extra room because one of the priests has not yet arrived, but you will have to move to another room tomorrow."

To Joseph, the words sounded like they were being spoken by a heavenly choir.

The monsignor invited Joseph to join them for dinner, but Joseph demurred. "For the last twenty-four hours I have had nothing to eat or drink, nor have I had the use of a bathroom. Please, may I borrow yours?"

That night Joseph slept the sleep of the dead, profoundly grateful to God, the Polish priest, the man at the furniture store, the taxi driver, and the monsignor who had been to Pakistan.

The next day, the monsignor asked if he would mind moving to a smaller room in the attic. "As long as I have a roof over my head, I don't care where you put me," Joseph replied. It was a small room, just big enough for a bed and two suitcases, but to Joseph, it was heaven on earth.

The priest in charge of the house gave Joseph some French francs for his Mass Intentions, as that was the only way they could offer him any financial assistance. Joseph then called his rector in Rome to let him know what had happened and that he would be late returning, maybe even a by couple of weeks.

Over the next few days, Joseph did a little sight seeing, returning often to the embassy to check on the progress of his passport. He saw more of Lyon than most tourists ever do. Finally, after twelve days, he got his passport.

He then took the new passport to the Italian embassy to get his visa for Rome. When he went to pay the fees, the clerk smiled and said "*Gratis.*" Free.

CHAPTER 23

New York

Lord, make me an instrument of your peace. Where there is hatred let me sow love; where there is doubt, faith; where there is despair, hope; where there is darkness, light; where there is sadness, joy. Grant that I may not so much seek to be consoled as to console; to be understood as to understand; to be loved as to love. For it is in giving that we receive, it is pardoning that we are pardoned, and it is in dying that we are born to eternal life.

—St. Francis of Assisi

Back in Rome, Joseph was two weeks behind on his coursework and had to catch up quickly. He also began work on his thesina— a shorter form of thesis. According to Joseph, "Writing a thesis is like writing a book; a thesina is about half a book." The subject of his thesina was (no surprise) "The Development and Role of the Catechist in Pakistan," the subject that had become his life's obsession. With every fiber of his being, Joseph still longed to do meaningful work to improve the lives and standards of the catechists in Pakistan, and so to advance the lives of his people.

Since Joseph lacked sufficient fluency in Italian, he was allowed to write his thesina in English. In May 1983, he completed the course and received his licentiate in Missiology.

In October, Joseph returned to Lahore and a grand reception. More than twenty family members had waited most of the night at the airport for his arrival at four o'clock in the morning. It was a memorable homecoming, with masses of flowers and money garlands draped around his neck. Mariam feasted her eyes on this apparition, her long-absent son whom she clearly adored and had not seen in more than two years. Because she could not read or write, there had been no real communication between them while Joseph was away in Rome, but Mariam had been ecstatic that Joseph was studying in Rome. She was, after all, the one who had so desperately wanted to go to school, and who had been so forcefully dissuaded by a machete-wielding brother.

During his absence, Mariam had saved every rupee she could in order to buy a small gold cross and chain, and it was her great joy to finally hang it around Joseph's neck.

Joseph's new post would be Mary Immaculate Conception parish just outside the city center of Lahore, near the legendary Anarkali bazaar. More than one hundred years old, the church had served as the Lahore cathedral prior to the construction of the new one. In 1983, the parish had a boarding house, a two-story rectory, a large two-story study hall and science lab, and a school. (During the 1970s, the school, St. Francis, had been conscripted by the Muslims, and remains under their control today.)

Joseph would serve as a parish priest at Mary Immaculate Conception for three years, without a break. Having gone to Rome to take courses to improve the situation of the catechists, Joseph found himself back in Lahore with a licentiate in Missiology, doing the same thing he had done before he left, teaching the catechists and conducting the annual refresher courses—without benefit of any new tools or resources. Joseph remained frustrated and deeply troubled that he lacked the skills to achieve his goal. Like a dog with a bone, he could not let it go.

During Joseph's absence, the local clergy had split itself up into several factions, seemingly according to age. Having been away, Joseph was the outsider. He belonged to no group. And he didn't particularly want to belong to any "group," believing as he did in the fundamental unity of one body of priests—one in Christ. He could not understand this apparent division in the ranks. "I had been away for two years," he recalls. "Suddenly I was a stranger—perhaps the color of my stripes had changed?" The situation rankled and contributed to Joseph's increasing restlessness.

* * *

On December 3, 1985, after a short illness, Joseph's beloved mother died.

A few months earlier, Mariam had complained of chest pain, and Joseph had taken her to the hospital in Lahore. Several days later, she suffered a stroke and was transferred to ICU, and from there the family decided to move her to the more familiar Bethania Catholic hospital in Sialkot, where Joseph's niece was a nurse. Bedridden, partially lucid, unable to feed herself, Mariam was nearing the end. Soon thereafter, the hospital administrator, Father Hubert, called the family together. "There is nothing more we can do for her here," he said. "It is time to take her home." Two months later, she was dead.

Joseph and the old family friend Father Fidentian concelebrated the funeral Mass in Pajian, the village of Mariam's youth. "Mama was buried in the Christian cemetery next to my father, and, unlike my father, she got a box [casket]," Joseph says.

In the last years before Mariam's death, feeble as she was, she would often go to see Joseph at the rectory, traveling on foot and by bus, whenever she needed company. But Joseph was not much company because of his busy schedule. "Mama would say to me, 'I am alone at home and I am alone here.' I will never forget, and will always regret, her comment. Even among family, she was alone."

* * *

In March of 1986, after three years as a parish priest, Joseph was appointed rector of Sacred Heart Cathedral, where he had been ordained eighteen years earlier. Fifteen years later, Joseph's nephew, Reverend Andrew Nisari, would follow in his footsteps as rector of the cathedral.

A few weeks later, the Catholic community in Lahore had a visitor—one that Joseph would never forget. The beloved spiritual icon and Nobel Peace Prize winner, Mother Teresa, came to town to visit the newly established convent for her order, the Missionaries of Charity.

Born in Albania in 1910 and christened Agnese Gonxhe Bojaxhiu, Mother Teresa was eighteen years old when she left home to join the Sisters of Loreto as a missionary. For almost half a century, she ministered to the poorest of the poor, caring for, in her own words, "the hungry, the naked, the homeless, the crippled, the blind, the lepers, all those people who feel unwanted, unloved, uncared for throughout society, people that have become a burden to the society and are shunned by everyone." After her death, she was beatified by Pope John Paul II and given the title Blessed Teresa of Calcutta.

At the airport in Lahore, Mother Teresa was given a special VIP room to receive her guests. Father Joseph, along with several nuns from her convent, a number of her followers, and the director of the Pakistan Department of Social Work were there to greet her.

Afterward, Mother Teresa, Joseph, and a government dignitary were taken by official car to Sacred Heart Cathedral. Along the way, large crowds of Catholics lined the streets, anxious for a glimpse of her famous, weathered face.

At the cathedral, Bishop Trindade, Mother Teresa, Joseph, and the guests shared a cup of tea and visited for about half an hour. Then the bishop asked Joseph to escort Mother Teresa to her convent, which was some minutes away. Because of the narrow, potholed streets, the official car could not get through, so Joseph walked with Mother Teresa to the residence. It was March and the weather still cool, so she wore a little blue sweater over her habit.

"Mother Teresa was a tiny woman, only about five feet tall, and I had to stoop a bit to talk to her," says Joseph. "She had a gentle, almost beatific smile and very penetrating eyes, as if she were looking into your soul."

* * *

In spite of his relatively lofty posting at the cathedral, Joseph's mind and heart were not at peace. He was still searching for that elusive "something" that would help him in his catechetical ministry. Three months later, in June, Joseph asked the bishop for some time off. He had not had a vacation in three years and felt that a change of scenery would give him time to clear his head, find his focus, and renew his apostolic zeal.

The bishop granted him a month. That month would turn into five years. Joseph would not return to Pakistan until June 1991.

* * *

In August 1986, Joseph traveled once again to the United States. After a brief visit to Hancock, he headed to Brooklyn, New York, to Immaculate Heart of Mary (IHM) Church, where his Irish friend Ed O'Connor was pastor. Father O'Connor offered Joseph a temporary spot as associate pastor and, sympathetic to his quest for anything that would strengthen his pastoral ministry, supported his desire to visit Iona College in nearby New Rochelle, which offered courses in pastoral counseling.

"I was grasping at straws, I suppose, but the opportunity was there, right in front of me, and I was not likely to get many chances to advance my cause," Joseph remembers.

Joseph soon discovered that the "courses" were actually a three-year master's program in Pastoral Counseling, and he didn't have three years. The bishop had granted Joseph a month. How he could stretch that into enough time for a three-year program, he had no idea. He decided to try for admission, and if successful, he would then approach the bishop.

Shortly thereafter, Joseph wrote Bishop Trindade with news of his admission to Iona and expressed his hope that a master's degree in Pastoral Counseling would make him a more effective priest and counselor. Not surprisingly, the bishop did not acknowledge the letter. Ever hopeful, Joseph continued writing to the bishop, and even wrote to his old friends in the Bishop's Council. He heard nothing.

Determined not to let this opportunity slip away, Joseph construed his bishop's silence as acquiescence, of a sort. Surely if he was needed at home, the bishop would ask for his return. He had every confidence he would receive good news from his bishop—if he just waited long enough. This had often been the case in the past, and with enough prayers and perhaps a little luck, it could be again. Didn't God help those who helped themselves?

Iona College was a religious institution run by the Christian Brothers, and they accepted Joseph on scholarship, on the condition that if he did not receive his bishop's permission within a year, he would have to leave. Eventually Joseph heard from Bishop Trindade, who did indeed grant him permission to attend the program—for two years. Two years was infinitely better than no years. Joseph would take his chances.

New Rochelle was twenty miles north of Manhattan in suburban Westchester County. Joseph lived in Brooklyn, so he had to go from Brooklyn to Grand Central Station by subway (one hour), from Grand Central Station to New Rochelle by train (one hour), and from there walk thirty minutes to the college—a five-hour round-trip commute.

Learning his way around New York City's labyrinthine subway system was a challenge, which Joseph transformed into an adventure. "I asked a lot of people a lot of questions, and eventually came to realize that it was important to know that 'uptown' is Manhattan and 'downtown' is Brooklyn," Joseph explained. "If I was going to Brooklyn, I took the F train; if I was going to Queens, it was the A train. I got lost more than once, and a couple of times, I slept through my stop, but eventually I got the hang of it.

"One of my first cultural miss-steps occurred on a subway train when I happened to bang into a lady (good thing to remember: HOLD ON TO SOMETHING). She glared at me and said, 'Watch out, you bumped into me.'

"No," I replied, "the train moved but I did not intend to bump into you."

"You should at least apologize," she huffed.

"In retrospect, this was an important lesson for me," recalls Joseph. "This was something I was not accustomed to. I had to learn when and how to apologize, and to say I'm sorry—regardless of whether I was at fault (which, apparently, was not the point). I also had to learn to say 'thank you' at the appropriate moment. These were cultural gestures, and common behavior in many countries. But in my culture, these refinements were taken for granted. For example, on a subsequent visit to Pakistan at Christmas time, a little girl approached her papa and said, 'Papa, where is my Christmas gift.' Papa proceeded to give her fifty rupees and she smiled and walked away. I stopped her and said, 'Don't you think you should say thank you?' (It was now a habit of mine.) She said simply, 'But that's my papa.' In Pakistan, that is the way, that is our mindset. In fact, until recently, there were no words in Punjabi that could be literally translated to mean 'thank you.'

"Later on when I was back in Pakistan at Shahdara, I would tell the people at St. Luke's that if they wanted to be regarded as civilized and respected, they should learn to say 'I'm sorry' and 'thank you.' When you make a mistake, you say 'sorry,' and when somebody does something for you, you say 'thank you.' Good manners in any culture are often a by-product of education, and most Pakistani peasants are uneducated."

* * *

Joseph made the trip to Iona College three times a week. Weekends, he helped out at the parish. Weekdays he would say the first Mass at six thirty in the morning, and by seven thirty he was out the door. When he returned in the evening, he had other pastoral duties. Early on he realized he needed to make good use of the time spent commuting, so he did much of his reading and studying on his trips back and forth from Iona.

Joseph did his fieldwork at Adelphi University on Long Island, working with immigrants who had sought asylum in the United States. He was also simultaneously supervising children at the Sisters of Blessed

Sacrament Community Center three times a week.

As an intern, Joseph was given the position of job coordinator. In addition to counseling and helping the new citizens find jobs, he was also charged with introducing the foreigners to American culture, something he was still in the process of doing for himself. He would also be learning to speak "American" English right along with his immigrant clients.

"My supervisor was Jewish lady. She would always take a few minutes before each session to ask me how I was doing. In our very first session, I told her about my adjustment to American culture. I explained that I had come from a male-dominated society, that, as a Catholic priest, I had been relatively independent for the past twenty years, and in my last position, I had supervised seven catechists, 150 villages, and more than fifteen thousand people. Although I had no problem with the irony of my situation, I found the role reversal interesting, if not amusing. She was a very nice lady. She smiled and said, 'OK, glad I asked.'"

Joseph's clients were five immigrants from the countries of Vietnam, Cambodia, Iran, Armenia, and Afghanistan. Five people from five different cultures, religions, and backgrounds. As their job coordinator and mentor, Joseph was responsible for helping to ease their transition into American society. Often, the agency would give him leads for jobs for his clients, and Joseph would have to call the prospective employers on the phone to arrange interviews.

"I didn't know if I should say 'May I speak with so-and-so' or 'Please, can I talk to so-and-so?' In my hesitation, they would often hang up," Joseph remembers. "Many times I went to my supervisor asking, 'What is the correct way to say this in America?' Then I would call again with more confidence and they would listen to me. I was lucky to be a part of the acculturation program. I knew that many immigrant doctors, engineers, and other professionals were working in gas stations and convenience stores, without benefit of any cultural acclimation, a situation that must have been very difficult for them, not to mention their loss of stature and dignity."

Joseph was able to find jobs for every one of his clients.

* * *

"In those days, visas and green cards were much easier to obtain because there was no real concept of terrorism as we know it today," Joseph recalls. "When I came to the US the first time, all I needed was a letter from my bishop and a letter of invitation from the United States. At that time, green cards were primarily the purview of teachers, nurses, doctors, and religious clergy. The green card was usually issued at the airport; however, Pakistani professionals entering the US had typically been given some kind of competency exam in Pakistan prior to their arrival in the US. Today, it is very difficult for most Pakistanis to get a visa to come to the United States.

"When I went for my interview with the judge who would issue my green card, I noticed a picture of his children on his desk and I asked about them. Immediately he began to tell me all about his family, and we chatted for about fifteen minutes. It seemed oddly as if I were interviewing him. Finally, he looked at his watch and our time was up. 'I'm sure you know all of the things I was supposed to ask you,' was all he said.

"My green card arrived in the mail two weeks later."

* * *

Meanwhile, as Joseph worked to improve the lives and dignity of his fellow human beings, the government of Pakistan was going down a different path. In 1986, Pakistan implemented Section 295C of the Pakistan Penal Code, more commonly recognized as the blasphemy law, which specified a mandatory death sentence for defaming the Holy Prophet Muhammad. (In 1982, President Zia ul-Haq had passed Section 295B, which punished desecration of the Quran with life imprisonment.)

In spite of the harsh punishments, there was no penalty for false accusation, so the law quickly became a powerful tool of intimidation and was frequently misused to resolve personal disputes, professional or political rivalries, or to escape debt. Even if the accused was exonerated, both he and the judge who acquitted him were at risk of death at the hands of radical fundamentalists. Some Muslims even took it upon themselves to carry out the death penalty, without benefit of the Pakistani legal system.

CHAPTER 24

Fordham University

Let us work as if success depends on us alone, but with the heartfelt conviction that we are doing nothing and God everything.

—St. Ignatius of Loyola

The registrar at Iona College had made it quite clear to Joseph that, without a letter from his bishop authorizing him to continue, he would have to abort his studies at Iona.

Although the bishop had eventually granted Joseph permission for two more years of study in order to complete the three-year program at Iona, the permission came too late. By then, the door at Iona had slammed shut, which actually turned out to work in Joseph's favor.

What to do now? At a virtual impasse, Joseph had another idea. "What's the difference between pastoral counseling and social work?" he asked himself. " Which would be more useful for me?" Since he now had the grace of two more years of study, he decided he would be better served to pursue a two-year master's program in social work at Fordham University, which, conveniently, had a branch in Manhattan. It would be a relatively short commute.

Joseph consulted several colleagues who assured him that many priests and bishops had degrees in social work, which had helped them significantly in their ministries; in the social work program, students also received counseling training.

It would be a rigorous and demanding program, requiring Joseph to write a ten-page paper every week, in English. Each week, the instructors would provide a topic and a bibliography for the dreaded paper. After classes were over for the day, Joseph would bring a load of books back to the rectory and start writing. He would take a break for supper, then write some more. There was an old typewriter at the rectory, but, having never in his life even seen such a machine, he had no clue how to use it. Nevertheless, he was determined to type his own paper. Surrounded by stacks of reference books, he would write everything out on a legal pad first before typing it up on the typewriter, an agonizingly slow process even if he hadn't been translating everything from Urdu to English.

"I would peck at that creaky old machine until about six o'clock the next morning, take a shower, and go to the six thirty Mass. By seven thirty, I was gone. My first class was at eight o'clock, and I was in class all day. On weekends, I attended to parish business."

Over time, the grueling schedule paid off. Joseph passed his exams and graduated in May of 1989 with a master's degree from Fordham University's School of Social Service. This would be a very special graduation for Joseph. All his life, whenever he had graduated—from middle school, high school, or seminary—there had been no celebration, no party, no congratulatory cards, nothing to mark his achievement. But Fordham had organized a grand reception, with music, food, and socializing. Joseph's family was, of course, unable to attend, but he invited an Italian family from Immaculate Heart of Mary parish in Brooklyn and a cousin from New Jersey to join him.

After Joseph graduated, he sent a letter to Bishop Trindade advising him of his graduation, as well as the student loan for which he was now responsible. "As a result," says Joseph, "we had a tacit understanding that I would remain in the US and seek employment to pay off the loan."

Joseph was now a bona fide, certified clinical social worker—with a bona fide student loan. In spite of his scholarships, Joseph owed many thousands of dollars in student loans. The arrangement he had with his bishop in Pakistan was rather wobbly; he would have to repay the loans but no specific time had been set regarding how long he was to remain in the US. The first loan installment was due in June, and the parish stipend Joseph received each month was nowhere near enough to cover his obligation. He would have to find a job. Fortunately, his agreement with the pastor at IHM only required him to serve the parish on weekends; during the week he would be free to work at an offsite job.

Joseph liked children, so the New York City School District seemed a good place to start looking for employment. There was an opening for a bilingual school counselor, which paid reasonably well, so Joseph decided to apply for the position. During the interview process, he chose to be tested in Hindi, which, in retrospect, was a stupid thing to do. In Pakistan, most people understand a lot of Hindi through television and movies, but written Hindi is very different from Urdu or Punjabi. Joseph thought his passing knowledge of Hindi would be enough. It wasn't. When he went to be tested, he was asked if he could write Hindi. He could not. The interviewer spoke excellent Hindi, which Joseph could barely understand. He thought his career as a bilingual counselor was over. However, he had done very well in Urdu and offered his skills in Urdu and Punjabi. Unfortunately, there was no need for the Punjabi language, but they did need Urdu-speaking counselors.

In a lucky turn of events, Kings County Hospital in Brooklyn was, at the same time, looking for a clinical social worker. One day Joseph was at home in the rectory along with Father Simon Joseph, another priest from Pakistan who had recently graduated from Yeshiva University in New York City, also with a master's degree in social work. The phone rang and the secretary said, "It's for Father Joseph." When Joseph heard this, he automatically picked up the phone.

At the other end of the line, a voice said, "This is so-and-so at Kings County Hospital. Last week, you interviewed with us for a position as a social worker, and we would like to discuss a job offer with you."

Joseph was stunned. He had not applied for such a job, nor gone for an interview, at Kings County Hospital. Nevertheless, without thinking any further, Joseph went straightaway for the second interview at Kings

County. He was after all, looking for a job. Maybe this was how that "networking" thing worked.

When Joseph appeared for the second interview, the administrator realized immediately that he did not look familiar. "I think we had another priest at the last interview," the administrator said. Nevertheless, they offered Joseph the job on the spot. Slowly it dawned on Joseph what had happened. That phone call had really been meant for Father Simon Joseph. "Had it been a possibility, I think he would have killed me," Joseph recalls. "But all ended well. The hospital needed two social workers."

Joseph was offered a position as a clinical social worker for the Department of Alcoholism, Drug Addiction, and Psychiatric Impairment. Father Simon Joseph was offered a job at the Alcoholism Clinic.

Thus, Joseph found himself a newly minted social worker, working with New York City's most miserable, not at all where he imagined his training would take him. He began work at Kings County Hospital the end of May. His first Sallie Mae installment would be a bit late, but at least he would be able to make it.

The first day on the job, Joseph was shown how to take a patient history. Shortly thereafter, he had his first new-patient interview. Afterwards, Joseph wrote carefully in his notes: "This patient is completely crazy."

"Later I came to know that the unfortunate man was schizophrenic and quite unable to connect the dots," Joseph says.

When his supervisor checked his notes, he exclaimed, "Oh my goodness, you never write that a patient is crazy! You have to say something like 'psychiatrically impaired.'" So Joseph began learning yet another language: medical speak. He would have to pay careful attention that his patient histories reflected a diagnosis rather than his personal opinion.

In due time, Joseph learned about all the pathologies, as well as about alcoholism, pharmacology, psychiatric impairment, drug addiction, and treatment options. He also had to learn to make the distinction between Spanish and Hispanic clients. "The Hispanics spoke Spanish but were not necessarily from Spain, while the Spanish spoke Spanish and were from Spain."

One afternoon, Joseph was making a home visit and noticed six or seven kids running around. "I don't understand, is this woman the mother of all these children?" Joseph asked his colleague. The counselor explained that the woman was seeking to increase her monthly welfare check. "The more children you have, the bigger the check. Every time she needs money, she goes out into the street and looks for a prospective man to father another child," he explained. "Most of those children have never even seen their fathers."

Working at the hospital introduced Joseph to a new level of culture shock. Most of the people he saw were substance addicts or psychologically impaired. Often they ended up in jail or in a grave. It was a pattern and the success rate was tragically small, maybe only two or three out of a hundred patients.

The patients were provided with a token lunch, usually a ham or chicken sandwich, nothing very gastronomically appealing, but rather intended to ward off hunger. They would open the sandwich, check the filling, and if they didn't like it, toss it in the trash drum, which mortified Joseph. "At least ten families could have been fed with all the food that was discarded every day." Joseph's supervisor put things in perspective: "What can you do?" he said. "If the patients don't want it, you can't force them to eat it."

During Joseph's tenure as a counselor, he came to realize that the reluctance of many patients to treat their own depression was a sign that they had succumbed to their helpless state. His own background of discrimination and oppression put him on level ground with his patients, able to empathize and understand—on a very personal level—how they dealt with oppression and depression in their own lives.

Over the years, Joseph would counsel many young people and community leaders never to succumb to poverty, helplessness, or discrimination. "Instead," he would tell them, "you must build your own fate through unity and hard work, with patience and perseverance, making use of all your resources. As a human being, you must protect your rights, fight for justice and equality, and never accept an existence of destitution and wretchedness."

* * *

In June 1991, out of nowhere, a call came to the chancery office of the Brooklyn diocese from Joseph's bishop in Pakistan. Joseph was summoned to meet with Father William Hoppe in the diocesan office.

Father Hoppe questioned Joseph as if he had committed a crime, which apparently he had. His crime was that he had overstayed his time in the Brooklyn diocese, and his bishop was threatening to remove his faculties if he did not return immediately to Pakistan. Faculties are basically a certification from the bishop of a priest's original diocese to the bishop of another diocese, authorizing him to accept you with full privileges as a priest and member of the diocesan family. Without faculties, Joseph would not be allowed to remain at the rectory or function as a priest.

Joseph had eighteen months left to pay on his loan.

* * *

After five years in the United States, Joseph found himself once again headed back to the country of his birth, the country that had given him so much joy—and so much frustration.

Back in Lahore, Joseph went to the cathedral to face his bishop, who happened to be away on vacation. The rector found a small room for Joseph, which was opposite the nun's bookshop and not a part of the bishop's residence. The room had no facilities for drinking water or washing up, and after eleven o'clock in the evening, the doors to the bishop's residence were closed and locked. Joseph's cousin arranged to bring him a small cooler with some ice and water.

A few days later, Joseph's sister Maria came to visit him. "How can you stay in this room?" she asked him. It was a very dirty place and only half the windows had any glass, Maria remembers. "There were no sheets and the mattress was soiled. I wanted to cry, so I asked him, 'Are you going to stay here?' Joseph replied, 'It is only temporary. When the bishop returns, I will have my assignment.'"

Joseph found it unusually difficult to adjust once again to the customs and rhythms of Pakistan and to re-establish his old routine. *How spoiled and petty I have become,* Joseph thought. *Why do they need me in Pakistan anyway?*

Meanwhile, Joseph's sister Maria was going through her own agony, having left her convent after many years of service, during which she had managed to earn a master's degree in economics, often studying by candlelight late at night in her little cubicle. But in the end, things had not gone well for her and she made the bitter and difficult decision to leave the convent.

Maria's decision was a shock for Joseph. He did not judge her, but her actions deeply troubled him. "She was one of the most senior sisters in her order," Joseph recalls, "and a very effective one, but apparently her superior had not supported her and had made her life very difficult. This I understood; it is difficult to be productive if you are not supported."

Joseph was eventually won over by Maria's plight and sympathized with her decision to go to America. "I had no place else to go," said Maria. "My parents were dead and I could not go to my brothers' or sisters' homes because, once you left the convent, it was a perceived dishonor to your family."

Her mind made up, Maria set out to obtain a visa to go to the US, but failed in her initial attempt. *No problem,* she thought, *I will try again in Karachi*—where Joseph had advised her to go. She had been told in Lahore however, that "once you are rejected, you are rejected forever." This in no way deterred Maria.

In Karachi, Maria went to see the Sisters of the Holy Cross, specifically one of the nuns who was known to the immigration authorities and routinely handled visas for members of religious congregations. In an hour, Maria had her visa. In Karachi in those days they did not have computers, so there was no exchange of information and no way to know that Maria had already been denied a visa in Lahore.

Maria received her visa on July seventeenth and left for the United States the next day. She arrived in New York City dressed in her religious habit (she had no other clothes), with little else besides a positive spirit, a six-month visa, and her language capabilities; she could speak Maltese, English, Italian, Urdu, and Punjabi. She went directly to the convent of the Sisters of Mercy in Brooklyn, where she would remain for about a month. "I had no idea what to expect in America," she recalls. "I had no plans, but I was sure that in spite of my difficulties, I would survive. America would give me that opportunity."

Maria did indeed survive and today lives in New York City, where she has worked as a para-professional in education in the New York City School District for the past sixteen years.

* * *

When the bishop returned to Lahore, he called Joseph to his office. "I am sending you to St. Xavier's in Gujranwala," was all he said to him.

Forty-two miles—an hour and a half drive—from Lahore, Gujran-wala was a major agricultural and industrial city and the seventh largest city in Pakistan, according to the 1998 census. Trying to spin the new assignment in a positive light, Joseph went off to check out his new parish, taking with him his sister-in-law Elvina and brother Peter. Driving into the church compound, it became harder for Joseph to remain positive. The church stood in bad repair, like a neglected monument. The rectory, only five years old, was shabby and tired, the paint peeling off the walls in great swipes. There were few signs that anyone had recently lived there.

The catechist came out to meet Joseph and show him around the compound. The inside of the parish house was as dismal as the outside, the walls stained with smoke. The office was bare, stripped of any furniture, and in the little bedroom there was no bed. The kitchen had a large table and chairs but no dishes, pots, or pans.

Joseph's predecessor, Father Rufin Julius, had lived there as a parish priest until he became a politician. Father Julius had had a rather checkered career as a clergyman, and during his transition from priest to politician, the parish house had been at the mercy of Father Julius' political associates. People came for various meetings and activities and when they left, they apparently took whatever they needed at the moment: a chair, a bed, dishes, whatever. Over time, the house was slowly dismantled; the church contributing more than just a priest to the community.

Father Julius succeeded as a politician because he was Father Julius; he used his position as a trusted priest to win elections. Since priests are prohibited by the church from entering politics, he eventually left the priesthood, married, and became quite successful as a member of the National Assembly, even serving as Minister of Minority Affairs.

Joseph decided to remain in his little room at the cathedral in Lahore—where at least he had a bed—while he refitted the parish house. Elvina made a list of items Joseph would need to set up housekeeping, and they went shopping together. His purchases came to nearly eleven thousand rupees (about two hundred US dollars), which did not include furniture for the second bedroom and or the office.

Back in Lahore, Joseph presented the bill to the bishop, who immediately forked over ten thousand rupees. When Joseph remarked that that amount was a thousand rupees short, the bishop sighed and said, "You should cut the cloth according to the coat," meaning you should only buy what you can afford to pay for. Chagrined, Joseph left the money on the desk and turned to go. "You keep it, I will manage," he said. "These things I have bought are for your diocese. I do not own them; I am only trying to reestablish the house. When I leave, everything will stay." The words tumbled out like water from an open faucet. He had not the luxury of deciding what the appropriate response should be.

Using small donations from family and friends as well as some of his own meager funds, Joseph managed to buy a bed and few other items. Meanwhile, the bishop called Father Mani, the vicar general, who had a second office in Gujranwala. "Father Nisari is upset, and I want you to take this money and give it to him," he told Father Mani. A few days later, Father Mani called Joseph and asked him to come over. Handing Joseph an envelope full of rupees, he said, "Please, take this money." Joseph swallowed his pride—pride can be fatal to spiritual progress—and accepted the money. By this time, he really needed it.

A couple of weeks into his new assignment, Joseph set out on his first daura in the area. The villagers were usually informed whenever a priest was coming, and typically made special preparations for his visit. So when Joseph and his catechist arrived at the first village, he was surprised to find the streets empty and no one around to welcome them. *How strange,* he thought. At the home of his host family, they set about spreading out the mats and getting everything ready for the service. After an hour, no one had come. After several hours, still, no one had come, and Joseph needed to leave soon in order to keep his schedule.

"What has happened? Why aren't the people here?" Joseph asked the catechist, who explained that the people were still angry over the actions and neglect of their former priest. "How can we believe that this priest is any different from Father Julius?" the people had protested, believing as they did that Father Julius had neglected his flock in favor of political pursuits.

Joseph was astonished. "But they don't even know me. How can they make a judgment without even meeting me? Please, go one more time and ask them to give me a chance."

After some time, a few villagers began to arrive; soon about twenty-five people were gathered in the small house, watching Joseph with wary eyes. One priest had already compromised their trust, and they were not sure they wanted to believe another.

While the English language had always been a major stumbling block for Joseph in the US, now, after so many years in the US, Joseph found himself struggling to renew the cadence of his native Punjabi. He began the service with a plea for tolerance and understanding: "Brothers and sisters, I understand that you need some time to decide if you can trust me. I apologize for the neglect you have suffered in the past, and I recognize your concern, but it is time to move on in God's mercy and love."

When it was time to return to Gujranwala, the catechist suggested that Joseph take a short cut. "After you leave my house, follow the road about eight kilometers until you come to a turnoff, then continue straight on," he advised Joseph. By now it was past eleven o'clock at night, so Joseph climbed into the jeep and took off down the road the catechist had suggested, headlights poking holes in the darkness. Traveling about forty-five miles per hour, he suddenly realized he was on a bridge with a big zigzag ahead, which, having no bright beams on his vehicle, Joseph had failed to detect. This was no ordinary turn; it required that the driver first anticipate the two consecutive jigs in the road ahead and then negotiate the sharp turns at a reduced speed.

Joseph hit the brakes hard, but he was going too fast. He slammed into the side of the bridge, flipping the jeep over on its side. Instinctively he reached over and turned off the engine, crawled from the driver's side to the passenger side, opened the door, and climbed out. He was unhurt, and because he had only gone about three miles he tucked up his cassock and walked back to his catechist's house. They had all gone to sleep. Joseph knocked at the gate and soon a very surprised catechist came outside.

"Do you have a tractor around here?" Joseph asked.

"Yes, I think the Christians have a tractor, what happened?"

"You didn't tell me about the bridge. I missed the turn and turned the jeep over."

The catechist felt terrible about the accident, even though it was clearly not his fault. He may have neglected to mention the bridge, but he was not responsible for Joseph's penchant for speed. The two men hiked off in the middle of the night in search of the Christian with a tractor. A couple of hours later, the jeep was righted, a bit bashed up, but drivable. Something was rubbing against the wheel and several parts were dangling off the chassis, so it was slow going on the way back.

The next day, Joseph went by bus to Lahore to retrieve a mechanic who could come back to Gujranwala and repair the jeep. It would then have to be driven to Lahore for more extensive repairs.

CHAPTER 25

AWOL

*Out of the depths I have cried to thee, O Lord: Lord, hear
my voice. Let thy ears be attentive to the voice of my sup-
plication. If thou, O Lord, wilt mark iniquities, Lord, who
shall stand it. For with thee there is merciful forgiveness,
and by reason of thy law, I have waited for thee, O Lord.
My soul has relied on his word. My soul has hoped in the
Lord. From the morning watch even until night, let Israel
hope in the Lord. Because with the Lord there is mercy;
and with him plentiful redemption. And he shall redeem
Israel from all his iniquities.*

—Psalm 129

Joseph had never stopped thinking about his unpaid student loan, left
behind in the United States when he was commanded back to Pakistan. And, quite coincidentally, Joseph had recently received a letter
from Kings County Hospital, offering him his old job back. After Joseph
had abruptly left their employ in June 1991 they had interviewed a number of social workers, but the position remained unfilled in the hopes that
Joseph would be allowed to return.

Joseph took his letter of invitation and his concerns to Bishop
Trindade, whose reply was brief: "If you stay in Pakistan, you won't have
to worry about your loan, they will not be able to collect the money."
Joseph was somewhat surprised at the position of the bishop on this matter. It was a debt that Joseph had incurred in good faith and promised to
repay, and besides, if he ever did return to the US, he could be in serious
trouble—maybe even considered a criminal.

Joseph attempted to convince the bishop of the possible consequences of neglecting the debt, the practical ones as well as the moral and ethical ones. The bishop then produced a book on scholarship information and education loans and said, "Write to these people and they will help you settle your loan."

Joseph wrote straight away to four of the listed organizations, three of which were in the US. He wrote under the bishop's letterhead and signature, and six months later had heard nothing. He reminded the bishop once again that his loan was due in full the following year. He had been able to secure a six-month extension, but he would have to start making payments again in February of 1992.

For weeks the bishop remained intractable. Then, a small crack appeared. Finally he called Joseph to his office and said, "The diocese is not able to repay your loan, so I believe you must go back and take care of it yourself." Joseph was both relieved and stunned at the unexpected turn of events. They agreed on a course of action. "Make your arrangements and when you leave, give your car keys to the bishop's driver and the house keys to the vicar general," the bishop said. Thus it was decided: Joseph would return to his old job in Brooklyn and the bishop's letter granting him permission to leave the diocese would follow.

The bishop's letter did indeed follow, but what it said would be totally unexpected.

Joseph still had some small savings from his work in the US, so he decided to buy his ticket himself, rather than charge the diocese. He said his goodbyes in Gujranwala, packed his clothes, and notified Kings County Hospital that he would be there in early February.

The bishop's letter, sent directly to the Brooklyn diocese, was waiting for Joseph when he arrived in New York. The letter explained that Joseph was "absent without leave and without faculties," from his diocese in Pakistan. And without faculties, he was officially persona non grata within his church, effectively stripped of his priestly duties and responsibilities, unable to celebrate Mass or even approach the altar.

The words hit Joseph like a train. He had no idea why the bishop had changed his mind, especially now, at this particular moment. But the bishop had undeniably played the trump card, and there would be no appeal. According to canon law, a priest cannot leave the diocese without the bishop's permission, and although Joseph believed that he and the bishop had an agreement, he had nothing in writing.

Joseph considered his options. He had an obligation to repay his loan, and he had made a commitment to Kings County Hospital. There appeared to be no compelling reason for him to remain in Pakistan. *I have to do this*, he told himself. *In my heart, I have no choice.* And in a church where he was already on shaky terms, it would be a precarious decision. Somehow, he would have to find a way to square things with the bishop.

And so it came to pass that Joseph found himself in the United States in January of 1992 with no letter of authorization from his bishop, no faculties, and no place to live. What he did have was a job.

His purpose and optimism diminished, Joseph descended into a sort of mental purgatory, and for the first time in his life, he despaired. He would soon realize how fragile his human nature was, and how much he would need God's grace and guidance. He was also acutely aware of how much of his very human pride remained. Of only one thing was he certain; he was ordained a priest, and he would die a priest.

Paul's second letter to the Corinthians, chapter 12, verse 9 says, "And he said to me: My grace is sufficient for thee, for power is made perfect in infirmity. Gladly therefore will I glory in my infirmities, that the power of Christ may dwell in me." For Joseph, this would become his mantra and his lifeline in the months to come. He would remain in Brooklyn for the next six years, as an AWOL priest.

* * *

Joseph desperately needed a place to stay, so he contacted some old friends, a sympathetic Italian family that was willing to provide temporary accommodations. Casting about for more permanent arrangements, Joseph remembered Sister Elizabeth, now known as Mariam, an ex-nun whom he had sponsored some years back for medical treatment in the United States. Severely crippled with rheumatoid arthritis and unable to care for even her basic needs, Joseph had arranged for her to come to the US for treatment. Having since left the convent, she was much improved and working with disabled children in New York City. And, quite coincidentally, she was living in a two-bedroom apartment in Queens—and one of her bedrooms was unoccupied. He decided to ask if he could rent a room from her. His ecclesiastic reputation was already toast, so it hardly mattered that he would now be living with an ex-nun.

* * *

Several months later, Joseph became a US citizen, something he never longed for but which was mandated by the terms of his green card.

"In those days, you had to complete your citizenship requirements five years after your green card was issued," he remembers. "If you passed the examination, you were given the opportunity of participating in a swearing-in ceremony held in a Brooklyn courthouse. I chose to go, and I was not alone. About four hundred other people joined me in the ceremony, where, for the first time, I pledged my allegiance to the American flag.

"It was with both sadness and joy that I took the oath of citizenship and renounced my native country. The oath states that 'I absolutely and entirely renounce and abjure all allegiance and fidelity to any foreign prince, potentate, state, or sovereignty of whom or which I have heretofore been a subject or citizen . . . so help me God.'"

Having previously held citizenship in two other countries, India and Pakistan, Joseph was now an American, filled with pride and gratitude for the opportunities and blessings his new country had to offer. A part of him, however, would forever remain Pakistani.

* * *

Joseph's spiritual life may have been in turmoil, but he had a job to do. Every morning he would go to work at Kings County Hospital in Brooklyn by train, and every evening he would return to his small rented room in Queens.

"It was rewarding but precarious work," Joseph said of his new employment. "Many of the patients had AIDS; others were victims of drugs, dementia, and/or alcoholism. Most patients appeared 'normal' but psychotic patients can be unpredictable, and if they were not taking their medication, they could become dangerous in the blink of an eye. You learned to keep one eye looking over your shoulder at all times. Once, when I was conducting a spirituality group, I closed my eyes for the opening prayer and the psychologist sitting next to me whispered, 'Never, never close your eyes around here. Anytime you look vulnerable, you are asking for trouble.'

"I remember a particular patient, a rather mild-mannered middle-aged man, who had killed his wife and five small children. In his mind, he believed the world was a very dangerous and corrupt place and everyone was going to hell. The deluded man decided he would send his family to heaven, and so he killed them—one by one—in an oven. How he did this I have no idea. He was obviously too ill to be tried in court so they confined him to a psychiatric facility. When I met him, he was in charge of a food bar in the hospital and appeared to be a normal, functioning person."

* * *

Back in Pakistan, Joseph's niece had married a Pakistani doctor who was also a very devout Christian. Dr. Justin Samuel loved to tell his patients that they could overcome their illnesses more quickly with faith. "In the beginning, I could say these things with impunity," Dr. Samuel recalled, "because a doctor was much respected and trusted, and no one would ever speak against a doctor who taught them about the things of God.

"I was just happy if I could offer my patients the joy of the Lord in their lives along with any medical help. Many times people would knock on my clinic door looking not for medical help, but to know more about God. I continued healing body and soul for another five years in various Pakistani hospitals. At the same time, I was becoming increasingly involved in sponsoring and working with interfaith meetings between Muslims and Christians. Then suddenly, there it was: my death sentence. I had been accused, under the blasphemy law, of crimes against Islam. Several weeks later, in the middle of a frigid December night, I sneaked out of Pakistan and escaped to Bangkok. I left behind a wife and two children. It was 1993."

Dr. Samuel eventually found refuge in Germany, where he would spend the rest of his life as a Christian evangelist. Some time later, his family was able to join him, but he remained a wanted man in Pakistan and dared not return. In 2005, a major earthquake occurred in the mountainous region of Pakistan-administered Kashmir, killing more than 75,000 people. Traveling in disguise and using an alias, Dr. Samuel returned to Pakistan, to Kashmir, with a team of doctors to offer medical assistance. While there, he was able to visit his aging parents, whom he would never see again. In August of 2009, Dr. Samuel and his wife—Joseph's niece, Angelina—were killed in an automobile accident in Germany.

* * *

One of Joseph's colleagues at Kings County Hospital was a Presbyterian minister. When Joseph shared his story, Reverend Mike invited him to visit his church, thinking Joseph might find solace in a place of worship, even if it wasn't Catholic. Joseph joined him several times, discovering that the Presbyterian service was surprisingly similar to the Catholic Mass. Except for the absence of the statues of the saints, the alter appeared the same. The canon of the Mass, even the Creed, except for a few words, seemed the same.

Both denominations share many of the same tenets, including belief in the Holy Trinity, the most obvious differences being the infallibility of the Pope and the status accorded to Mary. With regard to Communion, Catholics believe in transubstantiation, in which the bread and wine literally become the body and blood of Christ, while members of the Presbyterian faith believe that the bread and wine are representations of the body and blood of Christ.

Since Joseph had no parish and no bishop, Reverend Mike suggested that he might like to visit with the Presbyterian bishop about a possible spiritual "home." Joseph knew he was grasping at straws, but he made an appointment with the Presbyterian bishop. To get to the bishop's office, Joseph had to first take the subway, then walk three blocks to the train station and take the train to his final destination. As he walked toward the station, thoughts swirled in his head like a shaken snow globe. *Do you really want to do this? What do you expect to gain, when you have everything to lose?*

By the time Joseph reached the station, he knew he could not do it. All the years of studying, preaching, practicing, and believing his Catholic faith could not be erased, discarded, or rejected. His faith stuck to his soul like gum on a shoe. He suddenly thought of his father, the faithful catechist, so proud that his son was studying to be a priest. He knew his father would never have approved of any deviation in his faith; there could be no reason compelling enough to justify abandoning his Catholicism. His God, after all, had not abandoned him. His actions suddenly felt profoundly wrong; so wrong that their wrongness hurt him physically. He would have to find another way to return to the work he had been ordained to do.

* * *

In due course, "Mr. Nisari," as he was called by his peers, was promoted to the rank of Social Worker II and transferred to a nearby federal facility, Kingsboro Psychiatric Center. Social Worker II was a step up, signifying that Joseph had surpassed his training position.

One of the first people Joseph met at Kingsboro was Father Bob Frueh, who served as the Catholic chaplain at the center, and who would become a good friend and mentor to Joseph in the months ahead. (In 2010, Father Bob had been at the center for twenty-three years.)

"Joseph's priorities were relating to the patients and meeting their needs," Father Bob recalls. "I think paperwork and the attendant deadlines took second place, which, in my impression, caused some conflict with his supervisors, some of whom were intent on looking good and having their department look good, rather than having the patients' welfare as a main concern. The supervisors tended to be rather inflexible where written reports were concerned.

"To Joseph, the problems and life experiences of our clients must have been quite shocking, and quite a contrast to his life in Pakistan. Joseph was a people person, open, non-judgmental, empathetic, and a good listener. Most of our patients were mentally ill and suffered from related physical ailments; they had no money, no moral support from family members, and no competitive skills for the job market. They desperately needed a willing, understanding ear, and Joseph was able to provide that, having himself come from a simple background.

"Joseph told me about his history as a priest, but I was in no position to make any judgments about his situation, which was so different from mine. So I just related to him as the friend I saw him to be, a deeply spiritual, passionate, and holy priest. I was also impressed with his unflappability and his belief that all would turn out well. In fact, I can't recall a time when he ever lost his cool."

One afternoon, Joseph and a colleague were asked to visit a young Hispanic man who suffered from psychiatric impairment and was also in the last stages of AIDS. When they arrived at his apartment, the young man, a devout Catholic, was rambling incoherently about the Bible. But his manner changed abruptly, and he began to threaten the two men in broken English, promising to kill them both.

According to Joseph, "The skin around his nose and hands was badly blistered and swollen, and he was probably in severe pain. We asked him if there was anything we could do for him, but he would not talk to us. He continued behaving in a belligerent manner, then suddenly he climbed on a small table next to his bed, brandishing two kitchen knives. My colleague disappeared into another room and called 911, while I remained with the sick man, trying to calm him until the police arrived. In his demented state, the poor man was still shrewd enough that when he heard the police outside and saw the ambulance, he instantly put the knives away, and just as quickly transformed himself into the most benign of men, cool and calm. When the police came in with the paramedics, he was like a lamb."

"What's wrong with this guy?" one of the policemen asked Joseph, looking at the pitiful, docile creature before him. "Why did you call us?" Joseph could not tell the policemen—in front of the patient—that the man was psychotic, so he said simply, "Since you have arrived, he seems to be OK." They managed to convince the policemen to take the man into custody since he was, most certainly, a danger to himself and others.

Tom Meany was Chief of Service at Kingsboro, which, at the time, consisted of two adult male psychiatric wards. As the social worker assigned to the service, Joseph had a caseload of anywhere from eight to twenty patients, and was responsible for providing for all their social service needs.

"The wards were crowded and there was a lot of pressure to manage the census by discharging as many patients as were being admitted— or more," Tom recalled. "In order to successfully discharge a patient, a number of social services needed to be in place, primarily somewhere to live, as well as financial, psychiatric, medical, and social supports. The communities we were discharging these patients into had very few of these support services available, making for a tremendous creative challenge.

"My daily charge to the staff was: 'Team, we have to get the damn job done, no matter what.' This always cracked Joseph up, but he pulled together with his team to find creative solutions in connecting patients with the resources they needed in order to be discharged. He also worked directly with the patients, individually and in groups, providing therapeutic treatment interventions designed to smooth the healing process.

"Some of the most difficult challenges for Joseph were with the language and culture. He was like a duck out of water, always puzzled by idioms such as 'a day at the beach' or 'a piece of work.' His supervisor was a very proper lady and a strict task master. She had little empathy for Joseph's challenges, but he dutifully tried to meet her expectations. I remember that he had a Colorado Rockies baseball cap with their 'CR' logo. He insisted it stood for 'Christo Rex' [Christ the King].

"His greatest strength was the unconditionally positive regard he had for the patients and they understood this. He had a calm demeanor and a soft-spoken voice, which put patients at ease, and he was a great listener. The flip side of this was that some of our patient's had dual diagnoses of mental illness and drug addiction and many of the manipulative drug users tried to take advantage of his humble nature, but he learned fairly quickly from the rest of the team how to be more assertive in setting limits with them.

"Joseph and I often socialized with Father Bob. We would go on 'retreats' to Father Bob's house in the Pocono Mountains. After dinner we would sit around the fireplace and Joseph would astonish us with stories of his life in Pakistan, and the amazing predicaments he found himself in as he made his rounds of the remote villages on a motorcycle. One of the most memorable stories was when Joseph was riding his motorcycle through a small town and accidentally brushed against a pedestrian woman, snagging her burka and partially disrobing her. Fortunately, at that time, this was probably perceived as an accident and not cause for criminal prosecution."

In 1995, Joseph found himself in a rather unique position as supervisor of the women's floor at Kingsboro Treatment Center, a state-run outpatient center for the treatment of alcohol and substance addiction. There were two counselors on the staff, both female. Joseph was the only man on the floor.

Joseph would attend all the ADL [activities of daily living] group meetings, which taught basic hygiene skills. "The ladies would discuss all manner of personal and private things," says Joseph, "which had the effect of greatly embarrassing me, but they did not seem to have a problem with me being there. Nor were they aware that I was a Catholic priest (albeit a defrocked one), and that probably would not have mattered anyway. The women had more important things on their mind.

"One morning, a hefty, middle-aged black man showed up on my floor. He was clean-shaven and dressed in a skirt and blouse—shocking pink—with a lady's fancy hat on his head. It was my task to interview all new patients and obtain their personal data. As the lone social worker, I also had to provide a diagnosis of each patient's apparent problem, which was then given to the psychiatrist for further evaluation.

"I greeted the man and asked him, 'What kind of drama is this? Why are you wearing this costume? What are you doing here?' The man was a transvestite and probably also mentally ill. He later complained to the director that I had made fun of him, but in my defense, I had never seen a transvestite before, at least not up close, and I wasn't at all sure what I was dealing with. I didn't know whether this person was a genetic man or woman, and I was uncertain how to diagnose or treat him or her. Happily, and in spite of my apparent ignorance, the man went on to enjoy many more days dressed up as a woman."

In Pakistan, transvestites—*hijras*—are usually entertainers, male-to-female transgender people who dress as women and earn a marginal living singing and dancing at ceremonies, mainly weddings and the births of male babies. They usually live on the fringes of society, and often engage in begging and prostitution. Nevertheless, their presence at ceremonial events is seen as a sign of good luck and fertility, and their blessings—and their curses—considered potent.

The *hijra* society is deeply rooted in the Indo-Pakistani culture, and most are Muslims, some even descendants of the court eunuchs of India's Mughal Empire. During the days of Indian royalty, the *hijra* often served in royal palaces as trusted servants; poor families frequently converted a son into a eunuch in return for potential palace employment (and an income for the family).

* * *

At the treatment center, the residents suffered from a variety of illnesses and psychoses, including alcoholism and substance abuse, which was often the cause of their psychiatric problems. They were also the ones who, once freed from jail, would return to the streets, sin once again—mostly with drugs—and, hopefully, be arrested and returned to jail. However, instead of sending them back to jail, the authorities would often send them to the treatment center, where they would be kept for five days, during which time they would be diagnosed, prescribed medications, and referred to halfway houses and, from there, to job training and eventual employment. But jobs were often the last thing these people aspired to.

"Most of the staff had long ago come to the conclusion that all we provided was a revolving door," Joseph says. "For many of these patients, the ultimate destination was jail. Jail was their resort, their luxury hotel, complete with their own cell, a bed, a gym, TV, health care, heat and air conditioning, and three meals a day. Why would they want to be anywhere else? It became kind of a sick cycle; you committed a crime, then you went to jail—where life was basically good. I was not understanding this rationale, what kind of punishment was that?"

Since Joseph was not a fully functioning priest, he was also able to work nights and weekends. He spent his weekdays at Kingsboro Psychiatric Center. Three evenings a week, he counseled patients at a clinic for young handicapped adults who were psychiatrically impaired. Saturdays he rode with the Mobile Outreach Team (MOT) on a sort of "search and evaluate" mission. MOT provided psychiatric assessment, crisis intervention, medical prescriptions, and other related services. The team checked on patients who had been discharged from the hospital, those that had not kept their follow-up appointments, and those that might have run out of their medications. If a patient was in trouble, either physically or psychiatrically, the team would arrange for the police or an ambulance to take them to the hospital. The schedule was exhausting, but the experience—and the money—rewarding.

"In Pakistan and in many Muslim countries, these unfortunate people might have been considered as sent from God, as a kind of a blessing," Joseph explained. "Yet they were also often neglected, even disowned by their families. They would survive by begging, at the mercy of those more charitable. Medical or therapeutic treatment for these people wasn't even thought about."

Months passed in this manner, and although he was without a spiritual home, Joseph never missed Sunday Mass at St. Teresa's in Queens. Then one day, out of the blue, he suddenly thought of his friend, Father Oliver Weerakkody. Born in Sri Lanka, Oliver had worked in the Lahore diocese as a missionary in Pakistan in the early seventies. He and Joseph had become good friends. Joseph had followed Father Oliver to assignments in two different parishes, and when Oliver moved on, Joseph took his place. Father Oliver had even been transferred to Brooklyn and had worked in a neighboring parish while Joseph was also in Brooklyn at Immaculate Heart of Mary. And now, Father Oliver was once again in the United States, this time in Austin, Texas.

Father Oliver was about to become Joseph's deliverance.

* * *

As Joseph struggled with his demons in New York City, the Christians in Pakistan were dealing with demons of their own. On February 6, 1997, a mob of around twenty thousand militant Muslims attacked the Christian village of Shanti Nagar in retaliation for the alleged (and widely disputed) desecration of a copy of the Quran by a Christian from the area. Thirteen churches were torched and hundreds of homes sacked and burned. Pope John Paul II reportedly even took the extraordinary step of sending a personal protest to the Pakistan government.

Sadly, this incident was by no means an isolated one. Similar attacks against Pakistan's Christian minority were continuing unabated, and half a world away, Joseph feared for the future of his countrymen—Christian and Muslim alike.

CHAPTER 26

Austin

True holiness does not mean a flight from the world; rather, it lies in the effort to incarnate the Gospel in everyday life, in the family, at school and at work, and in social and political involvement.

—Pope John Paul II

On a sweltering morning in May 1998, Joseph's fellow seminarian, John Joseph, the charismatic bishop of Faisalabad and the first Punjabi Catholic bishop in Pakistan, took a loaded pistol and shot himself to death in front of the Sessions Court in Sahiwal, in protest of the death sentence handed down to a twenty-five-year-old Catholic convicted of blasphemy against Islam under the infamous Blasphemy Law.

Ayub Masih was condemned to death for allegedly speaking favorably of British author Salman Rushdie's controversial book, *The Satanic Verses*. According to Amnesty International, the real reason for Masih's indictment was an alleged land dispute in his village. For Bishop John Joseph, however, Masih's conviction symbolized the desperate plight of all Christians in Pakistan.

Profoundly saddened by the death of John Joseph, Joseph contemplated his own bleak and very uncertain future. He wasted no time in calling his old friend, Father Oliver, who was working as a hospital chaplain in Austin, Texas. Joseph explained his fall from grace and his unhappy situation in Brooklyn.

"I came to know Joseph back in the Lahore diocese in Pakistan when I was a missionary there," Father Oliver remembers. "He was a good man, an excellent preacher, and very concerned for his people. I was aware that he had had a disagreement with his bishop, but I did not know the specifics. I knew that he had been called back to Pakistan and that it had not worked out. I was concerned for his pastoral well-being as well as his personal well-being, and I knew that he would fit in very well in the Austin diocese. I also believed that Joseph would be better served in a pastoral setting, rather than as a social worker in a hospital, so I asked him if he would like to come and visit our diocese."

A few days later, Joseph got a call from Bishop John McCarthy of the Austin diocese. They talked for about ten minutes, and then, without ever having met Joseph, Bishop McCarthy said, "I am in touch with your bishop, and it looks like he will grant permission for you to join us."

God does indeed work through others, Joseph thought. It was not a miracle in the strictest sense, but it was most certainly an extraordinary thing.

Oliver was familiar with the bishop in Pakistan, so he had some idea of Joseph's frustrations. "When I went to Pakistan the first time, the bishop [Armando Trindade] told me not to bring anything," Oliver recalls. "'Everything you need will be supplied here,' he told me. But I brought my clothes anyway, which was a good thing. The bishop gave me 250 rupees and told me to buy whatever I needed, but you couldn't even buy a pair of shoes for that. Although Bishop Trindade was Pakistani, born in Karachi, he was also an English-speaking Goan from another culture, with an apparent lack of appreciation for, and sufficient understanding of, the pastoral and spiritual capabilities of the Punjabi priests. In the end, Joseph was promised many things according to his abilities, but none ever happened. I think the Holy Spirit moved Joseph after he had been in Rome and opened his eyes to other possibilities. His need was to be a pastor, to minister to the people. It was God's doing."

* * *

Joseph had planned to visit his family in Pakistan on his vacation, so he told Bishop McCarthy he would meet him in Austin in July. When he returned from Pakistan, he went straight to Austin. Father Oliver met him at the airport, and the next morning he met with Bishop McCarthy.

Bishop McCarthy recalls his first meeting with Joseph, who, at the time, was technically AWOL from his diocese in Pakistan: "I had dealt for the last ten years with an extraordinarily good priest, Father Oliver Weerakkody, who I trusted in every area, especially in his knowledge of priests coming into the US from his part of the world [Sri Lanka]. At the time that Joseph entered the Austin diocese, Father Oliver was a hospital chaplain in the Seton system, but he was much more than that. He helped me relate to the many Asian priests that were in our area. He also knew Father Joseph personally from their time together in Pakistan and had a lot of confidence in him. And so I agreed to meet with Father Joseph, review his situation, and extend the invitation. It was a good decision, and the fact is, Joseph has done great work in Texas and has been a blessing.

"When I interviewed Joseph the first time, his English was excellent, and he obviously manifested good horse sense and a commitment to hard work, so I said, 'Why are you doing social work in New York City? Why don't you come to Texas and do priestly work?'"

For Joseph, it seemed the end of his long nightmare was near. A few days later, Father Oliver flew to New York so he could help Joseph with the drive to Texas.

* * *

On September 5, 1998, at six thirty in the morning, Oliver and Joseph left New York City in Joseph's Toyota, headed for Texas. Joseph drove most of the time, stopping only for food and short breaks, and for the night at a motel in Johnson City, Tennessee. The next day was Sunday. Oliver had brought the host and wine, so the two priests celebrated Mass in their little motel room. For Joseph, it was a simple and emotional return to the priesthood he had never left. He had not celebrated Mass in almost six years.

The following morning, the two priests drove on until they arrived at the Texas state line, where Joseph turned the wheel over to Oliver, "You are a Texan, you know the way," he said.

The next day, Joseph met with Bishop McCarthy. "All right then, welcome to Texas," the bishop said. "I'm not going to give you a parish straight away because Texas is a different world. The culture, the language, and the people will take a little getting used to. Before we send you to the trenches, you need to get your feet wet, so I'm sending you to our Catholic hospital as a chaplain."

In his service as a chaplain, Joseph would celebrate Mass in the hospital chapel, visit and comfort the sick, and prepare the dying for their journey to life ever after. Catholic priests anoint the sick and the dying with holy oil and offer them Holy Communion if they are Catholic and if they wish to receive the sacrament. Catholics believe that anointing a person can also be a sacrament of healing, providing spiritual strength.

"The work at Seton Hospital was not difficult because I had already experienced working in a hospital environment," says Joseph, "but compared to the places I had recently come from, the people in Texas seemed exceptionally friendly. According to Bishop McCarthy, Texans had their own language, and he was right. It was all about 'you all' and 'I reckon.'"

In October, Joseph was temporarily assigned to St. Louis King of France Catholic Church in Austin. He would spend several months at the parish, also called IHOP, or the International House of Priests. The majority of the priests coming into the Austin diocese were sent there to get the flavor of the multinational, multilingual, and multicultural congregation.

At St. Louis, Joseph met Father Larry Heimsoth, a Lutheran priest who had converted to Catholicism and was waiting to be ordained as a Catholic priest. Father Heimsoth was in charge of evangelization and social work, while Joseph was doing counseling. What they had in common was that they were both waiting—Joseph to be assigned, and Father Larry to be ordained. Coincidentally, they would both end up serving at St.

Luke's in Temple a short time later.

When Father Larry converted to Catholicism, he was already a married man. In such cases, if a Lutheran or person of other faith decides that he would be better served within the Roman Catholic Church, he can apply to the bishop for candidacy. If accepted, he is not required to divorce or separate from his spouse, so the wife usually comes with him to his new ministry. (This exception to the celibacy rule was created in July of 1980.)

Three months later, Joseph received his first American parish posting. He would be an associate pastor at St. Luke's Church in Temple, about forty miles from Austin.

Monsignor Louis Pavlicek, the pastor at St. Luke's, was a congenial, bespectacled gentleman with an easy manner, a big smile, and a degree in electrical engineering. He recalls his first meeting with Joseph: "Bishop McCarthy called me and said, 'We've got a Pakistani priest here in our diocese who has been working in New York City for the past eight years, and I'm looking for a place where he can stay for awhile while we determine if he will work out in our diocese. Do you have a place for him?' I said sure. I had an associate who was being transferred to North Dakota, and he just happened to have a big U-Haul truck at the front door and four men helping him load all his stuff. So I thought to myself, if I'm going to Austin to pick up Father Joseph, I better take the parish van so I have enough room for all his luggage. I drove down to Austin and there he was, ready to go, with two or three boxes. That's all that he had—a few clothes, some books, and a car." The contrast in lifestyles did not go unnoticed.

"Among priests, there truly is a sense of brotherhood," says Monsignor Louis. "You can meet a priest from another part of the world and experience an immediate connection, a common bond that transcends nationalities. So I felt that even though Joseph was from Pakistan, we shared a common ministry, a common seminary experience, and to some extent, a common experience in our apostolic work. He struck me as being very open and receptive to new things, to going wherever the Holy Spirit guided him, and, as I would soon find out, he was very good at reconciliation.

"I remember one particular experience at St. Luke's that clearly demonstrated who Father Joseph was. A young man, sixteen years old, had committed suicide while his parents were on vacation, and his grandparents were staying with him. He had gone into his parents' room, found a gun, and shot himself. The funeral was huge; about 90 percent of the attendees were young people, and the atmosphere was profoundly sad. Another priest did the funeral Mass and I was the assistant. Father Joseph was also present. When the other priest gave the homily, it seemed very generic and, I thought, did not really seem to comfort the people. When the priest finished speaking, Joseph asked if he could speak. Then, very spontaneously, he addressed the mourners, as the Spirit moved him to speak: 'How do you cope with personal concerns and crises? You talk to your parents, talk to anyone who will listen, open yourself up, and become more transparent. Friendships must be filled with care and compassion, and whenever we are burdened, we must share our anxieties and learn to trust people.' Whatever he said was right on, an especially powerful message for the young people."

The despair felt by the people attending the funeral that day was probably also exacerbated by the ambiguous history of the Catholic Church's position on suicide. For Catholics, death by suicide has historically been considered a grave and mortal sin; the major argument being that one's life belongs to God and to destroy that life is to wrongfully take that which belongs to God. According to the 1997 Catechism of the Catholic Church, the person who commits suicide may not always be in full control of their mental facilities, and thus, not always morally culpable. Catholics pray for victims of suicide, knowing that God will judge them fairly and justly.

"The people at St. Luke's readily accepted Joseph because of his gentleness and spirituality," Monsignor Louis recalls. "He also brought along an international perspective. He didn't have a very good sense of direction, however. If you told him to go north for a mile and then take a particular exit, he would tend to get lost. There were quite a few times when he was supposed to be at a nursing home or a specific place, and people would call us expecting him, and we didn't know where he was. Eventually he would call, often from another town."

As a farewell gift when Joseph was later transferred to Granger, the people of St. Luke's gave him a map of the tiny city of Granger: population 1,331 in 2005.

* * *

In June of 1999, Joseph was assigned as pastor at St. Cyril and Methodious Church in Granger, a small farming community not far from Temple. In the early 1880s, Czech immigrants had settled the fertile blackland area, and in 1891 they built a wood-frame church on donated land, which they named after the Czech patron saints, Cyril and Methodius. Most of its residents had never heard of Pakistan.

"For the people of Granger, Father Joseph was probably a bit of a surprise," says Monsignor Louis. "When they heard rumors that a priest from St. Luke's in Temple was coming to Granger, they came to Mass at St. Luke's to check him out. Granger was primarily a Czech community. The people were strong in their faith, very devout, and very conservative, and they probably would have preferred a Czech priest as their pastor rather than someone from Pakistan, but they accepted Joseph, and I think it had a lot to do with his personality and his spirituality. They were able to see the man instead of the color."

To Joseph, St. Cyril and Methodius was vastly different from the relatively urban St. Luke's, where many of the parishioners were doctors, lawyers, social workers, and other professionals. Granger, on the other hand, was a rural community with strong Czech cultural influences and traditions, some of which had not changed in decades. "Getting a dark-skinned priest after decades of American priests, well, I might as well have been from the moon," says Joseph.

Initially, Joseph would find it difficult to gain a foothold in the ultra-conservative, insular community, but in Pakistan, he had faced bigger challenges. According to a longtime parishioner, "In the beginning, some of the congregation accepted him, and some didn't. Father Joseph was not white, nor was he Czech like most of our other priests had been, and he was often hard to understand. Although he could not always relate to a farmer's way of life, or to the old Czech ways, he was friendly and open, and his ability to understand and relate to people was a great gift."

Another parishioner, a Catholic convert with two children in St. Cyril and Methodius school, characterized Joseph as "one of the most spiritual people I have ever known, always smiling and very good at diffusing difficult situations." This assessment did not surprise Joseph. For most of his priesthood, he had had plenty of practice.

Some parishioners took exception to Joseph's efforts to promote "Missionaries of Hope," a project he had begun some years earlier to provide education and health care to the "poorest of the poor" in the rural villages of Pakistan. St. Cyril and Methodius had its own school, which was struggling to remain open in the face of dwindling enrollment and an economic downturn, and many parishioners felt that Joseph's support should be more committed to the church's own school. Joseph believed that while the Catholic school at St. Cyril and Methodius had a support system in place, the forgotten children of Pakistan had none, and he tried to balance the needs of the two as best he could.

Nevertheless, in spite of Joseph's "foreign ways," the people of St. Cyril and Methodius came to accept and embrace him, warts and all.

CHAPTER 27

Between Two Cultures

I knew nothing; I was nothing. For this reason, God picked me out.

—St. Catherine Laboure

In April of 2001, Joseph heard that his old friend, Father Larry Saldanha, had been appointed Archbishop of Lahore by Pope John Paul II. His ordination was scheduled for September eleventh. When Joseph called to congratulate him, Father Larry invited him to the ordination. Joseph decided to arrange his vacation schedule so that he could be in Pakistan for this most important occasion.

Destined to be one of the darkest days in American history, the morning of September 11, 2001 started out like any other. It was the day of Father Larry's ordination.

"The ordination had gone beautifully and everyone was rejoicing, the mood very jubilant," Joseph recalls. "After the ceremony, we were invited to Jesus and Mary Convent for a special meal. There was a TV in the dining hall and someone turned it on. Suddenly, unbelievably, there it was—the twin towers of New York City's World Trade Center were burning, falling, disintegrating before our eyes, half a world away. The atmosphere in the room changed to shock, disbelief, and profound sadness. Later, I told the archbishop that the date of his ordination would be forever burned into my memory.

"In Lahore, there was no immediate or obvious reaction to the tragedy, although I later heard that the Muslim community had celebrated the disaster as 'a victory of Islam.' Presently news came that many Muslims who worked in the towers, including some Pakistanis, had also been killed in the attack, and the mood suddenly changed from rejoicing to mourning."

Later Joseph—and the world—would learn that Islamic terrorists had hijacked four commercial airplanes, crashing two of them into the World Trade Center and a third into the Pentagon. The fourth plane went down in a field near Shanksville, Pennsylvania, after passengers and crew members had attempted to take control of the plane, which had been headed toward Washington, DC. There were no survivors.

In addition to the nineteen hijackers, 2,974 people died in the attacks, including nationals from more than ninety countries.

* * *

Several days after his ordination, Archbishop Saldanha called Joseph into his office. "I want you to stay in Pakistan and work with me," he told Joseph. He then wrote an official letter to the Austin diocese, requesting Joseph's presence back in Pakistan. Bishop Gregory Aymond had just replaced Bishop McCarthy, who had retired, and since Bishop Saldanha was now an archbishop, his rank trumped that of Bishop Aymond.

Joseph had been happy in Granger and was reluctant to leave a post where he felt accepted, needed, and fulfilled. He was not eager to make yet another transcontinental move back to the country of his birth, but perhaps this time it would be different. This time, maybe he could make a difference. He told Archbishop Saldanha that he would go back to Granger, pack up his things, and return to Pakistan.

"Bishop Saldanha was a good friend," says Joseph. "I had served with him during my first assignment in Anarkali, back in 1968, where he had suffered through my motorcycle ministry. Later, when I went to Narowal, he followed me there. But my pleasure at serving with him in Pakistan was tempered with serious misgivings about the mission. Returning to the country of my birth after spending so many years in the US would prove to be a difficult adjustment. Most of Pakistan's infrastructure and commerce still remained about fifty years behind the times, and it would take some time to re-acclimate myself in my own culture."

In the end, the assignment would test Joseph's integrity, his moral righteousness, and his priesthood, and end forever his ecclesiastical ministry in Pakistan.

* * *

Meanwhile, Pakistan was becoming an increasingly dangerous place, especially for Christians. On October 29, 2001, Islamic extremists armed with AK-47 rifles attacked St. Dominic's Catholic church in the town of Bahawalpur during a morning service, killing fifteen Christian worshippers and a Muslim policeman. The assault was perceived as apparent revenge for America's recent bombing of Afghanistan.

December 28, 2001, was a Friday and the day of Joseph's farewell Mass at St. Cyril and Methodius Church in Granger. During the week, he normally celebrated Mass in the chapel, but this was Christmas week with all the beautiful decorations and lights in the church, and, being his last Mass and also the Mass of the Holy Innocents, he decided to celebrate in the church.

"I expected the regular crowd of around fifty people," says Joseph, "and as the faithful began the rosary, I joined them. After the rosary, I went to the sacristy and put on my vestments. When I came out on the altar to celebrate Mass, the church was nearly full. 'Wow,' I thought, 'where did all these people come from?'

"After Mass was over, I said my own goodbye. 'I came here as a missionary from Pakistan, and you accepted me and made me part of your parish family. Now that I am going back to Pakistan, I will be your missionary to Pakistan, and I ask you to bless my mission. I knelt down and everyone stood and gave me their blessing. It was a beautiful moment."

* * *

In January of 2002, Joseph returned to Pakistan and was assigned to the cathedral for three months. In April, he was appointed pastor at St. Luke's in Shahdara, a district of Lahore, where his sister Teresa and her family lived, and where he had served more than thirty years ago, back in 1969, when he had organized the first Mela to the Blessed Virgin Mary. History had a way of repeating itself.

At St. Luke's, Joseph found himself responsible for more than a hundred villages and seven catechists. He also served as editor of the Catholic magazine, *Naquib*. There was no priest's residence near the church; instead, the "rectory" was a small house in a nearby neighborhood, surrounded by Muslim neighbors, several of whom were Wahabi Muslims, members of the conservative, fundamentalist sect of Sunni Islam. Joseph's predecessor had had a good relationship with his neighbors, and so would Joseph.

In retrospect, he would have fewer problems with his Muslim neighbors than he would have with the congregation at St. Luke's. However, his introduction to his new neighbors was less than inspiring.

There would be two priests living at the rectory, and when Joseph met his housemate, it was a reunion of sorts. Father Paul had been a little boy in Kasur when Joseph was transferred there in 1975. His father had been a gardener and a janitor for the parish, and his mother had cooked for the priests.

The rectory was about a ten-minute walk from the church and five minutes by car. Late one afternoon, an associate from the parish showed Joseph how to find his new home. In spite of its proximity to the church, it was not an easy place to find. The streets were unmarked and arranged in a sort of maze, and you really needed to have a specific landmark to know where to turn.

The former resident of the rectory, Father John Francis, had been many things, including something of a technological wizard. He had installed a very newfangled item for the time, an electronic gate. At the press of a button inside the rectory, the gate would open automatically. When pulled closed, it would lock. And if the electricity went out with someone caught inside, he had to know exactly where to push on the gadget that opened the gate. A key was needed to open the gate from the outside.

One evening soon after he arrived in Shahdara, Joseph decided to move some of his things to the new residence. He did not yet have the parish jeep so he borrowed an old car—a most unreliable old car—used by visitors to the parish. About ten thirty that evening as he drove into the neighborhood, there was a sudden electrical blackout, more commonly referred to as "load-shedding." All at once, the entire area was plunged into darkness. Traveling slowly, following the dim light from his headlights, Joseph finally located the house and stopped in front of the high wall that surrounded the courtyard.

"I opened the gate by the light from my headlights and it swung slowly shut behind me. I probably should have driven the car into the garage right away, but it was locked from the inside with a padlock and I did not have a key, and was thus without access to my rooms. So I went back out to the gate to wait for Father Paul. However, because of the blackout—no electricity—the gate did not open when I pushed the button. I, of course, did not know how to manage the gadget that opened the gate manually, so I was locked in and with a nine-foot wall surrounding the house, I couldn't even climb my way out. By then it was after eleven o'clock at night, so I decided to make some noise and perhaps someone would hear me. I picked up a piece of wood and started banging on the gate and soon enough some people came out calling, 'Who's there? What's going on?'

"I am Father Joseph," I called out. "I am your new neighbor and have only just arrived here, but I can't open the gate from the inside. I need to get out, but I don't know how to open the gate without electricity, so I'm stuck."

"It is eleven o'clock at night—why do you want to go out?" a voice in the dark replied.

"My car is in the middle of the street with the engine running"—*I had suddenly realized this*—"so I must move it somewhere.

"Someone asked if I had the keys to the gate. I said yes, so they told me to throw the keys out, saying, 'We will open it.' All the time I am thinking . . . *I don't know these people and they don't know me. I haven't seen them and they haven't seen me.* But it did not seem the right time to evaluate my neighbors' trustworthiness, so I tossed the keys over the wall and they managed to open the gate.

"About this time, I decided to go back to Lahore for the night, thinking maybe I could get my old room back. Suddenly I realized that, in my nervousness, I had locked the keys inside the car. Locked out of my house and now out of my car, I was looking quite stupid in front of my new neighbors. One fellow suggested that his car key might work on my car—sometimes they did, apparently. Luckily, his key opened my car door and I was able to shut the engine off."

It was now about midnight and Father Paul finally arrived in his car. He greeted his neighbors, curious as to why they were gathered in the street in front of his house in the middle of the night. Joseph explained his predicament, and Father Paul went immediately to unlock his garage. There were two garages; one was used by Father Paul, and was next to the stairs that went up to his bedroom; the other garage provided access to Joseph's living quarters.

Father Paul put his car in his garage, Joseph put his car in his garage, and the two men went inside—to a very dark house.

"I knew nothing about load-shedding, so I was not prepared—no flashlight, no candles, no light. A week earlier, I had asked some workmen to make some repairs to the bathroom, but they apparently had not finished the job. The bathroom was full of construction debris, so I looked around for a broom and, finding none, picked up two pieces of wood to remove the rubbish—by the light of the moon. Just about that time, the electricity returned and the light came on. Quickly, I filled up a bucket so I would have water for washing the next morning, when I would say my first Mass at St. Luke's.

"I climbed into bed, and when I touched the cupboard next to the bed, it fell apart, eaten up with termites. All the woodwork in the house was eaten up as well; it had not been whitewashed or painted in many years. Finally, I turned off the light to go to sleep, lulled by the sound of scurrying cockroaches. About ten minutes later, I heard a thump in the bathroom—which had no door—and then some scratching. A large rat had fallen into the water bucket and was trying to get out. I said 'I can't kill you, but I will let you out,' so I tipped the bucket over with my foot and it spilled out the door onto the little veranda. 'If you live, you live,' I told the rat. In the morning, the cook came and told me that he had thrown a big, dead rat into the street.

"All in all, it was a very unremarkable house, but it was home, and it would do well enough. This was, after all, how many of the better-off people lived in Pakistan."

In Joseph's defense, however, most of the Catholic parish houses of the day had been built years earlier by the Belgian missionaries and were quite nice, some even elegant.

Joseph ended up spending quite a lot of his own money (about two thousand US dollars) on repairs. He also bought an air conditioning unit—he was quite spoiled by American amenities—did some painting, and put a new water tank on the roof. He did not ask the diocese to reimburse him. He had been away for many years and had not contributed to its well being. Now it was his turn.

* * *

While Joseph was getting his feet wet at St. Luke's, his brother Peter was teaching nearby at St. Anthony's school. Peter had remarked to Joseph several times that the new principal, a lay Catholic, seemed to have no idea what a Catholic school was about, and had set about removing all the signs and symbols that identified the school as a Catholic institution. But worst of all, Peter said, was the fact that he had taken away the statue of St. Anthony and put it in a storeroom.

"I just can't bear to have St. Anthony hidden away like that," Peter told Joseph. "Maybe you could use it somewhere?"

Joseph said of course, he could put it in the church, so he called the principal who immediately agreed to let him have St. Anthony.

Joseph recruited a couple of men to help him load the life-size statue into his jeep. The only way they could get it into the jeep was to lay the statue front to back, across the top of the seats. And so off they went, Joseph in the driver's seat, St. Anthony sprawled unceremoniously across the seats. As he drove along, he noticed people staring at his car, curious about his passenger. Was it real? Was it a body? Where was he taking it?

At a traffic stop, Joseph became aware of a police car behind him. "The policemen were paying a lot of attention to my passenger, but by then, I was having a good laugh."

The parish was thrilled with their new statue, which they could never have afforded to buy outright. Now, every Tuesday night when St. Luke's had their devotion to St. Anthony, the faithful had a life-size statue to inspire them, instead of the small picture they had previously used.

In May, there was a crowning celebration for the Blessed Mother in Shahdara Colony, where Joseph lived. In Shahdara Town, five miles away, there was also a Catholic church and, apparently, there was some rivalry between the Colony people and the town people. If you had a crowning in Shahdara Colony, there must also be one in Shahdara Town. So Joseph decided to keep the peace and hold a second celebration in Shahdara Town.

"Father Simon invited me to be the main celebrant on that day, so I would be the one preaching the sermon," Joseph remembers. "In retrospect, since Father Simon was in charge of that church, he should have given the sermon, especially since my problems in Shahdara would begin with that sermon.

"I had read somewhere that while Mary was betrothed to Joseph, she would often bring him water from the well and, after drinking from the pitcher, he would open the upper part of his shirt and cool off. Whenever he exposed any part of his body, Mary, being very modest, would turn her head. So I decided to use this story to illustrate my sermon on modesty. 'In today's world, how much modesty do we really practice?' was the question I posed to the congregation.

"To understand what happened next, you need to know something about Father John Francis, my predecessor. Father Francis had apparently been a troubled man, a priest first, but a man nevertheless. The parishioners had often used his various weaknesses to blackmail him. 'Give us five thousand rupees and we will not tell anybody what you have done,' they would say. I never actually knew what his sins were, nor if they were even sins at all, but he had his own ways and the people had often taken advantage of him.

"So, during the first three or four months of my ministry in Shahdara, these same people were listening, watching, and measuring me, looking for any weakness that they might turn to advantage. I'm sure they thought that I was loaded with dollars, having just come from America. And when they heard my sermon on modesty, they said, 'We have him, he has committed blasphemy against Mary.' The story they spun went something like this: 'Father Joseph said in his sermon that when Mary was betrothed to Joseph, she used to bring him water to drink, and he would take his clothes off and she would give him a bath.' My detractors thought they had a point, so the rumors and accusations began, but I refused to acknowledge that I had in any way disrespected Mary."

A few days later, Mr. Naseer, an area councilor, telephoned Joseph. In the local communities, the councilor held considerable status. Mr. Naseer also happened to be a member of St. Luke's church. When Joseph answered the phone, Mr. Naseer said, "Do you know who is calling?"

"Yes, you are Councilor Naseer," Joseph replied.

"Have you heard what the people are saying about you?" he asked. "People have come to me and reported that you made a blasphemous remark about the Blessed Mary."

"Did you hear it?" Joseph countered.

Mr. Naseer said no.

"Do you have a recording?" Joseph continued.

Mr. Naseer did not.

It was a pointless conversation, but Joseph was nervous neverthe-less. "I knew these people could do a lot of harm by just spreading the rumors," says Joseph. "But this was by no means my only transgression. The litany was growing ever longer.

"There was no sacristy in the church, only a cupboard in the sanc-tuary for the vestments. When the priest changed into his vestments, he did so in front of the entire congregation, so unless you came with your cas-sock on, you had to change your shirt in front of everyone, which is what Father Francis had been doing for many years."

So, one of the first things Joseph did at St. Luke's was to build a sacristy on the left side of the altar. The cupboard was shifted and a table added so the priest could prepare his books, and the priest and altar servers would have a private place to dress. From there, they would go in proces-sion to the back of the church and enter with the opening song.

Letters began to go out, one even went to the bishop. Another was from a very well known and respected gentleman who had known Joseph in the past, and who had even donated land for the church. He was now an old man in his nineties and, although illiterate, had managed to get a letter written in his name. Joseph recalls the letter, which said essentially, "Since you have come here, there is no peace in our parish. You never visit the homes of the poor; you go only to the rich houses, those who offer you a good meal. Your behavior is very rude . . . "

The letter mentioned several other complaints; one being that Jo-seph had changed the Mass ritual. Apparently, Father Francis never began the Mass himself, but would arrive around gospel time, read the gospel, and then give the homily. Sometimes he would ask his catechist to give the homily. His congregation had come to believe that this was the accepted practice because for eighteen years; this was the way it had been. Father

Francis' rationale for this practice was that he was a busy man and this saved him time. The congregation was by now used to the catechist starting the Mass, so they thought that Joseph's changes were unacceptable, possibly even decadent.

Joseph had replaced a priest who, although he had done some good work, had also damaged and undermined the parish. The changes Joseph was making were not really changes at all, but rather things that should have been in place in any parish.

When the bishop received these disparaging letters, he merely laughed. He had already heard the rumors and he merely dismissed the letters without even reading them. Joseph, however, took them much more seriously.

"Bishop Saldanha was only two years into his bishopric and was probably still finding his way," says Joseph. "For him it was just the usual stuff. Priests were often blamed for things that weren't remotely their concern, so he advised me not to worry. But it was not easy to dismiss the complaints or the hostile situation."

Eventually, Joseph held a community meeting with the parishioners and they reached a kind of forced reconciliation. "We will stop all our complaints if you give us money for a new sound system and put carpets in the church," they told him.

Joseph agreed to support their effort, but explained that the community would have to come up with 20 percent of the expenses. "OK, we will give two Sunday's worth of collection money to you," they said.

Joseph responded that that money was already coming to him. "You have to collect 20 percent *extra,* and then we will get the sound system and the carpet."

"The situation I found myself in was frustrating in the extreme, but also profoundly sad on many levels," recalls Joseph. "I concluded from all this that it is the priest who is responsible for instilling respect, educating and nurturing his people, and strengthening their faith. To that end, I also believed that my predecessor had failed his people and his mission. I also began to wonder if the archbishop had not sent me to this parish because no one else would go?

"I'm sure many viewed me as an outsider because I had been living in the US. 'You had a good life in America, but where were you when we were going through our troubles?' they would ask me. And my thinking, my whole approach had been influenced by many years in the US, in a more tolerant, liberated, and educated society. For whatever reason, I seemed to have lost my connection not only to the people, but also to my country. Even my own language sounded strange to me. I had committed myself completely and totally to my mission at St. Luke's, but too much had changed, both in Pakistan and in me."

Joseph began to feel that his assignment to St. Luke's was 100 percent wrong, the situation at Shahdara beyond his control. It seemed that every time he was transferred to a new assignment in Pakistan, it was to a troubled parish in need of reconciliation. And St. Luke's needed more than he had to give. Even though Archbishop Saldanha had made a personal appeal to the people of St. Luke's in support of Joseph, it was not enough.

CHAPTER 28

Stranger in His Own Land

*Let nothing disturb you, nothing frighten you. All things
are passing. God never changes. Patient endurance at-
tains all things. Whoever possesses God lacks nothing.
God alone is sufficient.*

—St. Teresa of Avila

In June, Joseph returned to Texas for a much needed vacation. He desperately needed a positive environment to recharge his spiritual batteries, so he went back to St. Cyril and Methodius Church in Granger,
where he had spent two and a half happy years in 1999 through 2001.
Their pastor was on vacation, and Joseph was glad to fill in for him.

"When I came back to Granger, everyone said, 'Welcome home!'
This was ironic because I was beginning to feel more and more that the
country of my birth was no longer my spiritual home, and that my work
there was often misunderstood."

While Joseph was in Texas, he met with Bishop Gregory Aymond,
who had replaced his friend, the retired Bishop McCarthy, and they dis-
cussed his situation in Pakistan. Bishop Aymond remembers counseling
Father Joseph: "Joseph mentioned that his ministry in Pakistan was not
working out as he had hoped, and he expressed an interest in returning to
do pastoral work in Texas, so I told him I would write to his bishop. As
bishops, we work together. Our philosophy is that if a person feels that
his gifts for the ministry can be best used and he can be happier in a place
other than where he is currently serving, we try to accommodate them.
Joseph had originally been incardinated in the diocese of Lahore in Pakistan, and had technically been on loan to dioceses in the United States. But

now, since he obviously felt that his ministry would be more effective in the Austin diocese, his bishop and I agreed that it would be appropriate for him to change his allegiance to the Austin diocese, and so I incardinated him in the Diocese of Austin. (Incardination basically means that a priest has been officially released from the jurisdiction of one bishop, and transferred to that of another.)

"Joseph is, in my opinion, a holy man, quiet and thoughtful. He takes his priestly ministry very seriously, serving God's people with great integrity. Although he had adapted to the culture in the US quite well, he had not lost the quiet, reflective spirituality of the Pakistani people."

Joseph returned to Pakistan a month later. Bishop Aymond did indeed send a letter to the archbishop in Lahore, but the archbishop did not respond. Nor did he say anything to Joseph, who would not find out that the letter had even been sent until weeks later.

Over the next few months, Joseph continued to agonize over his loyalties and his ministry. He met several times with the archbishop, fellow priests, and finally, with his family. His sister Theresa, who lived in his parish—just five hundred yards from the church—said to Joseph, "Although we have enjoyed you and you are an asset to us in all ways, we cannot bear the insults you are receiving. I would be selfish to ask you to remain here." Even his nephew, the priest Father Andrew, said, "Uncle, this is not the same Pakistan or the same people you lived among before. Much has changed."

All of which convinced Joseph that his situation at St. Luke's was untenable. He felt out of place, no longer needed, a stranger in his own country. It was time to find more fertile ground for his work.

"In my heart, I knew that I had done my best. I had no more to give. I had remained at my post for two long, difficult years, and more and more, my heart was no longer in Pakistan. I had become disconnected. I wasn't speaking their language and wasn't thinking their thoughts. I had become an alien in my own land."

Eventually, Joseph heard that Archbishop Saldanha had received the letter from the bishop in Austin, and went to see him. "Bishop Aymond has written to me that they are opening an office for family counseling in his diocese," the archbishop announced, " and since you have a background in pastoral counseling and social work, you could be useful to them. But," he continued, "these are rich people, they have a rich diocese and can get someone from anywhere. We, on the other hand, are a poor country and a poor diocese, and we need you here."

Patiently the archbishop continued, explaining his position to Joseph as if Joseph were a problem child. "You should know that your people love you; look at all you have accomplished in Pakistan, at Mariamabad, in the villages, even at St. Luke's. You must pray and trust in God. Everything will be OK."

Although the archbishop's argument was painfully hard to ignore, it did little to inspire Joseph to continue his ministry in a country where he felt increasingly inadequate.

News of the murder of his friend Father George Abraham only depressed Joseph further. On July 5, 2003, Abraham had been gunned down at his parish house at Renala Khurd. According to Archbishop Saldanha, the motive for his death seemed to be related to the government's decision to return the school to Father Abraham's parish after thirty years of state control. After the court-ordered denationalization of the school, the Muslim headmistress had apparently refused to leave, in protest of the expected loss of her job.

His countrymen's code of honor had begun to mystify Joseph, their souls seemingly bereft of the ancient tribal traditions of honor, integrity, and decency. Crimes could be committed with impunity, so long as they were done in the name of family, village, or religion.

Around Christmastime, Joseph approached the archbishop again and said, "This isn't working out, for me or for the church. I would like to return to the US where I have a job waiting and can be more useful."

The archbishop seemed disappointed but resigned, his response predictable. Joseph had hoped for an amiable parting, but knowing the archbishop's sentiments, felt that he would be lucky to get a letter of ex-cardination, which would release him from the Lahore diocese and allow him to be accepted by another. Without that letter, he would be in the same position he had been in before: spiritual limbo.

Archbishop Saldanha wrote the letter—a very short letter—and that was that.

Joseph would not see Archbishop Saldanha again until he visited Pakistan in April of 2008. A few weeks before his visit, a suicide bomber had driven a vehicle loaded with explosives into the eight-story Federal Investigation Agency, blowing himself up and killing more than twenty people. Across the road from the FIA building, several Catholic institutions were also damaged, among them Sacred Heart Cathedral (where he had been ordained forty years ago), several schools, and the hundred-year-old bishop's residence. A cathedral security guard and the three-year-old daughter of Archbishop Saldanha's driver were among the casualties.

Joseph was distraught by news of the tragedy and went to see his old friend and adversary while he was in Lahore. He gave the archbishop a sizable donation from his own funds to help with the restoration effort.

Joseph also made his peace with another old adversary, Armando Trindade. In 1994, Trindade had been appointed archbishop of Lahore. Joseph met with him just a few years before the archbishop's death in 2000. "It was his birthday, and he seemed glad to see me. 'I hope you have forgiven me,' he said. I told him that I don't keep such things in my heart."

Joseph's battles with his bishops were finally at an end.

Joseph returned to America in December of 2003. As his plane took off from Lahore's Allama Iqbal International Airport, he stared out the window, watching Pakistan fall away below him into the night. He would never live in Pakistan again.

CHAPTER 29

Coming Home

While faith makes all things possible, it is love that makes all things easy.

—Gerard Manley Hopkins

Back in the United States, Joseph was assigned once again to St. Luke's in Temple, where he had been posted back in 1999. He would serve as associate pastor until May, when he would be named pastor of the parish, succeeding his old friend, Monsignor Louis Pavlicek, who was being transferred to another parish. While Pakistan had rejected him, he would find a home at St. Luke's—but acceptance into their culture would once again come slowly.

Father Joseph would be remembered at St. Luke's for many things, not the least of which was his seemingly total lack of navigational skills. He was, in his own words, "directionally challenged."

"From the time I was able to walk, I've had a problem with directions. In the villages, of course, you can't get lost. Whenever I traveled to a distant village to visit someone, the only directions I needed went something like this: 'When you get to the village, look for the mosque and you'll find so-and-so's house on the right,' or 'once you come to the big tree, there are Christian people living beside it, and they will show you where to go.' When I arrived in Temple and had to drive myself around, I got lost quite often. Many times I had to call someone and ask how to get there from wherever I found myself. This is still a problem for me. I've noticed that in the US, people often say that a man will never ask for directions. I will tell you that this man does. Every time."

In September, Joseph was transferred back to Granger, to St. Cyril and Methodius church, where he had served as pastor just three years earlier. He would be replacing Father Isador Ndagissimana from Uganda. "It was, once again, a homecoming for me," says Joseph. "I was happy to be returning to a welcoming and friendly flock."

Looking out from the altar as he celebrated his first Mass back in Granger, Father Joseph was comforted by the familiar faces of the congregation, many of them old friends. "I am back home," he told them.

Joseph is a hugger, and every Sunday after Mass, he looks forward to greeting his parishioners in the back of the church, happily accepting great bear hugs from the children (and many of the adults).

Rejected in Pakistan, Joseph found another home when he returned to St. Cyril and Methodius. The people of Granger understood his message.

EPILOGUE

"I have made numerous trips back to Pakistan since closing my ministry there in 2004," says Father Joseph. "Much has changed, and yet much has stayed the same. Brick homes have replaced many of the mud houses, large Walmart-type stores and Western-style shopping malls have appeared in the larger cities, many of the restaurants and movie theaters are now air conditioned, and roads have improved, although traffic has not. On the other hand, electricity remains sporadic, poverty extreme, and conditions for minorities remain difficult."

Pakistan is the first country in recent history to be founded on the basis of religion, with a democratic style of government. But today, Pakistan's increasingly restrictive Islamic culture continues to create problems for minorities, especially Christians. Like so many other religions, the message of Islam has been exploited and corrupted by fundamentalists and militants, compromising the opportunity for peace and tolerance. However, amid all the unrest and fanatical rhetoric, there are supporters of reason and tolerance. Not all Muslims are terrorists, and many would like to live in a tolerant society. Unfortunately, fundamentalism remains a global problem, and is not strictly the purview of Islam.

In the last ten years, militant groups like al Qaeda, Lashkar-e-Jhangvi, the Islamic Dawa Party, Sipah-e-Sahaba Pakistan, and other radical organizations have overshadowed the political, social, and religious life of the citizens of Pakistan. Hundreds of Pakistanis have died in sectarian violence and suicide bombings. Christians have suffered significant and particular hardships: murder and mutilation, their homes and churches burned, their schools destroyed. Education and employment opportunities remain limited, under vague and unwritten government mandates.

"The Muslims and their government are caught between a rock and a hard place," says Father Joseph. "On the one hand, they are challenged to remain true to the principals of Islam; on the other hand, the militant groups are attempting to thwart the government in the name of pure Islamic law, or *sharia*. My question to the fundamentalist Muslims is this: If Islam is a religion of peace and compassion—and many Islamic prayers and most chapters in the Quran begin with, 'In the Name of Allah, the Compassionate, the Merciful'—then where is the mercy and forgiveness?

"Often in my dialogues with prominent Muslims, I have heard it said that the militant terrorists are not regarded as true Muslims, and that acts such as terrorism and suicide bombings are counter to the teachings of the Quran. The Quran even encourages Muslims to respect the people of the book (both Christians and Jews). That being said, it seems that little is being done to stop these 'unIslamic' factions."

Samir Khalil Samir, Jesuit priest, Islamic scholar, and world-renowned expert on Islam, writes of the "ambiguity" of Islam.

When some fanatics kill children, women, and men in the name of pure and authentic Islam, or in the name of the Quran or of the Muslim tradition, nobody can tell them: "You are not true and authentic Muslims." All they can say is: "Your reading of Islam is not ours." And this is the ambiguity of Islam. From its beginning to our present day, violence is a part of it, although it is also possible to choose tolerance; tolerance is a part of it, but it is also possible to choose violence. (Samir Khalil Samir 2008)

One might say, then, that Islamic principles are a matter of interpretation, or of choice.

In her book, *On the Fence: A Woman Between Pakistan and the West,* Magda Khan offers an interesting perspective on democracy in underdeveloped nations. Khan maintains that Western-style democracy cannot easily succeed in these countries. Religious issues notwithstanding, the majority of the people, says Khan, are largely ignorant of the countries' political situations and, in elections, tend to vote for their landlords or village headmen because they do not want to lose their livelihood. And the people they elect are generally incompetent leaders, seeking only personal gain and caring not at all for those they are elected to serve. Typically, Khan says, residents of these nations are happy if they are allowed to earn an adequate living, and it does not seem to matter who is running the country.

"On my trip back to Pakistan in 2008," recalls Joseph, "I had an opportunity to observe the kind of 'slavery' that is endemic in the brick kiln industry and in many other industries in Pakistan. One of the workers complained that the Muslim owner of the kiln would not allow him to take time to say his morning and evening prayers. In Pakistan, as in many countries, enough money and power can corrupt absolutely. And to ensure that these men did not complain—or escape—they were chained to their cots at night.

"Poverty and oppression remain a cruel fate for many Pakistanis. Children are still being sold in the marketplace because their parents cannot afford to care for them, and a recent article in a local paper referred to one desperate woman who threw herself—along with her three small children—under a train because of the hopelessness of her situation.

"I have always believed that education is the key to overcoming poverty and oppression, and to enriching hearts, minds, and souls," says Father Joseph. "Education has made the difference in the lives of my brothers and sisters, all of whom were able to obtain good jobs, which enabled better lives. Eventually, I came to realize that it was time to share our blessings with those less fortunate, especially the impoverished people in the villages of my native country.

"And so, after abandoning my goal of improving the lives of the catechists in Pakistan, I am now pursuing another dream—that of uplifting and improving the lives of the poorest of the poor in the rural villages of Pakistan. And that dream has become a reality. In 2004, I established "Missionaries of Hope," a non-profit organization created to provide education and healthcare to the impoverished people of the villages of Pakistan."

The organization began modestly, establishing two schools: Holy Family School in Bhai Pheru, in the district of Kasur; and Jesus, Mary, and Joseph School, in the village of Pajian (district of Lahore). Holy Family currently has two teachers and about forty-five students in first and second grades, while Jesus, Mary, and Joseph School has more than one hundred and fifty students in grades 1 through 5. The schools are open to all children, regardless of religion.

A third school will open in 2011 in the village of Mall, District of Lahore. The village elder, a man who was converted to Christianity by Joseph's father more than sixty years ago, donated part of the land on which the school will be built. "Your father brought me the light of faith," he told Joseph, "and now you bring us the light of education."

A niece of Father Joseph's, Joan Nisari, has started a branch of Missionaries of Hope in Australia. Another niece, Angelina Samuel, established a branch in Germany. (Angelina's husband, a doctor, received political asylum after being accused of blasphemy against Islam in Pakistan.) Although Angelina and her husband were killed in an automobile accident in 2009, the German branch of Missionaries of Hope continues its support today.

"When we started the schools in 2004, we needed considerable funding," says Joseph. "I had no idea where it would come from, but God provided and continues to provide. When I mentioned this program to Bishop Gregory Aymond [then bishop of the Austin diocese], he was eager to provide financial and moral support, designating the program as one of the beneficiaries of the Ashes to Easter Lenten program in the diocese."

The following year, Bishop Aymond granted Father Joseph permission to make mission appeals in three local parishes, which gave the organization a significant financial boost.

"The schools have been a real blessing to the people," says Father Joseph. "They have energized and transformed the children, the parents, and neighborhood. Ignorance and illiteracy are the biggest hurdles to progress, so having Muslim children attend our schools is a positive bridge-building experience. If they are educated in Christian schools, then we can have a dialogue that can lead to brotherhood and friendship.

"As long as there are caring and generous people who partner in our crusade against ignorance, poverty, and oppression, we will continue to bring hope to the forgotten children of Pakistan, who, unlike children in the United States and much of the Western world, have no hope at all."

* * *

Many of Father Joseph's family members remain in Pakistan, living in communities where they have resided for many years and have long-standing relationships with their neighbors. Half of the original family still lives in India, estranged from Pakistani relatives they never really knew.

Joseph has nine living siblings. His oldest brother, Peter, lives in Lahore, where he worked for the Pakistani government as a registrar in the Office of Marriages and Deaths until his retirement. After his "retirement," Peter taught English for the next twenty years at St. Anthony's High School in Lahore. His son, Michael Nisari, is a physician in Lahore, and is also chairman of the board of directors of Missionaries of Hope.

Another of Father Joseph's brothers, Benjamin, was employed as an officer for the Pakistani Employees Old Age Benefits Institution until his retirement in 2006. His son, Andrew, also a Catholic priest, is the current vicar general of the Archdiocese of Lahore. Joseph's oldest sister, Teresa, an ex-member of the Franciscan Sisters of the Heart of Jesus of Malta (and later the Franciscan Sisters of Christ the King) eventually married and worked as a teacher and headmistress until opening her own school in Shahdara, Lahore, where she worked until the school closed in 2004.

Sister Sabina (of the Franciscan Sisters of Christ the King) is a nurse, currently posted to Sanghar Hospital in Sindh province. Joseph's younger sister Justina married and worked as a teacher and headmistress. Today, she teaches at Holy Family School in Bhai Pheru, which is sponsored by the Missionaries of Hope.

Paul, Joseph's youngest brother, married and had three children. In 2010, he retired from the Pakistan Old Age Benefits Institution. His oldest daughter, Sonia, married a Pakistani American and works for the New York City School System. Paul's son and another daughter remain in Pakistan, where his son is a secretary for St. Anthony's School, and his daughter is studying for her MBA at Kinnaird College for Women in Lahore. Siblings Mary Rose and Maria work for the New York City School District; Mary Rose with blind children, and Maria with the disabled.

Father Joseph's long-time friend Sister Elizabeth, whom he lived with in New York when he arrived without faculties in 1992, works with disabled children and still maintains the home she shared with Father Joseph. She is actively involved in Missionaries of Hope as a program director, responsible for federal registration, tax status, and marketing activities.

Today, as pastor of St. Cyril and Methodius Church in Granger, Father Joseph is happily involved with his parish family and the many activities associated with maintaining a Catholic church and school in a rural Texas town. Working as dean of the Georgetown/Round Rock Deanery of the Austin diocese keeps him connected with his fellow priests and other parishes in the area, as well as the diocesan administration policies.

"But the great joy of my ministry at St. Cyril and Methodius," says Joseph, "continues to be our parochial school. Established in 1899, our school has been offering a quality Catholic school education to elementary school students for one hundred and ten years."

In January 2008, Father Joseph celebrated his fortieth anniversary as a priest. To honor the occasion, his family came to visit: Sister Sabina from Pakistan; sisters Mary Rose and Maria from New York; niece Angelina and her husband, the physician, evangelist, and Pakistani refugee, from Germany; and niece Sonia and her husband Younas, also from New York. Sister Elizabeth, with whom Father lived so long ago in New York, also came. Bishop Gregory Aymond (now Archbishop of New Orleans), Bishop John McCarthy (Bishop Emeritus of Austin), Msgr. Michael Mulvey (then Vicar General of the Diocese of Austin, now Bishop of Corpus Christi, Texas), Msgr. Louis Pavlicek (pastor, St. Helen Church, Georgetown, Texas), and Reverend Oliver Weerakkody (associate pastor, St. Louis King of France Church, Austin, Texas), along with many friends and members of Joseph's beloved Granger parish, also helped to celebrate this special milestone.

For more information on the Missionaries of Hope, please visit **www.godsforgottenchildren.org**

ACKNOWLEDGMENTS

Father Joseph:
There are so many friends, relatives, and associates—too numerous to mention—whose contributions and support have made this book possible, and to whom I am most sincerely grateful. I am especially indebted to my long-time friend, Reverend Oliver Weerakkody, associate pastor, St. Louis King of France Catholic Church (Austin, Texas), who introduced me to the bishop of Austin. I also owe my heartfelt gratitude to the Most Reverend John McCarthy, Bishop Emeritus (Austin diocese) who accepted me with open arms, and to His Excellency, Archbishop Gregory Aymond (New Orleans diocese), who graciously supported me. I am also most grateful to Monsignor Louis Pavlicek (pastor, St. Helen Church, Georgetown, Texas), who accepted me as his associate pastor and offered his kind support along the way.

My grateful appreciation to my dear friends in New York, Thomas Meany and Reverend Bob Freuh; my sisters Maria and Mary Rose; my good friend Justin Sharaf (retired Pakistani army major); and most especially, the members of my parish family at St. Cyril and Methodius in Granger, who gave—and continue to give—so unselfishly of their time and support.

And finally, my sincere appreciation to Rosemary Colgrove—for writing my story and for having the patience of Job—and to Millie Heine, who transcribed so many, many interviews. Without them, this book would not have been even a remote possibility.

Rosemary:

In the process of writing this book, I had the good fortune to meet many amazing people, who were unfailingly accommodating and have most certainly enriched my life. My deep appreciation to all of them, especially to Maria and Mary Rose Nisari, Sister Sabina, and Sonia and Younas Masih.

I am forever grateful to Robbin Colgrove for her awesome creative talents; to Katie Gutierrez Painter, my copyeditor, for her indispensable help; and to Millie Heine for her invaluable assistance and the treasure of her friendship.

And finally, my deep admiration and thanks to Father Joseph, for his friendship as well as his unlimited patience and candor. Without him, there would be no story.

ABOUT THE AUTHOR

A writer/editor for more than twenty-five years, Rosemary has published articles in *Austin Home & Living* magazine, written marketing materials for commercial markets, and co-authored an account of the Peace Corps experience in Romania, titled *Bread, Salt & Plum Brandy*, published in 2009. She lives with her husband Dean in Georgetown, Texas, and between them, they have five grown children and twelve grandchildren.

CPSIA information can be obtained
at www.ICGtesting.com
Printed in the USA
FFOW02n0149050418
46160283-47358FF